Praise for *Agile Innovation*

"*Agile Innovation* promises to profoundly transform businesses and institutions. By bridging the worlds of Agile and traditional innovation, the authors enable the transformation of self-organizing toward self-optimizing teams, and offer a map for the journey to the self-actualizing organization. This book is a strategic imperative for anybody aiming for success in a brutally competitive, digitally accelerated business world."

—**Errol Arkilic**, CEO, M34 Capital and co-creator
of the Innovation Corps

"This thought-provoking and inspirational book is a must-read for anyone seeking to master the art and science of innovation and accelerated business development. Simply put, it's a map that will lead you and your organization to exponential breakthrough success in the new Digital Gold Rush."

—**Jack Canfield,** Coauthor of *The Power of Focus*
and The Success Principles

"Innovation is about speed. Agility. The old methods of innovation are slow and rarely involve those who matter most: front-line workers. This book absolutely changes the game and it will change the way you innovate. Don't delay. Read it now!"

—**Stephen Shapiro,** Author of the bestselling *Best Practices Are Stupid* and *24/7 Innovation*, and former Director of Accenture's Global Process Excellence Practice

"*Agile Innovation* is a must-read for anyone interested in what will become one of the major stories of the next few decades. The global innovation landscape is undergoing profound changes and companies challenging the traditional innovation concept are poised to win. No one is better placed than this team to provide key insights about the blend of agility and innovation."

—**Tan Yinglan,** Author of *Chinnovation* and Partner, Sequoia Capital

"As an advisor to hundreds of startups, I'm very interested in learning all I can to help foster innovation in rapidly shifting markets. *Agile Innovation* is a game changer. The authors have brought to us a valuable resource that is filled with pertinent case studies and practical advice. It's one of the best innovation books I've read in years and I think its approach can elevate the art and science of innovation at any organization."

—**Akira Hirai,** CEO, Cayenne Consulting

"This book is an outstanding addition to the 'bible of best practices.' It is certainly a unique treatise on successful, high impact innovation in the explosive new global digital age. More universities around the globe should be offering courses centered on this book's valuable content."

—**Dr. Dixon R Doll,** General Partner, DCM Venture Capital, Past Chairman, U.S. National Venture Capital Association

"Finally, a comprehensive book has been written to narrow the gap for companies seeking to make innovation a core driver of sustainable growth and positive financial impact. Today's corporate leaders must build a culture of agile innovation and this outstanding book is the perfect manual for business today."

—**Harry W. Kellogg,** Vice Chairman, Silicon Valley Bank

"Nothing has been written about more in the business world over the last decade than Innovation. However, the authors have brought something quite new to the discussion by weaving together many of the threads into a complex and colorful fabric that will aid any organization in fostering and utilizing innovation to grow and prosper. This idea-packed book will provide valuable lessons for those thoughtful business leaders who realize, as the authors note, the risks of innovation are far less than the risks of not innovating."

—**Elliot E. Maxwell,** Director of the Internet Policy Project at the Aspen Institute, and former Special Advisor on the Digital Economy to the U.S. Secretary of Commerce

"*Agile Innovation* is a tremendous leap forward in innovation thought leadership. The authors first synthesize the best prevailing innovation practices of today and then take it to a whole new level. This groundbreaking book has just the right mix of examples and advice, including hands-on methods and detailed management practices. As a result, this book is an absolute gem."

—**Jacob Hsu,** Chief Executive Officer, Symbio.com

"There really is no option but innovation. The authors teach you the art of innovation: building the right innovation processes; reducing innovation risks; amplifying innovation through collaborations; and developing innovation leaders. An insightful and practical methodology for winning through *Agile Innovation*."

—**George Bickerstaff,** Managing Director, M.M. Dillon & Co

"Morris, Ma, and Wu have taken what are on reflection two blindingly obvious bedfellows and put them together in a story that makes sense, and just as important, is a fascinating read. The Agile Innovation concept is not just a good one for start-ups to consider, it also presents a disciplined approach for managing what a great many large corporations currently do not manage well.

—**Larry Campbell,** knowledge management expert

"Innovation is too often discussed in the abstract, almost as a spiritual totem. The authors of *Agile Innovation* demystify innovation, and lay out a thoughtful road map for readers to understand how to create innovative organizations. It should be on the reading list of anyone who wants to prepare their companies for the rest of the twenty-first century. All our portfolio companies will certainly receive a copy!"

—**Gary Rieschel,** Founder and Managing Director,
Qiming Venture Partners

"Finally, here's a book that pulls far away from the me-too peloton of innovation tomes. Enlightening, energizing and execution-oriented, *Agile Innovation* should be at the top of the reading list for professional services firms leaders."

—**Andrew Dietz,** CEO of Creative Growth and author of The Opening Playbook: A Professional's Guide To Building Relationships That Grow Revenue.

"*Agile Innovation* is an essential survival guide for businesses large and small in what is an ever-changing but always fiercely competitive 'innovate or die' environment. A clear and thought-provoking synthesis of the principles of Agile development that have revolutionized software development, extrapolated to a set of best practices for innovation generally."

—**Gordon Davidson,** Fenwick & West

"*Agile Innovation* is more than a wake-up call! It is about survival issues in a fast changing, highly complex world. A 'real must-read' for all leaders and managers who are responsible not only for the further development, but also for the survival of their organizations."

—Mark Schmid-Neuhaus, MD, German Fairness Foundation

"*Agile Innovation* pours a very potent brew of innovation insight and wisdom. This is required reading for anyone hoping to thrive in the highly competitive international marketplace in the twenty-first century. It distills the essence of the innovation spirit into an agile process."

—Jerome Conlon, Former Global Director Marketing Insight, Nike, VP Brand Planning Starbucks and Sr. VP Marketing & Program Development NBC, President Brand Frameworks, LLC

"Sustainable Innovation: the speed to innovate and the ability to foster a culture or constant creativity is becoming a critical function for organizations given the fast pace of today's global business. *Agile Innovation* captures the essence of this domain in a succinct, informative and highly engaging manner."

—George Thomas, Partner and Director, IBM Corporation

"*Agile Innovation* is a very creative and practical book. It borrows very sharp, useful and pertinent learnings from the AGILE methodology to make the innovation process effective and agile. The book has important lessons for all—senior leaders, middle managers, and young managers."

—Ravi Arora, Vice President, Tata Sons

"A true masterpiece! *Agile Innovation* is taking us in our journey to a whole new level of innovation. The powerful collaboration between three talented experts has brought out the best book on innovation ever!"

—Signe Gammeltoft Frantzen, Partner, SandS Design

"If there is one book to read on Innovation, we would strongly recommend this. It is an innovation on innovation with a fully integrated approach. It provides a complete guide from plan to implementation, with the agile approach to manage the process and mitigate risk. This is must-have for management to achieve higher chance of success."

—Alfred Pang, CEO, TSM Singapore

"*Agile Innovation* provides wisdom, framework, process, and tools that guide people accomplish great innovation results through collaboration, quick response to change, and iterative working philosophy. It's really a great book about implementing innovation."

—**Arthur Lok,** CEO, China Institute for Innovation

"Agility meets Innovation. This is a concept blend that will thrive in facilitating exponential value creation in years to come. The book harmonically covers people, leadership, methodological, technological, implementation, and even philosophical aspects related to this novel integration. It's a great book and I strongly recommend it!"

—**Fabián Szulanski,** Director, Learning Lab, Instituto Tecnológico de Buenos Aires.

"Langdon Morris, along with Moses Ma and Po Chi Wu, have produced Agile Innovation when it is most needed by the market. As we continue to see an evolution from 'we must innovate!' to 'how do we innovate?' this commonsense approach to moving your organization from simply talking about innovation to actually achieving innovation breakthroughs is simply elegant."

—**Brett Trusko,** President, The International Association of Innovation Professionals, Texas A&M University, New York University

"This book is a must-read for practitioners of innovation. The principles of *Agile Innovation* can unleash the transformative potential from every corner of an organization, creating sustainable competitive advantage."

—**Annie Donovan,** CEO, CoMetrics

"*Agile Innovation* has the potential to move the entire field forward, through the clarity of its writing and the importance of its message. If you are going to read only one book on innovation this year, make it this one."

—**Pascal Baudry,** Founder, WDHB Consulting Group

AGILE
INNOVATION

THE REVOLUTIONARY APPROACH
TO ACCELERATE SUCCESS, INSPIRE
ENGAGEMENT, AND IGNITE CREATIVITY

LANGDON MORRIS
MOSES MA
PO CHI WU, PhD

WILEY

For general information about our other products and services, please contact our Customer Care Department within the United States at (800) 762-2974, outside the United States at (317) 572-3993 or fax (317) 572-4002.

Wiley publishes in a variety of print and electronic formats and by print-on-demand. Some material included with standard print versions of this book may not be included in e-books or in print-on-demand. If this book refers to media such as a CD or DVD that is not included in the version you purchased, you may download this material at http://booksupport.wiley.com. For more information about Wiley products, visit www.wiley.com.

Library of Congress Cataloging-in-Publication Data:

Morris, Langdon.
    Agile innovation : the revolutionary approach to accelerate success, inspire engagement, and ignite creativity / Langdon Morris, Moses Ma, Po Chi Wu.
        pages cm
    Includes index.
    ISBN 978-1-118-95420-1 (cloth); ISBN 978-1-118-95421-8 (ebk);
    ISBN 978-1-118-95422-5 (ebk)
    1. Organizational change. 2. Creative ability in business. 3. Success in business. I. Ma, Moses, 1956- II. Wu, Po Chi, 1948- III. Title.
    HD58.8.M653 2014
    658.4′063–dc23
                                                                    2014023093

Printed in the United States of America

10 9 8 7 6 5 4 3 2 1

For Elizabeth

With love always, and deep appreciation for all you do.

—Langdon

For Qian

Who is both agile and innovative in the ways of love. Thank you so much for helping me see how beautiful life can be.

—Moses

For Mary

Without your loving support and encouragement, my life would have no meaning. Your innate entrepreneurial spirit has taught me the essence of agility and focus.

—Po Chi

CONTENTS

CONTENTS

ABOUT THIS BOOK

Charles Darwin said it quite well:

"In the long history of humankind (and animal kind, too) those who learned to collaborate and improvise most effectively have prevailed."

Innovation, collaboration, and improvisation are essential forces shaping all of business and all of modern life, and they've become vitally important for the individual, for the organization, and indeed for all of society.

The significance and importance all three and their close cousins, adaptation, leads us to some essential questions:

How well are you and your company prevailing in the current environment of accelerating change?

How well positioned are you and your company to benefit from the countless new opportunities that change is bringing?

Does your organization have a rigorous innovation process?

Are you sufficiently agile to survive and to succeed?

These questions matter so much because the scope of the challenges that every organization faces today is nothing less than enormous. Threats are everywhere, technology is accelerating, and success clearly belongs exclusively to those rare organizations that have the capacity not only to adapt to change, but also to thrive on it, and indeed to create it.

How do they do that?

> The great companies disrupt industries by reshaping entire market ecosystems. The market is forced to adapt to them.

Perhaps your organization is among these exemplars?

If not, then it's likely that Agile Innovation can benefit you. That is the promise of this book.

MASTERY OF INNOVATION

The art and science of creating change is really the mastery of innovation, but innovation takes many forms: new products and services that turn customers into evangelists; new sales channels that dominate markets and confound competitors; accelerated product development time frames that amaze and delight customers, investors, and stakeholders; and novel technologies that inspire wonder.

Agile Innovation asks:

> How can these outputs be achieved not just once, but consistently?

Our answer, and the essential argument of this book, can be summarized in this way: The market is becoming brutally competitive. It is much like a war, and to survive, your organization must become proficient in innovation, which, of course, could become one of the most powerful weapons in your arsenal. In fact, given the accelerating rate of change, *there really is no other option but innovation.*

What is required, then, to master innovation and to become an agile, adaptive, winning organization?

First, design the right business processes that enable you to out-innovate your competition, combining quality and speed.

Second, reduce the inherent risks in innovation while making the right investment decisions in new ideas.

Third, generate ideas that are better than everyone else's by effectively engaging a larger group of people—the entire organization as well as its broader ecosystem—as effective co-ideators.

Fourth, develop and demonstrate exceptional leadership skills, because making this all happen will probably require that you provoke and lead a genuine revolution in how your organization operates.

These principles constitute Agile Innovation, which is a blend of great advances in technology development (Agile Software Development) with the leading-edge practices and principles of innovation management.

How easy to do is all this?

Well, it may not be so easy at all, and it's probably going to be a big challenge. But it is definitely achievable, and the rewards from doing so will be great.

Anyway, what's your next best alternative to innovation? Is there even any alternative? Probably not.

WHY DON'T LARGE FIRMS INNOVATE?

The development and refinement of Agile Innovation has been the focus of our work for quite some time, and it is a passion that the authors share wholeheartedly. As a consultant (Langdon), technologist (Moses), and investor and educator (Po Chi), we've been deeply engaged in developing, practicing, and sharing the principles and practices of effective innovation management over the past two decades.

Underlying this work has been a constant theme: Large organizations, by their very nature, have difficulty embracing a culture of continuous innovation, and they struggle to adopt the necessary practices.

But this is neither necessary nor inevitable. The belief has to be changed, or there are going to be a lot of unpleasant consequences.

> Why don't most large firms innovate well?

Many of the root causes are related to the challenges inherent in managing a large enterprise: the need for coordination, scale, efficiency, and sustained profitability in a brutally competitive, global marketplace, and an equally brutal securities market.

Further, the modern corporation is typically built on structures, rules, and processes that may also inadvertently stifle innovation, or even kill it outright. Whether intentional or not, the premature mortality of ideas and innovations occurs regularly. The logic behind suppressing innovation may even make sense, in a limited, short-term context, such as when senior executives try to exercise control over unwieldy organizations so that critical objectives can be achieved.

In so doing, however, they often sacrifice important long-term benefits. Hence, one of our goals in this book is to show how *short-term objectives and long-term needs can be balanced,* and how operating units and innovation teams can work in close and effective partnerships rather than as bitter rivals that compete for resources.

During the years that we've been applying and refining these concepts, we've also been nurturing new enterprises (as entrepreneurs, consultants, and investors) and new technologies (as scientists and technologists). Through this work, we've come to appreciate the value of the methods widely known in the tech sector as Agile.

Agile refers to a set of principles and practices that software programming teams have developed with two major goals: to accelerate their work and to reliably produce work of the highest quality. By reducing the burdens of bureaucratic project management, they also free programmers to work more productively and with much greater satisfaction. This effort has been amazingly successful, and a robust methodology has emerged since "The Manifesto for Agile Software Development" (www.agilealliance.org/the-alliance/the-agile-manifesto) was published in February 2001.

In this book, we are delighted to be able to bring the two concepts together into a unified, effective, and practical methodology. How are Agile and classical innovation management related? One way to think of it is this: Agile is a speedometer that allows you to know your speed, and therefore gives you the ability to calculate when you'll reach your destination. Without a speedometer or odometer, reliable measurement, in other words, you have to guess, and the longer and less familiar the route, the worse your prediction will be.

Agile Innovation, in complement to your Agile speedometer, is the global positioning system (GPS) that helps you stay on course. Even without plotting your course in detail ahead of time—or developing comprehensive documentation and specification—you can get started right away, and if you make a wrong turn or hit a traffic jam, your Agile Innovation GPS makes a course correction. Whether the journey is 10 miles or 10,000, you'll always know the estimated arrival time.

In the applications of Agile Innovation we have completed to date, the approach has proven to be a powerful enabler of success, and we hope that as you traverse these pages you'll find the blend of Agile with Innovation a valuable speedometer and GPS for innovation in your own enterprise.

Agile Software, Agile Innovation, and Agility

Please note that in this book when we capitalize the word *Agile,* it refers to the formal practice of Agile Software Development methodology. We use the terms *Agile* and *Agile Software* when we're referring specifically to the movement that has grown out of the Agile Manifesto. You will also notice the term *Agile Innovation,* which refers to the overall innovation management model that we develop throughout this book.

When we don't capitalize it, we mean the more general concept of agility, which refers to a more general capacity to adapt to change.

David versus Goliath

Many practitioners and advocates of Agile tend to see themselves as Davids, small, lean, and determined, standing toe-to-toe on the battlefield and fighting an enormous bureaucracy of Goliaths, whose sole function is to suppress their creativity, their innovativeness, their productivity, and even the joy they find in their work.

Consequently, in much of the Agile literature, there is an undertone of rebellion, and determination to defend the capacity of programmers to self-organize because they love their work and are fully committed to performing to the utmost of their abilities.

In this respect, the Agile movement reflects a profoundly important and meaningful inner drive.

(*continued*)

(continued)

Inner motivation is the root system that supports great works of genius. External motivation, on the other hand, is based on reward and punishment and can achieve, even at its best, only compliance.

This burning desire to achieve greatness is reflected in the creation of Agile, and this principle of inner drive is also a key premise of our work. By extending this same energy, the same drive, beyond a group of programmers or a research and development team to other parts of an organization, tremendous value can be created and captured.

Although our passion is to direct this marvelous innate creative force specifically toward innovation, this book will show you how the same concepts and principles can be applied in a great many aspects of your organization.

What is the story of Agile Innovation?

The shift we are proposing is from traditional, top-down, control-oriented management to self-organizing, customer-driven Agile Innovation. This is, of course, nothing less than a revolution.

In Part 1 you'll learn what this new way of working entails and why the powerful forces that are driving the economy and society will most likely require your organization to engage in this type of revolution sooner (better for you), or later (procrastinating will come with lots of adverse consequences).

In Part 2 we'll help you design the specific work processes that are necessary to create change and empower innovation throughout your own organization.

In Part 3 we'll suggest the critical factors for you to consider as the leader of your organization's revolution, putting your plans into action.

Innovation is a great journey of creation, and Agile Innovation is the same, only faster and perhaps better. Thank you for joining us!

PART I

THE INNOVATION REVOLUTION

A new movement is emerging.

Product and technology development teams all over the world are now quietly engaged in a highly effective revolution that is changing business forever.

They are self-organizing to adapt to the accelerating rate of change and the complexities of the global digital age. Industry after industry, from Internet software, to aviation, to digital health care, to mobile telephony, is using a process called Agile to turn out better results in less time.

> Agile is fundamentally changing the way that business works.

Soon Agile will move beyond the technology world because the insights it reveals are applicable across the entire organization.

> This book describes Agile Innovation management, a radically new and eminently practical approach to the challenge of survival.

When this happens, a true revolution will begin—not something limited to the self-contained world of software development, but instead spreading geometrically, catching on in every industry.

The revolution we speak of isn't the kind where people wear berets, wave banners, and hope for a coup d'état. The revolution we mean is a paradigm shift, as described by a modest book published 50 years ago, *The Structure of Scientific Revolutions* by physicist Thomas Kuhn, which went on to be one of the most influential books concerning the history of science.[1]

His core idea is that a paradigm is an intellectual framework that makes research possible, but which at the same time bounds knowledge and results in resistance to the development of new frameworks. A scientific revolution occurs, according to Kuhn, when scientists encounter anomalies that can't be explained by the current paradigm. When enough anomalies have been collected, the discipline is then thrown into a state of crisis, until eventually a new paradigm is formed, which then gains its own followers. An intellectual battle then ensues between the followers of the new paradigm and those clinging to the old.

These insights have been so influential because they describe how the world works—instead of steady, cumulative progress, we actually experience discontinuities and periods of turmoil, uncertainty, and angst, until in the end such a crisis is resolved by a revolutionary change in worldview, in which a new paradigm replaces a now-deficient one.

> We are going through such a change today. The old way of working has become swamped by the blinding speed of change, and its bureaucratic structures cannot keep up, leaving organizations of all types struggling for breath, struggling to keep up. The new, emerging paradigm is characterized by the concepts and principles of agility, and thus the Agile Innovation Revolution is a manifesto to guide you toward your future.

It's a new world coming, and by using these techniques and methods to achieve new levels of productivity and collaboration; by empowering and leveraging self-organizing teams; by increasing insight, innovation, continuous learning, and knowledge sharing; and by forging the innovation culture, your organization can speed up its internal clock to survive and to succeed.

In these first four chapters, we will explore the genesis of this revolution:

Chapter 1, "Starting at Sprint Zero: A Better Way to Innovate," is an introduction to the current state of Agile project management and classical innovation theory.

Chapter 2, "Becoming Agile Rapidly and Painlessly," explains Agile theory and then presents the basic concepts of Agile Innovation management.

Chapter 3, "Transforming How We Work," delves into the process of transforming both innovation and execution.

Finally, Chapter 4, "Thriving in Change," reiterates why innovation is imperative for any twenty-first-century enterprise or organization.

1

STARTING AT
SPRINT ZERO

A BETTER WAY TO
INNOVATE

The software industry is turning around and radically improving. The
uncertainty, risk, and waste you are used to are no longer necessary.
—Ken Schwaber and Jeff Sutherland[1]

How is Agile changing the world?
Let's begin with a bit of background.

If you are new to Agile Software technique, then the term *sprint zero,*
as used in the title of this chapter, may not mean much to you, but for
Agile practitioners it means the initial phase of work where you sort the
project out to make sure you start properly when you're about to tackle
a large programming endeavor.

In Agile terminology, the word *sprint* refers to a one- to two-week chunk of work, during which a programming team sets specific goals for itself and then works swiftly to achieve those goals.

When work is organized this way, in small and manageable chunks, brilliant and remarkable results have been achieved in the development of large software systems, the kind that run banks, airlines, health care systems, and even governments.

This is in direct contrast to the well-documented inadequacies of non-Agile approaches, which have led to extensive delays, cost overruns, and sometimes brutally terminal failure.

Epic Software Development Failures

You would hope that the technology industry has learned its lessons by now. But you might be wrong about that. The state of Oregon, for example, recently cancelled work on its massive online health care exchange, Cover Oregon, and switched over to the federal government's system, but not before paying $134 million to Oracle for its years of work on the failed project.[2] This certainly qualifies as an epic failure, but it is by no means unique in its epicness. Studies by Standish Group published in its annual CHAOS Report regularly find that nearly two out of every three information technology projects fall short or fail entirely for various reasons, most of which are related to the use of a dysfunctional process. This is an amazingly bad performance rate across an entire industry.

But this may be just the tip of the iceberg. Numerous reports and studies have looked at failed IT projects costing hundreds of millions of dollars, and even billions, including an $8 billion failed project for the U.S. government's taxation agency (the IRS), a $170 million project for McDonald's that was completely abandoned, a $600 million baggage-handling system for the new Denver airport that never worked, and a project for the London Stock Exchange that was originally budgeted at £6 million and was ultimately cancelled after 10 years and £800 million.[3]

Hence, the intent of Agile to find a better way to organize IT projects is not a trivial exercise, but could in fact be significantly important.

The Agile movement was born in response to millions of dollars wasted in failed technology projects and the horrors of even bigger multibillion-dollar disasters. The movement was nurtured and refined by programmers and project managers who were fed up with the ignominy of it all, and who knew there simply had to be a better way. Not finding one ready at hand, they invented it.

Now Agile is being used everywhere, and for very good reasons: It works brilliantly well.

At the same time, the innovation movement has also been evolving, and it's been having a clear and definitive impact on corporate strategy, and particularly on corporate results. Companies that have mastered the art and science of radical innovation and empowered ideation, collaboration, and corporate transformation are deservedly recognized worldwide as market leaders. They've got the magic and the mojo. They've got the market share, too, and the enviable stock prices.

We could cite the usual American exemplars: Apple, Google, Facebook, Starbucks, Procter & Gamble, and Tesla, companies that seem to have taken over the world with out-of-the-box thinking, novel products, and cool new business models. There are many examples in Asia as well, such as Alibaba, Baidu, Tata Group, Samsung, and Toyota. Europe, of course, has many as well—EasyJet, L'Oréal, Unilever, and SAP among them.

We also must note the very long and sad list of firms that were not able to sustain their presence at innovation's leading edge, fell behind, and suffered greatly. Nokia (swamped by Apple's iPhone), Yahoo! (displaced by Google), Kodak (which invented the digital camera and then missed the revolution), Xerox (missed the small office and home office copier market), Lucent (once Bell Labs, the pinnacle of technological prowess), and Sony (which fell from the heights to also-ran status) are only a few of the most famous disappointments.

What causes these companies to lose their mojo? What causes their innovation efforts to falter?

One of the main reasons, sadly, is reported by various studies and research groups ranging from the Product Development and Management Association (PDMA), to McKinsey, to IBM, which variously estimate that newly launched products continue to experience astonishing failure rates of anywhere from 30 percent to around 60 percent. In other words, between three and six out of every 10 innovation projects do not succeed, and even worse, this is happening at the tail end of an innovation pipeline process that was supposed to weed out the losers and focus scarce resources only on the winners. What a sad story of disappointment, what a tremendous waste of resources, and what an indictment of the innovation processes and methods that so many companies are using, which, obviously, are not working.

There has to be a better way.

WAIT, IS THERE . . . RESISTANCE TO CHANGE?

So why hasn't every company made the shift to new and better methods?

Perhaps you've heard some of these excuses in your organization . . .

- We already have too much on our plate.
- We just can't afford an innovation [fill in the blank].
- The boss will never go for it.
- They don't pay me enough to take on this kind of [fill in the blank].
- Why should I bother? Someone else will get all the credit.
- It's way ahead of its time.
- Maybe next year.
- Too much chance of failure.
- We'll try it after the merger.
- I'm not compensated for being innovative.
- The return on investment isn't good enough.
- It's not my job.

This is only a small sampling, of course. A Google search of the phrase *idea killers* will show some amusing but also painful and poignantly biting lists, including a collection of 103 different phrases offered on a website called freedom-school.com (if the website still exists when you read this book). Based on the sheer number of sites uncovered by our search for idea killers, it would seem that the sport of idea killing is quite a popular one, and indeed we've all witnessed this in meetings at one time or another.

So, given the prevalence of idea killing, how could we be surprised that people hesitate to take on the challenges of innovation? How unpleasant is it to be humiliated in a meeting by a sly zinger, meant precisely to derail your innovative spirit? Innovation is certainly filled with risk, uncertainty, and ambiguity, and these are definitely not characteristics that modern organizations are built to love. Quite the opposite is true.

On the other hand, given the tidal wave of change across society and the economy that has occurred over the past 20 years, how can any organization's leaders believe that they can survive, or thrive, without adapting, and thus without innovating?

> Simply put, only organizations that innovate have a chance of survival in the long run. Those that don't . . . will not.

One of the major reasons for the explosion of change has been the technologies of the Information Age, a steady flow of innovations that have resulted in a miraculous 98 percent reduction of the costs of computing and communication during the past two decades.

Technological changes, however, arrive like tsunamis in wave trains, one after another, boom, boom, boom! Although what we've just experienced was certainly massive, it's important to note that it was only the first wave, and bigger ones are on the way.

Such as? Another 100-fold increase in the performance/cost ratio for computing and communications will arrive during the next two decades, bringing with it even more disruption. This is roughly equivalent to taking all the power of every supercomputer that exists in the world today and stuffing it into your video game machine; it will be like turning your smartphone into a personal genius companion.

The impact on every industry, every company, and every one of us will be enormous and unstoppable as we experience unimaginable improvements in all the products and services we use across all aspects of our lives.

In the face of this impending onslaught, how can linear thinking, shifting the blame, idea killing, stalling tactics, static business processes, or even what we consider today's best practices in innovation help us maintain our competitiveness? Alas, they can't.

What's already required today, and what will be absolutely essential tomorrow, is a rigorous process of innovation management that reliably creates better ideas, and effectively and efficiently turns those ideas into both tangible and intangible business value. This process will involve nearly every aspect of the organization, and thus everyone, so participation by the many rather than the few will be inescapably necessary. Everyone from the executive boardroom to the creative geniuses in the labs, to those who provide their deep expertise in a particular aspect of business, all the way down to the rank and file—in the real-time enterprise of the twenty-first century, innovation has to come, and will come, from everywhere. (As we will shortly discover, this brilliant innovative expertise will come from outside, too.)

It is therefore time for new thinking, focusing especially on how we can successfully redefine how we're going to survive and thrive in the face of such tremendous competitive pressures.

That's what we mean by Agile Innovation. Are you ready? Good, then let's go.

The Secret Sauce of Innovation

There's a saying among venture capital investors that "Entrepreneurs are like tea bags—you never know how strong they are until you put them in hot water."

Companies, and their leaders, are the same. In today's demanding business climate, there's plenty of hot water for everyone, in the form of new technologies and new competitors that are providing plenty of challenges for your leadership team.

Despite the grumbling that accompanies a capital crunch or eco-nomic austerity, lean years are actually good for young companies. With people, challenges can build character; with companies, it can bond teams, enhance innovation, and instill operational efficiency. Many of today's highly respected brands, including General Motors, IBM, Hewlett-Packard, Microsoft, and Apple, started during the lean times of recession. GM was founded during the panic of 1907, IBM was founded during the panic of 1910–1911, HP was born during the Great Depression, and both Microsoft and Apple were founded during the depths of the oil shock era when the U.S. gross domestic product plunged a daunting −3.1 percent.

One of the reasons that great companies emerge during bad times can actually be explained by the way learning occurs in the human brain. Neurophysiologists use the term *plasticity* to describe the brain's capacity to modify its own organization, essentially the acquisition of new skills and learning. The concept of being *plastic* refers to something that can be easily shaped, or molded, meaning that it is not fixed. Hence, the plasticity of your brain refers to its capacity to learn, to be reshaped by experiences.

Interestingly, as recently as several decades ago, most neurologists believed that the brain's neocortical areas were fixed after a certain stage of development, nonplastic. But recent studies have found that environ-mental conditions can alter behavior and cognition in adults as well as in children.[4]

This is big news. Science confirms that the adult brain is not static but that it, too, is constantly reshaped by experiences. The Agile Innovator therefore seeks to know precisely what types of experiences can be leveraged to accelerate learning, because learning is, of course, critically valuable to future success.

Stress can also be a powerful driver of change. Not overwhelming, paralyzing stress, but moderately high levels of difficulty and challenge actually do facilitate learning. Apparently, the brain admits to itself, "My survival is at risk. I'd better start paying more attention and focus on adapting, learning, and coming up with new ideas . . . right now."

> When you're at risk, when you have skin in the game, then you're motivated to focus and come up with genuinely brilliant ideas.

So our point is that starting a company when the entire economy is experiencing a higher-than-normal level of stress can lead to great outcomes over the long term. We see this clearly in the story of Southwest Airlines.

The 10-Minute Turn

When Southwest Airlines was just being established, numerous obstacles had to be overcome, not the least of which was that its basic business model was illegal in Texas, its home state, and new legislation was required for the company to commence operations. After some years of lobbying the company was within days of running out of cash when the legislation was finally passed and signed. After that, the frantic work began to create an airline.

Airplanes were bought, staff were hired and trained, advertising began, and then they started carrying passengers.

In the early days, the company operated four aircraft and served three cities, Dallas, Houston, and San Antonio, on a flight schedule that offered high frequency at a very low cost compared with its competitors. However, as is common with young businesses, it was not long before there was a cash crunch, and it became necessary to sell one of the four aircraft. This would necessitate cutting back on the fight schedule, which would in turn signal to customers that the company was in trouble and drive customers back to the competition, resulting, they realized, in a death spiral.

Consequently, it became necessary to accomplish something that was considered impossible: to fly exactly the same schedule with just three aircraft instead of four. This required that planes land, be unloaded, be reloaded, and depart all within 10 minutes, rather than the existing industry standard of 1 hour.

A SWAT team was formed and was given 72 hours—a weekend—to figure out how to do it. "Most of us, not having an airline background, had no idea that we couldn't do this, so we just did it. We knew our survival was at stake."[5]

Without the pressure of imminent collapse, the transformation probably would not have happened, and certainly not in the decisive way that it did.

Also, as it turned out, there was an additional benefit that had not been part of the initial thinking. When aircraft are flying with passengers in the seats, they generate revenue, but when they are on the ground, they do not. Putting the aircraft back in the air quickly and flying a full route schedule with 25 percent fewer aircraft meant higher fleet utilization, resulting in a better return on assets and increased profitability.

During the 1990s, Southwest flourished while many other airlines were descending into bankruptcy, and its market capitalization kept growing, too. At one point, the combined market cap of American, Delta, and United was less than Southwest's, even though in terms of revenue and assets Southwest was tiny in comparison. The 10-minute turn was a big part of its success.

The success of this innovation-under-duress also contributed significantly to the dynamic, innovative culture that pervaded the company. People throughout the organization continued to seek and to find new ways to reduce costs and expand revenues, not only at the behest of management, but often also following their own initiative.

Unfortunately for Southwest, its amazing run to greatness was interrupted by the events of 9/11, which indeed put all airlines into a defensive mode. And just at that point the other shoe dropped, in the form of rising fuel prices, which further hammered Southwest's profitability. It has not escaped these pressures, and while the innovative spirit of the company persists, its

(continued)

(continued)

competitive advantage has significantly eroded while the larger airlines have finally recovered their footing in the market and on Wall Street.

What Southwest needs, perhaps, is a new generation of innovators to figure out how to differentiate the brand yet again and further develop the once-innovative business model. But it's also possible that Southwest's performance has regressed to the mean of the industry, and its days of superlative performance are in the past. It may indeed continue to be a great company, but without a brilliant innovation or two, it will no longer be an outstanding leader in the industry.

Under stress, groups respond just as the human brain does: they react with fear, they learn . . . and they innovate. Although the initial reaction may be an immediate urge to withdraw and resist, some advanced circuitry eventually activates. As people expand their creative capacity to solve problems, this invariably strengthens their long-term skills at adaptation and agility, thus providing manifold benefits.

And even better, you, in your role as Agile Innovator and leader, can promote, facilitate, and accelerate this kind of transformation. (More about that later.)

So, back to our point about starting a business in a time of stress— this era is one of those times of stress. The exploding Information Age, and all the change and chaos it's creating, presents a real and significant threat to every organization, but at the same time it brings a remarkable opportunity for innovative thinkers to create or find brilliant new opportunities. The next Google, the next Southwest Airlines, the next Amazon.com, the next Facebook . . . they're all out there.

But when will they make their move?

It could be that the strategy used by world-class bicycle riders to win races such as the Tour de France is the right strategy: Many of the best make their move when they're climbing the toughest hills.

It works like this. In competitive bike racing, the riders begin in a single group, the *peloton*, or large mass of riders who are grouped together during most of the race. (*Peloton* is French for "ball," as in a large ball of riders.) Because most of the riders remain tightly clustered in the peloton, only the few who are in the front face the full effects of wind resistance. Those drafting behind, much like in a school of fish, the V formation of birds in flight, or an auto race, don't have to work nearly as hard to maintain the pace. Consequently, it's very difficult for the lead riders to escape the peloton, because they're already working so much harder than the other riders behind them and thus they simply lack the energy, a root problem related to the very nature of human physiology, and the factor that makes the sport of bicycle racing so very interesting.

The peloton effect is reduced, however, on hills, especially on steep ones, because everyone has to work much harder to ascend.

> Steep hills give the strongest riders the opportunity to break away and outdistance the crowd because they put all the riders under more stress.

Hence, this is the tactic elite riders work so hard to perfect, that of timing the breakaway correctly, and then relying on superior conditioning to sustain the immense individual effort required to maintain a lead so that the peloton does not catch up. The greatest riders throughout the history of bike racing have been the very few who could do this consistently.

The same principle applies to business. During stable and good times the business environment is like flat ground. Under these conditions it's very difficult for any firm to break away. The majority of contenders are content to remain in the peloton, reaping comfortable profits, conserving their energies, and waiting to pounce on any rider silly enough to try to break away. But great business executives take advantage of the hills, the major challenges, and they use those opportunities to make their break for leadership.

Hence, when there's a recession or a major economic transformation occurring, such as the current digital revolution, it can be much easier to break away from the peloton, from all those firms that are content to ride along in a large pack with everyone else.

Does this sound like an overly simplistic interpretation? A study by McGraw-Hill found that firms that advertise during a recession, those gutsy enough to make their move, receive an amplification of sales growth compared with competitors who cut back. The gain, or lift as they refer to it, was found to be an improvement of 135 to 275 percent during bad economic times for firms that stepped up their advertising. In other words, advertising packs twice the wallop during a recession (as long as you actually make it through the bad times).[6]

From Eighth Place to First

Another stunning example of stress-induced contrarian success is the story of Adolph Ochs, publisher of the *New York Times* from 1896 to 1935.

When he acquired the *Times* in 1896, it was the eighth-largest newspaper in New York City, with only about 8,000 readers. There was a brutal newspaper war going on at the time, and one of Ochs's first moves was to reduce the price of his paper from three cents to one cent. Under his astute ownership, the paper grew by focusing on high journalistic standards at a time when most newspapers were still fiercely partisan, and the *Times* developed a very positive reputation for its objectivity.

By the 1920s, readership had grown to 780,000, but then came the crash of 1929. Ochs, however, did not succumb to the pessimism raging throughout the city, and at one point he issued this memo to his staff saying that "We must set an example of optimism. Please urge every department to go ahead as if we thought the best year in the world is ahead of us."[7]

Despite Ochs's optimism, major advertisers cancelled their contracts and the paper's revenues plummeted. Ochs avoided layoffs only by opting to spend the $12 million surplus he had accumulated during the roaring 1920s, using it to pay salaries, keeping the staff intact despite steep losses. Perhaps more important, he insisted on continuing to improve the editorial quality of the paper even as advertising revenue was falling significantly.

When the Great Depression finally ended at the outbreak of World War II his strategy had paid off, as the *New York Times* had more readers than any other newspaper in the country, which meant that it could also charge higher advertising rates. Ochs's vision, commitment, and risk taking were all validated.

Ochs is a great example of a visionary leader who breaks away from the peloton by using a steep hill to put his competitors at a disadvantage. This move takes courage, perhaps great courage, as well as self-confidence, and a clear view of the future. Ochs had all three. So can you.

Remember, when you're ready to try to break away from the peloton, the steeper the hill is, the more likely you are to succeed. This is true, that is, as long as you're the best-conditioned athlete in the race *and* you have a brilliant plan.

Our hope is that this book can help you get in tip-top racing condition and inspire you to prepare and execute a magnificient plan.

Today's pervasive bad news, the news that causes everyone else to moan and complain—the economic malaise, the chaos that the digital revolution created, the impacts of outsourcing, political instability, global competition—all of these offer amazing opportunities to outdistance your competition.

> When you know how to leverage bad times and use the right amount of stress to enhance your creativity and to exploit the complacency and fears of your competitors, then you can indeed surge ahead.

BE YOUR OWN REVOLUTION

Is it your goal is to learn how to become a true innovator—that is, to develop both the personal mind-set and the organizational culture that embraces disruptive innovation as a core value, practices continuous innovation as a core methodology, and produces breakthrough innovation as a consistent output?

The key characteristic of genuine innovation is the intent to avoid copying anyone else's innovation process . . . because if you imitated somebody, you've already failed. Genuine innovation is all about finding your own voice, your own path to a new kind of creativity that you can call your own. It's all about becoming your own revolution.

As Jobs said in his now-famous Stanford commencement address, "Your time is limited, so don't waste it living someone else's life. Don't let the noise of others' opinions drown out your own inner voice. And most important, have the courage to follow your heart and intuition."[8]

So, what does it take to become your own rebellion? World-renowned dancer and choreographer Twyla Tharp shares her view, similar to Jobs, that you have to go with your gut: "Dance is a tough life . . . and a tougher way to make a living. Choreography is even more brutal, because there is no way to carry our history forward. Our creations disappear the moment we finish performing them. It's tough to preserve a legacy, create a history for yourself and others. But I put all that aside and pursued my gut instinct anyway. I became my own rebellion. Going with your head makes it arbitrary. Going with your gut means you have no choice."[9]

That's the key to success—allow your intuition and inner brilliance to lead you, like an unseen hand, to your own path, and if that's in defiance of the dominant paradigm, so be it.

It's sometimes not so easy to believe in yourself so fervently, however. Sometimes even your own education holds you back, as the sad fact is that our education system is a remnant of the Industrial Age, created in response to the need to fill factories with compliant workers. This was not an unintended consequence but a specific objective, which we know because in the 1880s, when the movement toward compulsory schooling began, some railroad magnates opposed public education for fear that they would lose the workers who did the hardest jobs, clearing roadbeds and laying track. However, the first U.S. Commissioner of Education, William Torrey Harris, reassured railway baron

Ellis Huntington that the emerging American public education system was "scientifically designed not to overeducate" but to produce socially compliant workers.

Does that sound like an extreme interpretation? We thought so, too, until we looked a bit deeper. In his book *The Philosophy of Education*, Harris wrote these highly depressing but also very influential words: "Ninety-nine [students] out of a hundred are automata, careful to walk in prescribed paths, careful to follow the prescribed custom. This is not an accident but the result of substantial education, which, scientifically defined, is the subsumption of the individual."[10] Alas.

Hence, when you set yourself on the path to become an innovator this is part of the repressive legacy that you must overcome. Although the robber barons of the nineteenth century had no desire to cultivate among their future workforce the ability to think differently, twenty-first century organizations hunger desperately for creative thinkers and innovators.

Conventional schooling, however, often remains a genius killer, which even Thomas Edison noticed: "Somewhere between the ages of eleven and fifteen, the average child begins to suffer from an atrophy, the paralysis of curiosity and the suspension of the power to observe. The trouble I should judge to lie with the schools."[11]

It is perhaps for this reason that in 2013 PayPal cofounder Peter Thiel created 20 antischolarships for promising kids. He gave 20 youths under 20 years of age $100,000 each to drop out and start their own companies.[12]

While we're not recommending that you drop out of college, we do recommend that you relentlessly strive to improve everything about everything you do, including, if you choose, Agile Innovation. In the mastery of innovation you must, at some point, let go of all the textbooks and techniques and allow yourself to innovate your own approach to innovation, and thus to become your own revolution.

Courage, preparation, confidence, and exceptional skills—all of these are vital ingredients that will help shape your success.

We hope that you'll also make great use of Agile methodology, which we'll explore in depth in the next chapter.

Welcome to the revolution!

Questions to Reflect Upon

At the end of each chapter we offer a short list of questions for you to consider as you think about the themes and topics we have just covered. We hope you find them to be thought-provoking and therefore useful.

- How do you define innovation?
- How do you define agility?
- Like emptying a teacup in Zen practice, to make space for new knowledge, what can you *unlearn* from this book?
- If you could express the innovation culture of your organization in three words, what would they be?
- Who are your innovation heroes?
- What is it that you seek to learn from this book?
- Why are you reading this book, really?

2

BECOMING AGILE RAPIDLY AND PAINLESSLY

The Agile philosophy simply asks you to work collaboratively as much as possible with your teams and client to build products with quality, shipping early and often, while learning and relearning along the way.
—Peter Saddington[1]

To take advantage of today's and tomorrow's unique opportunities, and to rise above the intense existential challenges your firm will face in the months and years ahead, it will be supremely helpful and confer enormous advantages if your operations embody the Agile essence: quick, responsive, dynamic, innovative.

You've got to learn to recognize opportunities and to act on them faster than your competitors do. Hence, in this chapter we explore what Agile means in detail, with a focus on the roots of the Agile movement and its many insights and implications for today's organizations.

• • •

The Agile Software movement was initiated in 2001 by a group of 17 programmers, who, it turns out, have significantly changed the world by inventing a new way of organizing work.

They wrote a humble but ultimately wildly influential document called "The Manifesto for Agile Software Development."[2]

Composed of four simple statements, these axioms express the core values of their system for getting work done:

We are uncovering better ways of developing software by doing it and helping others do it. Through this work, we have come to value:

- *Individuals and interactions* over processes and tools
- *Working software* over comprehensive documentation
- *Customer collaboration* over contract negotiation
- *Responding to change* over following a plan.

While there is value in the items on the right, we value the items on the left more.

From this simple vision the Agile Movement was born.

It is, in essence, a social phenomenon, and it has proved to be a brilliantly simple way to organize people to get useful work done.

Because Agile was invented to help manage software programming projects, you might logically infer that its principles and practices are useful only or primarily in technology, but in fact the relevance of Agile is much broader. Its insights and principles are applicable to nearly every kind of complex project that involves creativity and uncertainty, which exactly describes what innovation is all about.

So, what can we learn from Agile about getting innovation work done faster and better? Agile offers insights across the full scope of innovation management themes, ranging from generating ideas to managing people, monitoring progress, assigning work, tracking work, optimizing time, structuring work, defining roles, and even facilitating the process itself.

Furthermore, there are also broad implications across the full range of operational issues that relate to the way we think about and operate entire organizations.

Consequently, in the sections that follow we deconstruct the four major axioms of Agile to explore a set of social conventions that explains how individuals, teams, and entire organizations can produce the very best outcomes across an enormously broad range of work processes and roles in the domains of innovation and beyond.

INDIVIDUALS AND INTERACTIONS

The first axiom reflects the view that the success of any project depends on the quality of the team, both as individual team members and in their capacity to work effectively through efficient and productive collaboration.

Although processes and tools can provide guidance and support for competent people to work effectively, nothing is more important than solid thinking and meaningful collaboration when it comes to creating something new.

But why did the Agile creators put this axiom first?

Agile was created as a response to business trends of the 1990s, a time when business leaders focused on process improvement as a panacea for all the ills that afflicted large corporations. A new term was invented, *business process reengineering,* and the associated acronym BPR became an accepted and widely used buzzword.

The BPR approach was hugely popular, and author and consultant Michael Hammer even persuaded Peter Drucker to provide a gracious quote for the cover of his mega-best-selling book about how important reengineering was.[3]

The pendulum went a bit too far in this direction, however, as some business leaders came to have more faith in their processes than in their people, and tried to reengineer, automate, and outsource their way to ultrastability and ultraprofitability. This was a cheerful way of saying that it didn't matter if your people were marginally (or significantly) incompetent, as long as your process was correctly structured.

That path might have worked out just fine if business conditions at the time had perpetually stayed the same. However, busts followed booms, new technologies emerged, globalization accelerated, and now, two decades later, we've seen wave after wave of disruption in many industries, while the search for process-driven excellence and stability has proved fruitless. How did all those perfectly reengineered companies fare? Some, especially the innovators, did very well; many of the others, particularly the noninnovative ones, collapsed.

The harsh lesson from the reality of the rapidly changing world was, and is, that survival and success are based on brilliant new ideas and the capacity to build and market great products and services much more than on engineered and reengineered processes. Success also requires dedicated and motivated people—engineers, designers, craftspeople, managers, executives, everyone in every functional role—who are filled with genuine passion for greatness, who possess the intrinsic competence and character to pursue it resolutely, and who work in ways that allow their talents to flourish and produce results quickly.

> The Agile movement was born precisely from such passion and commitment. Its essence is the resolute determination to return power to the people with the right stuff, from whom great ideas and great steps forward can, will, and indeed, do come.

Who Has the Right Stuff?

Logic and experience both tell us that having the right people involved in the right projects is critical to success. But who are the right people?

In our view, they're the ones with both exceptional technical ability (domain expertise) *and* who demonstrate effective, self-disciplined behavior.

In his marvelous book, *Software Engineering Economics,* Barry Boehm proposes the principle of top talent: "Use better and fewer people." He summarizes: "The top 20% of people produce about 50% of the output."[4]

Hence, Agile Innovation suggests that you seek out the 20 percent and consider leaving the rest entirely behind and that you take very seriously the aphorism that in the long run, and even in the short run, every less-than-competent person on your team will end up costing you a lot of time and even more money.

This is precisely the reason that Steve Jobs had zero tolerance for any but world-class talent. There was no gray scale for Jobs— either you were A-team material, or you were a complete bozo who should be kept as far away from Apple as possible.

WORKING INNOVATIONS

The second axiom of the manifesto— *"Working software* over comprehensive documentation"—moves the effort away from the production of voluminous documentation and specifications of questionable value and instead toward rapidly and continuously delivering actual value and working software.

The conventional approach—the massive design documentation effort ahead of any actual programming—originated from management's need to exert control over massive software projects that carried commensurately huge risks. To avoid huge mistakes, project teams were tasked to spend months, sometimes years, front-loading a monumental design process. They exhaustively gathered requirements, proposed elaborate system architectures, and designed and then redesigned the associated business processes (and reengineered them). Teams worked by proceeding in a logical and linear fashion and with little to no feedback from the front line, or from customers and users.

Despite these efforts, many projects were still resulting in massive failures, such as the acutely painful ones we noted in Chapter 1.

Even when the products did work, many of the ones intended for commercialization were completed long after the market window had shut, long after customers had become frustrated to the point of fury, and long after the analysts had totally lost faith. By then, the company's credibility had evaporated.

The Agile Innovation variation on this axiom requires the change of but one single word—from *software* to *innovations* and becomes "*working innovations* over comprehensive documentation."

In the innovation world, voluminous business cases are much less useful than prototypes of actual working products or services or new business models.

Why is this?

When customers and stakeholders can see your offering, or even a prototype of it, with their own eyes, touch it with their own hands, and experience it with all their senses, then they can give you the meaningful feedback you need, enabling you to learn the most about what's ultimately going to work and what's not.

- Does it work the way you intended?
- Will it change the customer's life?
- What is appealing and not appealing?
- What needs to be improved?
- What's the next step in design?
- In development?

Learning quickly, the most quickly, is the core and essential goal, particularly in highly competitive markets where speed often wins.

Thus, do we prefer spending six months on research and program planning, followed by six more months of architecture, and then a year or two of coding, product design, or business model construction, all to find out that the product concept doesn't appeal to customers? Or are we much better off finding out what is critically important within two months?

Of course these two-month prototypes will be very rough, and a great deal of further refinement and development will be necessary before they can be considered in any way ready for the market. Because Agile Innovation is about rapid-cycle, iterative development rather than getting it perfect the first time, this trade-off makes perfect sense.

Getting quickly to working products does not preclude the need for some degree of documentation, of course. But preparation of exhaustive administrative documentation must never be a substitute for clear thinking and quick action. Documents do indeed support communication and collaboration, and they are essential tools to enhance knowledge transfer, preserve historical information, assist ongoing product enhancement, and fulfill regulatory and legal requirements. Administrative processes are also necessary, but they have a lower priority than the imperative to get something working, test it, learn from it, and move forward.

NEW HABITS

A big challenge to implementing this rapid prototype approach is overcoming the habits and practices of organizations that are accustomed to the slow route. Hence, we recognize full well that what we're proposing may require a massive shift in corporate culture.

First, an education effort will be essential. This shift from being slow and risk averse to agile and innovative definitely requires everyone to understand the new rules of the game.

Second, the structure of the work process has to be modified to emphasize delivery of incremental versions of actual products for early and continuous market testing. This means changes, possibly massive changes, to the workflow.

Third, the benchmarks and incentives for everyone's performance need to be aligned with the new objectives. Human Resources will thus be involved.

Fourth, we shift from comprehensive business cases prepared up front to incremental business cases that are developed in the same iterative fashion as the products. The structure of innovation funding therefore also changes.

These are some of the key elements of Agile Innovation.

CUSTOMER COLLABORATION

Although this principle seems to be forgotten much too often, the essential role of every business is that it must serve the needs of its customers. Because Agile Innovation focuses on learning from customers' direct experiences in an iterative development process, there is a similar shift from contract negotiation to customer collaboration, which is the third element of the Agile manifesto.

The imperative is to establish productive and collaborative relationships with individual customers (for consumer markets) and organizational customers (for business-to-business markets), because doing so enables us to learn in depth about their values, motivations, behaviors, and attitudes, all of which will help us understand how to achieve success in the broader market.

Some will tell you that the best way to discover the future is to co-create with your customers, and we think they're right. This is the core message of the Fourth-Generation R&D approach pioneered by William L. Miller in his work at Intel and Steelcase and documented in his book of the same name. Bill's insights have been quite enduring and very influential in the global R&D community for the past 20 years.

So how does Bill tell us that can we collaborate in a deep and meaningful way? Part of the challenge is that the word *collaboration* is often used as a synonym for three other words that also start with *c*: communication, coordination, and cooperation.[5]

Some clarification of the different meanings of these words may help:

- Communication is about *messages,* sharing information from one person or group with another person or group.
- Coordination is about *organizing* activities so that people can work together effectively.
- Cooperation means *working together* for a shared purpose.

Collaboration is different from each of these because it means creating something new, which means that it's inherently more complex. The act of creating, when it involves more than one person, certainly requires effective communication, good coordination, and gracious cooperation and, in fact, integrates all of these at a high level of sophistication.

In both social and economic terms, effective collaboration is essential for creating value, and at the highest level the emergence of civilization occurs only as a result of collaboration, because what is civilization but the result of effective collaboration? People form tribes, villages, teams, and corporations to accomplish things that individuals alone cannot do.

Establishing a new corporation, for example, requires tremendous creativity across many types of activities, including legal, organizational, and financial dimensions, as well as an endless stream of design decisions about product, service, brand, etc. Extensive collaboration is the norm for these activities.

Indeed, research at MIT has shown that large teams are often the most successful. MIT educator Bill Aulet tells us, "There are many misconceptions about what entrepreneurship is and what is required to be an entrepreneur. The first myth is that individuals start companies. While the entrepreneur as a lone hero is a common narrative, a close reading of the research tells a different story. Teams start companies. Importantly, a bigger team actually adds to the odds of success. More founders = better odds of success."[6] To increase the likelihood of reaching your goals, assemble a team of more innovative minds.

However, as organizations grow, the focus tends to shift from the intense collaboration and inherently creative acts of the early days toward more narrowly defined functions in narrow disciplines, or silos, where the goal is attaining and then sustaining a stable state. As we will discuss later in this chapter, the current pace of change makes this approach essentially suicidal, because the attitude that underlies a quest for stability is often anti-innovation and thus, self-destructively, anti-adaptation.

A significant element that gives power to the Agile Software methodology lies in the ways that it nurtures effective collaboration through invoking both the spirit and the effective practice of creative work. In addition, the focus on customer interaction is inherently productive, adaptive, and collaborative because interacting with customers is the fastest way to learn about their attitudes, needs, and behaviors, and also how these are changing. This is therefore a most efficient way to learn how an organization needs to adapt.

Furthermore, many specific practices that fall within Agile Methodology are, in fact, techniques explicitly intended to foster collaboration, and to overcome the barriers to collaboration that emerge in all human activities. With conflicting needs and goals, it is hardly surprising that collaboration is not always easy. A humorous quote from Adam Kahane describes South Africa before the end of apartheid and illustrates the difficulty of collaboration quite nicely. "Faced with our country's overwhelming problems we have only two options: a practical option and a miraculous option. The practical option would be for all of us to get down on our knees and pray for a band of angels to come down from heaven and solve our problems for us. The miraculous option would be for us to talk and work together and to find a way forward together."[7]

As you know, South Africans did indeed learn how to work together, and they did end apartheid without the much-anticipated civil war, leading to the presidency of Nelson Mandela and a transformed nation. Kahane describes all of this quite eloquently in his book *Transformative Scenario Planning*, and he talks at length about the process of dialog that contributed to possibility of genuine collaboration.

This has informed our work to a considerable extent, and among the techniques that we will explore in coming chapters are the scrum, the sprint, the use of visual information display, and standup meetings that all support a uniquely effective teaming environment, virtual collaboration, facilitation, and personal growth, all of which are intended to subtly and not so subtly evoke behaviors that are conducive to effective collaboration. At its best, work organized according to these methods, many pioneered by Agile innovators, becomes fun, and great results are created, each participant learns and grows through the process, and the organization adapts, all at once. Everyone wins and prospers.

ADAPT OR DIE

The fourth axiom reminds us that companies that thrive in today's turbulent economy do so because their processes and the mind-set of their leaders are proactively oriented to managing change. This axiom reflects this need, stating that "*responding to change* over following a plan" is the preferred way of working. This directly addresses the need for adaptation, both with regard to projects and throughout the organization as a whole.

Given that the accelerating rate of change is one of the most pressing external forces that is affecting every organization, behaviors based on conforming to the plan may therefore be obsolete well before they even have time to occur. This doesn't mean that planning has no utility, but it does mean that in work where there is inherent uncertainty (i.e., innovation), slavish adherence to a plan is not a success strategy.

THE CHALLENGE

So, those are the four axioms in the Agile Software and Agile Innovation contexts. Taken together, they compose a simple, concise, and powerful framework that has broad application, and as you consider the insights that Agile offers, remember that it was invented specifically to overcome a brutally dysfunctional situation, one in which talented people saw their heroic efforts squandered in massive and excruciating failures. This happened because many corporate leaders believed that the need for structure, control, and process was more important than the exercise of talent, discovery, and thoughtful adaptation.

The lessons learned bear repeating:

> The instinct to control is likely to be, in a world of increasing uncertainty, self-defeating.

Former GE CEO Jack Welsh expresses this very well: "The old organization was built on control, but the world has changed. The world is moving at such a pace that control has become a limitation. It slows you down. You've got to balance freedom with some control, but you've got to have more freedom than you ever dreamed of."[8]

In summary, Agile demonstrates that the way to achieve success is through the cleverly organized efforts of individuals in effective interactions, by producing immediate value instead of writing lengthy explanations of what you *might* be able to produce on some glorious day in the distant future, through intimate knowledge of and commitment to meeting genuine customer requirements, and as the result of a dynamic learning process. The Agile movement is thus a social construct, one that recognizes that collaboration among large groups is essential to success.

Although the Agile movement has built momentum since these axioms were first articulated in 2001, the economy has continued to evolve such that today it's no longer just individual companies that face huge challenges. Instead, in industry after industry the rate of change requires reconsidering the structure and operations of entire sectors.

For example, between 2001 and 2011, nearly all the players in the airline industry leveraged the bankruptcy code to restructure the entire industry by dumping liabilities, changing their operating models, and finding new sources of revenue. Similarly, the U.S. auto industry transformed during the depths of the 2008 recession. Telecom has fundamentally changed during the last decade, as have retail, manufacturing, and health care, and now the energy sector is in upheaval as well. In the end, no industry, and no company, will be spared from massive disruption.

Hence, this brings us to the critical challenge: Can your organization learn to transform itself into a sustainable market leader?

Yes, it can. The principles described here, and in the following chapters, are intended to help you achieve such a transformation.

Questions to Reflect Upon

- What are the unshakable beliefs in your industry that you'd like to shake up?
- If you were CEO for one day, which three things would you change?
- If you could work on only one project for a year to transform your business, what would it be and why?
- What suffers more breakdowns at your organization: products, processes, or people? Honestly, how can you fix this?
- Which parts of your job would you like to kill or eliminate?
- What would your dream testimonial from a customer say?

- What can your company offer for free that no one else does?
- How can your company's services be turned into physical products? How can your company's products be turned into services?
- If you could hire five more people, what unconventional skills would they have and why?
- Where are my blind spots?
- How do I know if my idea is good?
- How can I create a safe space for innovation at my company?
- How do I inspire innovation throughout my organization?

3

TRANSFORMING
HOW WE WORK

*Do not repeat the tactics which have gained you one victory, but let
your methods be regulated by the infinite variety of circumstances.*

—Sun Tzu[1]

Sun Tzu was the renowned fifth-century BC Chinese military
strategist and philosopher who wrote the classic treatise on
strategy, *The Art of War*. Rediscovered in the past two decades, the
concepts and principles are now standard references for business
students and especially for business leaders. Two examples of his
insights are:

1. Whoever is first in the field and awaits the coming of the enemy,
   will be fresh for the fight; whoever is second in the field and has to
   hasten to battle will arrive exhausted.
2. Do not repeat the tactics which have gained you one victory, but let
   your methods be regulated by the infinite variety of circumstances.[2]

A contemporary interpretation of this wisdom applied in the business context would suggest that continuous innovation is a major competitive advantage. For if you are not the leading innovator, how can you be first and freshest to the field?

Hence, are you going to repeat the same old operating formula long beyond its utility, or are you prepared to adapt to the profuse variety of new circumstances with new tactics (and strategies)?

The principles of Agile that we examine in this chapter will help you understand what you need to do.

The 12 Principles of Agile

The website on which the Agile Manifesto is published is a paragon of simplicity. Its home page presents the four axioms described in the previous chapter, and one of the very few links on that page takes you to the following set of 12 principles (italics added)[3]:

- Our highest priority is to *satisfy the customer* through early and continuous delivery of valuable software.
- Welcome changing requirements, even late in development. Agile processes *harness change* for the customer's competitive advantage.
- *Deliver working software* frequently, from a couple of weeks to a couple of months, with a preference to the shorter timescale.
- Business people and developers must *work together daily* throughout the project.
- Build projects around *motivated individuals.* Give them the environment and support they need, and trust them to get the job done.
- The most efficient and effective method of conveying information to and within a development team is *face-to-face conversation.*
- *Working software* is the primary measure of progress.

(continued)

(*continued*)

- Agile processes promote *sustainable development*. The sponsors, developers, and users should be able to *maintain a constant pace* indefinitely.

- Continuous attention to *technical excellence* and good design enhances agility.

- *Simplicity*—the art of maximizing the amount of work not done—is essential.

- The best architectures, requirements, and designs emerge from *self-organizing teams.*

- At regular intervals, the team *reflects* on how to become more effective, then tunes and adjusts its behavior accordingly.

These guiding principles are entirely logical and sensible, and in that respect it's quite interesting that anyone ever had to write them down. They are central to the implementation of Agile Software methodology and its goal of delivering working code, and they're also hugely useful in helping innovation teams work effectively and meet the primary goal of Agile Innovation: delivering working innovations.

INNOVATING IS LEARNING

Did you notice the degree to which all 12 of the Agile principles presented in the sidebar center on various manifestations of learning? This makes perfect sense, of course, because the essence of agility is precisely the ability to respond to new and different conditions, just as Sun Tzu recommends. Because the appearance of a new condition means it has not been seen before, then old, rote, or standardized rule-based procedures, by definition, may not work (that is, they probably won't work). Hence, in a more general way it's clear that innovation is the organized search for *the better way.*

This notion of adapting is central to understanding why Agile methodology is so effective and why it's such a good model for innovators. When we consider this on the scale of an entire organization, we're talking not only about *change* but also about a much richer and more robust process of *transformation.* Hence, the title of this chapter is "Transforming How We Work," because as an Agile Innovator this is exactly what you intend to do.

Accomplishing this will require you to discover and create an entire repertoire of behaviors that are effective at encouraging and nurturing innovation, so naturally the question arises as to what constitutes *effective.*

The effectiveness of a tool depends on the context in which it is used. For example, recognizing what practices will now be appropriate, figuring out new ways of working when old methods fail, and adopting new ways to maintain and even to accelerate momentum will depend on your objectives, capabilities, and constraints.

The metric of effectiveness in Agile is working code product per effort invested, which has the virtues of simplicity and immediacy. To define a comparable metric for effective innovation methodology requires some adjustments because the context and demands are slightly different.

Agile Innovation is oriented around three critical performance categories into which the 12 principles can be logically grouped:

- Learning how to come up with truly great visionary ideas that deliver outstanding and lasting customer value, that is, transforming the process of ideation.
- Learning how to substantiate those visions with great execution and technical excellence, that is, transforming both execution and the use of time as the critical innovation resource.
- Translating these accomplishments into actions and attitudes that support the transformation of the culture of the organization.

Taken together, these three performance dimensions—vision, time, and action—are essential to realize the promise of Agile Innovation, and by combining them into an integrated system of management, we define a pathway to create innovative new products, services, and business models effectively. Isn't this the goal of any well-constructed and genuinely productive innovation process? Of course.

TRANSFORMING IDEATION

Suppose that you'd like your organization to become the next Google, Apple, Tesla, Alibaba, WhatsApp, Facebook, or any other company that you greatly admire (and who wouldn't?). Then you'll definitely want to implement these two principles:

- Customer insight must be expanded to discover unarticulated customer needs.
- Creativity must be amplified through continuous brainstorming.

The first means that to envision truly great products and services, we have to change the way we explore, see, and think. The words are easy to say, but putting them into action requires specific types of initiatives.

The wonderful successes of design consultancies and industrial or product design firms, such as IDEO, Frog, Method, and Dyson, and the growing influence of Stanford's d.school (*d* for design) are outstanding role models. The d.school is recognized as the world's academic home of the method known as *design thinking*, an approach that's based on the premise that enabling us to see differently is a necessary first step based on a formal and rigorous process of exploration and discovery.

The principles related to design are universally practiced by the best marketers and industrial designers, who know well the importance of studying intended users of the products and services they're designing. This often involves the practices of observational field work and ethnography, which are used to detect and decode unarticulated needs, providing the basis upon which innovative products and services can be envisioned and created. Furthermore, designers know that they have to do the research *before* they start developing design concepts.

A wide range of companies have begun practicing these techniques, and their successes are legendary. Intel, for example, is using ethnography to study the behavior of the aging population, with the goal of identifying how technology can help people sustain their health while growing older. A Google search for "Intel ethnography" will take you to a fascinating video about this work (if the website is still up when you happen to be reading this book).[4]

Intel also used ethnography to study computer users in China, reasoning quite astutely that China is an important future market for its chips. Intel's People and Practices Research Group described itself this way:

Through the People and Practices Research (PaPR) Group, Intel has established an important and unique capability: to engage the techniques of social science and design in order develop a deep understanding of how people live and work. This knowledge is then translated into insights for guiding corporate strategy and technology development. The ultimate goal is to ensure that future Intel products satisfy people's real world needs.

Another leading ethnographic research firm is Silicon Valley's Point Forward. It describes its work this way:

Your customers are trying to tell you something. But they don't tell you much directly. Participating rather than spying on people changes the whole digging process. Give them a chance to weave a story and you'll find out more, especially about what doesn't work in their lives. It's the narratives that are revealing. Finding the gaps, the disconnects, the things they keep coming back to, the things that don't exactly make sense. Learning as much from what isn't said as what is. When the talk doesn't match the behavior, then you really know you're on to something.[5]

This is the art of *need finding,* often the first stage in a larger art of creating products that brilliantly satisfy tacit (i.e., latent or hidden) needs. Great designs often build on ethnographic analysis and insights and then shapes them into breakthrough products and services. In the process, great designs also differentiate the companies that produce them, for they inspire, provoke, validate, and entertain.

From Insight to Disruption

> Innovation is the act of discovering new opportunities by looking beyond commonly held views, by questioning rather than accepting the limitations that conventional wisdom imposes.

There's an often-repeated expression in American culture that says, "If it ain't broke, don't fix it." Often when people say that, however, it's a sign of habitualized lack of perception and ritualized behavior. In fact, the secret of innovation is to perfect the subtle art of seeing things that actually are broken even when everyone else thinks they're just fine. This empowers you to perceive opportunities that are hidden in plain sight, and why, after something very cool is invented, many people think, "Man, that's so simple! Why didn't I think of it first?"

It's precisely this ability to see deeper that differentiates innovators, and enables them to create new business opportunities that disrupt established business models. Both the fine arts and technological innovation train us to perceive in new ways, more clearly and free of convention. Painters develop a more accurate sense of color matching and resolution, sculptors develop an increased capability for spatial perception, and innovators start to see what's broken in everything around them, and suddenly a wellspring of creativity erupts.

From such insights, great companies are born:

- Mr. Bell invented the telephone, and although the naysayers at the time did not recognize any utility in his invention, it turned out that long-distance communication really is important to people.
- Lumberyards were doing just fine until Home Depot combined the hardware store, the appliance store, and the lumberyard and quickly came to dominate the industry.
- The 50-cent cup of coffee was fine until Starbucks found a much better business model based on providing much higher quality cups of coffee for five dollars.
- Local bookstores were doing pretty well until Amazon.com blew up the entire industry with a much better business model.
- Nokia was the runaway cell phone leader until the iPhone was introduced.

- Airlines were luxury businesses until the 1970s, when deregulation and Southwest Airlines came along to turn the industry upside down.

There are countless additional examples to cite, but you get the idea. So you must ask yourself, *Has my industry been transformed?* If so, it's likely that until that happened, things were also just fine.

Perhaps it hasn't happened you, and things still are just fine now. If so, watch out—the list of industries that have recently been through major disruption is long and growing, and it will eventually and inevitably include yours also:

Advertising
Airlines
Autos
Banking
Book selling
Encyclopedias
Manufacturing
Music
Retail
Telecom
Transportation
Etc.

Hence, the more pertinent question is: "What industries are *not* on the list?" If you can think of one, then it's probably ripe for disruption—and someone may be working on that right now. Perhaps that should be you.

THE WORLD IS CHANGED

Part of what is so fascinating about this process is that, once successful examples are revealed, almost everyone immediately grasps the significance, and the world is changed. It's a paradigm shift.

Even after the telephone was invented, quite a few people thought it had no value. Many companies, quite contented with the communication tools they already had, shortsightedly turned down the opportunity to own Alexander Graham Bell's technology, and indeed a memo written at Western Union in 1876 said, "This 'telephone' has too many shortcomings to be seriously considered as a means of communication. The device is inherently of no value to us." An enormous opportunity was missed.

This is but one example among a great many. A humorous list of similar comments is circulating on the Internet, in which very smart and famous people reveal their incapacity to imagine the usefulness or the possibility of new technology.[6]

They Said What?

On a Web page titled "They Really Ought to Have Known Better," you can view a very long list of comments that are humorous in hindsight, such as[7]:

"Drill for oil? You mean drill into the ground to try and find oil? You're crazy."
—*Drillers who Edwin L. Drake tried to enlist to his project to drill for oil in 1859*

"Stocks have reached what looks like a permanently high plateau."
—*Irving Fisher, Professor of Economics, Yale University, 1929*

"Louis Pasteur's theory of germs is ridiculous fiction."
—*Pierre Pachet, Professor of Physiology at Toulouse, 1872*

"The abdomen, the chest, and the brain will forever be shut from the intrusion of the wise and humane surgeon."

—*Sir John Eric Ericksen, British surgeon, appointed Surgeon-Extraordinary to Queen Victoria, 1873*

"We are probably at the limit of what we can know about astronomy."

—*Simon Newcomb, 1888*

Noted computer industry pioneer (in mainframes and minicomputers) Ken Olsen pronounced in 1977 that no one would ever want a computer in his or her home. (Today, not so many years later, my home has more computer chips in it than I can count.)

Lord Kelvin, quite a talented scientist, nevertheless revealed his own ignorance when he proclaimed the heavier-than-air flying machine to be impossible. He made this remark just a few years before the Wright brothers proved him wrong.

Speaking of airplanes, Sir Sam Hughes, while Canadian Minister of Defence, commented in 1914 that "The aeroplane is the invention of the devil and will never play any part in such a serious business as the defence of a nation." Marechal Foch of the French War College said something quite similar around the same time, because it was a commonly held opinion.

These are examples of people making predictions based on their experiences of the past. This phenomenon is notable only because it's so common—people constantly assume, incorrectly, that tomorrow will be like yesterday. When business leaders make this mistake, the outcomes are generally bad because opportunities are lost. Later on, when things do change, we wonder why we didn't see something so obvious and simple, something that was staring us in the face all along.

> Once you master the ability to see when things really are broken, countless innovation opportunities will unfold before you. You'll then start asking questions such as, "How could this be improved through a different approach, a new process, or a new technology? How could this be *radically* improved?"

This way of thinking, of course, goes to the roots of the very process of learning, and developing skill in this way of seeing differently becomes a core competence that you can apply over and over in many contexts. The power of your new competitive advantage will be the ability to transform insights into useful innovations by seeing the unseen (understanding unarticulated needs), translating unseen needs into innovations (anticipating future or hidden requirements), and bringing them to market.

Furthermore, these competences must be developed at every level of the organization, not only in innovation or in research and development teams. In fact, the sales staff may be the most important group, because when they understand what hidden information is, then they can recognize it and use it to become better at selling, and when they know what good design is, they're also better at selling. They have done this quite successfully at Wells Fargo Bank, a top-five U.S. financial services company.

Ethnography Achieves $20 Million in Top-Line Growth at Wells Fargo

Wells Fargo embraces the power of ethnography and uses it extensively throughout its operations. For example, the bank conducts ethnography studies at client sites to uncover innovation opportunities both internally and for its clients, and to provide feedback to improve products and services.

Steve Ellis, EVP at Wells Fargo, along with EVP Pam Clifford and senior vice president Kim Pugh, had a brilliant idea to do a technology transfer project with coauthor Moses Ma and Michael Barry, a professor at Stanford's legendary d.school.

The objective was to teach the bank's customer insight group how to do ethnographic research.

Ellis, an extreme snowboarder, explains:

> When you go heliskiing, it's about the feel of the mountain and reacting to the texture of the snow and the hill. It's about intently listening to yourself, your body, and your emotions. In business, it's about listening as closely as you can to the customer. So it made sense for us to learn ethnography, which is all about listening harder. We created a small team to literally camp out at a customer site for several days to observe how customers do their jobs and interact with financial services. I felt this would give us a fresh approach to look for ways to reshape our services.

Vice president Paul Kizirian was tapped as the first official Wells Fargo ethnographer because of his keen skills as an analyst, paired with a remarkable level of empathy. He manages client studies in the Southwest and special projects. Kizirian explains the correlation between listening harder and being innovative:

> Listening more intently to our customers was both our objective and our greatest challenge. We needed to find a way to sit with the individuals who do the actual work in a customer's back office. To do that we needed to align the interests of several key people: the bank's relationship manager, the customer firm's leadership, and the individuals with whom we'd be sitting.
>
> At first the program was a hard sell because nobody had heard of ethnography. Relationship managers were hesitant: "Let me get this straight, you want me to introduce your ethnography service to the CFO [chief financial
>
> *(continued)*

(continued)

officer]?" And customers would say, "Okay, what is that . . . and does it hurt?" So we quickly realized that we needed to give something of value to our customers so that they would let us sit and observe their back-office operations. The service was free of charge, and we threw out the notion that they would only *get what we paid for* by wrapping up each study with a top-shelf consulting deliverable. The customer received insight into how they could improve business performance; relationship managers gained a much deeper understanding of their customers; the lives of customer employees were improved; and the ethnography team analyzed the data to identify opportunity areas for Wells Fargo."

After a careful start, the group's first few studies were so successful that news spread quickly through Wells Fargo's grapevine. Before long, relationship managers were calling to put their top customers into the pipeline. Even though the group could manage only a handful of studies at a time, the service gave leadership something to talk about as not only a source of innovation but also an expression of the bank's commitment to listening to its customers' needs.

Customers and relationship managers started having deeper conversations, and although customers are, of course, never obligated to implement anything that is recommended, the team tracked results and found an unanticipated so-called side effect—every customer that participated in a study subsequently bought more solutions from Wells Fargo.

One customer, a global sugar manufacturer, invited its long-time relationship manager to its global banking roundup meeting for the first time, marking the first time that Wells Fargo had a seat at the proverbial table. Its CFO commented about Wells Fargo: "This is a bank that really cares about us and wants us to succeed—it's not just a bank, but a partner."

Listening harder has also led to many other successes. Here are two.

Ethnography Drives Better Innovation

Ethnography studies are powerful at accurately identifying previously undiscovered customer needs, and in one case, ethnographers identified an unmet need that kicked off a new service for the bank. Today, this service helps hundreds of large corporations manage billions of dollars in cash around the world.

It all started with cash managers, who log on to various portals to aggregate account information for their firms. Then they call, e-mail, and fax others within their company to ask about their cash needs and put all of that into an Excel spreadsheet to assess how much cash they will have and need in their accounts after all transactions settle at the end of the day. At one company, the CFO mentioned, "Every day we end up in both a borrowing and investing position." One cash manager who works fast within a limited period refers to this deadline as a ticking time bomb, because daily she hunts down information from 15 people across 10 subsidiaries and three time zones.

This turned out to be a very consistent need across many customers, so Wells Fargo developed a next-generation treasury management workstation. Understanding the core needs accelerated product delivery by 12 months, saved millions by avoiding unnecessary features, and elicited customer responses, including "How did you know this is what I'd need?"

Creating a simplified solution that also solved customer needs meant that the service could be offered at a price one-tenth that of the nearest competitive offering.

Empathy Drives $20 Million in Top-Line Revenue Growth

Ethnography studies also led to new ways for Wells Fargo to sell its services. After each study, customers described the shift in the

(continued)

(*continued*)

relationship between customers and the bank as "being on our side." The studies and final presentations were not a sales effort, yet customers bought services they had resisted for years, surprising the relationship management teams.

At one point the head of Wells Fargo's Treasury Management sales asked a sales consultant, "What? They finally bought what we've been telling them for years?! I've been out to meet them for two to three years and they've never budged. What was it that did it for them?" to which the sales consultant replied, "It was an ethnography study."

Because of these successes, Wells Fargo's sales leadership asked the ethnography team to train the entire sales force of more than 800 to perform scaled-down versions of ethnography studies to give Wells Fargo an edge in the market.

The key learning is that sales professionals put aside their expertise so that they could listen, have empathy, be humble, and be curious about what it's like in their customers' shoes. By doing this, salespeople were able to transform their conversations, and Kizirian estimates that for Wells Fargo's 1,000 relationship managers, empathy and ethnography drive a contribution of $20 million in new sales each year.

In summary, ethnography at Wells Fargo identifies the right problems to solve, and then innovation helps find the right solutions. It helps increase customer satisfaction, customer loyalty, and ultimately new revenue, and it is as effective with new product development as it is in the sales process.

One of the keys to success is that listening and empathy aren't just buzzwords or marketing gimmicks; they're skills practiced throughout the Wells Fargo organization. At the top, Ellis practices what he preaches—he regularly studies what the ethnographers hear from customers, and he acts on it. From the front line to the back office, it is now a cultural norm for people within Wells Fargo to listen to their customers actively.

TRANSFORMING EXECUTION:
FROM ASSUMPTIONS TO EVIDENCE

Agile Innovation is an execution-based model, not a control-based model. This means that the focus is on what you do (execution) rather than on what you are instructed to do. Hence, this approach requires inner motivation, and it's not going to thrive in environments characterized by extrinsic, hierarchical, or fear-based motivational schemes.

Agile Innovation generally takes as its goal to turn product visions into reality as soon as possible, not by developing voluminous plans and schedules to explain, defend, justify, or comply with the demands of external authorities. To enable this shift from compliance to perform-ance, consider the next three principles:

- Constructive leadership takes appropriate risks by adopting incre-mental business cases to enable faster product cycles.
- Collaboration happens more effectively in smaller Agile teams and stand-up meetings than in monolithic project teams and tradi-tional death march meetings.
- Continuous learning is implemented through retrospective reflec-tion, analysis, and feedback. We learn from what we did, and we conduct sincere and open dialog to maximize the learning.

The shift from focusing on comprehensive documentation to deliv-ering software that works resulted in programmers who were liberated to get better at execution. Programmers were freed from death-by-meetings and could instead concentrate on the thing they loved (programming). However, accomplishing this required a new social contract, a new way of organizing, because it changed the nature of accountability and coordination.

Because coordination is still necessary, the Agile movement addresses this with a single daily meeting. To keep it from becoming a long and drawn-out affair, it's a very brief stand-up session, lasting about 10 minutes. Programmers also agree to daily self-reporting of their work results, which enables daily tracking of their progress. This approach provides much greater visibility into their work, which as a side benefit is also a very effective way to identify which programmers really produce and which are the laggards.

The result is an increase in both productivity and accountability, and programmers themselves gain a welcome sense of autonomy and control over their own time.

From this perspective, which shows us Agile as the design of a *social system,* one has to admire the subtle and effective use of logic and innovation. A process that was clearly broken—writing large-scale software systems—was transformed from within by people who had direct experience with what worked, what didn't work, and what they wanted to achieve. The phenomenon of Agile and its rapid growth is, in fact, a great example of the power of design thinking to transform work and life.

Applying these same insights to the broader process of innovation leads us to these key insights.

First, moving from advance preparation of comprehensive business cases to the progressive development of incremental business cases that evolve during a project liberates innovation teams to move faster and with greater agility to deliver working prototypes, prototypes that can then be tested to gain genuine market insights.

Second, from such insights can then come much better business cases, more accurate market assessments, and substantiated revenue models. This is enabled because—and this is important—instead of working from assumptions and desires, the innovation team has accumulated real data, real prototypes, real experience, and real evidence from actual customers about their genuine behaviors, attitudes, and willingness to buy.

> The transformational shift from assumption-based decisions to the evidence-based decisions is a fundamental theme in Agile Innovation.

TRANSFORMING TIME: FROM MEETINGS TO PRODUCTIVITY

A similar transformation concerning time management is also embedded in the Agile approach. In particular, Agile is adamant that meetings are generally undesirable time wasters, so the Agile approach consistently strives to minimize time spent in meetings. (The same concept is applicable not only for software developers, but also for employees throughout the organization, particularly by using techniques that we describe later.)

Evidence suggests that typical American managers have an average of three meetings per day, and many who deal with complex and inter-disciplinary projects are often forced to handle five or six. This means that essentially the entire day is spent either in meetings, or responding to e-mail, which is, in fact, a form of virtual meeting.

What are the consequences?

For one thing, it's a very reactive work style. Proactive initiatives are rare if not impossible when we spend all day reacting to the constant stream of new inputs and requests. Where is the thinking time? It's gone.

Not long ago we worked with a manager, someone exceptionally talented and overseeing massive and steady growth, who organized her schedule into 15-minute blocks. Because her associates had access to her calendar, 9 hours of her 8-hour day were regularly booked. This was obviously not sustainable, although she had somehow managed to survive with this schedule for about three years. We suggested she take the radical step of reserving 2 hours each day for no meetings at all. Stress went down, and somehow all those important decisions still got made.

However, is reducing meeting time sufficient?

We don't think so. What's really needed is not just fewer meetings and shorter meetings but *an entirely different way of working,* and Agile shows us this is possible and desirable and can be entirely effective.

How about conducting quick stand-up meetings instead of grueling sit-down meetings?

Why not measure all work with burn down charts (please see the sidebar) that show what's been done, what remains to be done, and the rate at which progress is being made?

What work can be better organized in teams?

Can we use brainstorming sessions more productively?

What organizational functions should be shifted to project teams?

Are we engaging enough people in the role of facilitators to expedite the work?

The Burn Down Chart

A burn down chart is a tool that's typically used on programming projects to forecast completion. Simply put, it shows how much work is left to do. By plotting the work done each day, over time it tracks the progress rate and is therefore quite useful for predicting when all the work will be completed. However, burn down charts are also useful beyond software programming, because they can be applied to any project that achieves measurable progress over time. (See Figure 5.12.)

Agile methods do, in fact, require documentation, because the need for it is inevitable and it can provide significant value, so it's really a question of emphasis. Agile methodology also calls for the tracking of progress, which is certainly a necessity. The answer is to approach both from a simplified, lean, good-enough-for-now (GEFN), just-enough, and just-in-time perspective, rather than creating a massive overhead-driven bureaucracy. Streamlining compliance processes and being aware of the difference between compliance and delivery activities is the key to success.

TRANSFORMING ORGANIZATIONS

Not surprisingly, organizations exhibit behaviors similar to that of people. Corporations even age like people do. When they're young, they're willing to take risks and follow their dreams. But with age they slow down, gain weight, and become risk averse out of sheer habit, and in the name of stability and order they actively resist change and make excuses to protect their illusions. Bye-bye agility, hello stagnation.

From this we take away the awareness that an innovation culture is very hard to sustain.

To help your company maintain its youthful spirit, you can implement these three principles:

- Compensation models must incentivize business creativity and accountability.
- Comprehensive software tools and systems must be deployed to enable management and measurement of idea creation, idea sharing, and idea execution (because you cannot manage what you do not measure).
- Cultural norms must encourage leaders to inspire new behaviors and new competencies.

Because they are very smart, employees have the astute and well-known tendency to organize their work according to what is measured and what is rewarded. So, if we measure activity, then people will find ways to stay active, whether they're producing anything of value or not.

How to Appear Productive and Get Nothing Done

When I was young and working on a large construction project, I was surprised to see that a few members of the crew could spend hours looking for a particular power tool that was highly specialized and relatively scarce. In fact, they could pass nearly an entire day wandering around and asking if anyone had seen it. They didn't get much work done, but they did spend a lot of time hunting for these rare tools. It took me a while to realize that their goal was to be highly visible and appear engaged, even if they were actually doing as little as possible and accomplishing nothing of value to the larger goal of the construction project itself. But by showing up at various places on the job site, and catching the attention of the project supervisors during the course of the day, they could continue their masquerade.

Of course, this story is interesting only because it's a common behavior not only on construction sites but also in all types of organizations. Some people are adept at getting next to nothing done while maintaining the appearance of engagement and productivity. We've got to root those people out.

As we noted earlier, Agile solves the problem of measuring productivity and actual work accomplished, as opposed to busy-ness that accomplishes little or nothing, by defining specific production targets weekly and then tracking each person's progress toward his or her individual and team goals.

However, the downside of this causes Agile to be not quite so brilliant on the creative side of things. Because once people know that their productivity really is being tracked, and they get grooved into production mode, they tend to be a little less willing to pause and come up with new ideas.

This is a key issue, because *rapid prototype development* often translates to *time pressure* to kick out the next thing, even if it's not the right thing, because people strive to deliver something tangible and measurable instead of taking time to think or collaborate more deeply. One way to address this is to focus on the step between iterations, the reflection phase.

In the reflection period after an iteration has been tested, which Agile refers to as the *retrospective,* the time to look back and learn, a team should conduct an extensive and intensive debrief process. This can be conducted like a brainstorming session, where everyone adds his or her input without critiquing or judging. After this input is recorded, a second session is held to sort through the feedback and determine what direction the next iteration *might* take. The focus is on *might,* because the goal is to entertain multiple options rather than merely selecting the next idea that comes along.

In this context, Agile Innovation is therefore subtly different from Agile (Software) development. For the software developers, the kind of creativity necessary is different, because they are typically working with known tool sets and discovering clever, new ways to assemble and apply their tools, whereas for Agile Innovation we often have to discover and invent new tools. This underlines the importance of the continuous learning step, because the tool set itself continually evolves.

SUMMARY: EIGHT ORGANIZATIONAL PRINCIPLES

Throughout this chapter we've been discussing the approaches necessary to transform organizations to achieve innovation actions and outcomes. These can be summarized in eight principles, the eight Cs of transformational change:

- *Customer insight* must be expanded to discover unarticulated customer needs.
- *Creativity* must be amplified through continuous brainstorming.
- *Constructive leadership* takes appropriate risks by adopting incremental business cases to enable faster product cycles.
- *Collaboration* happens more effectively in smaller Agile teams and stand-up meetings than monolithic projects and traditional death march meetings.
- *Continuous learning* must be implemented through retrospectives.
- *Compensation* models need to be modified to incentivize business creativity and accountability.
- *Comprehensive* software tools and systems that can provide measurement and management of both ideation and execution must be deployed.
- *Cultural norms* must encourage leaders to inspire new behaviors and new competencies.

Although these principles are straightforward, it's important to remember that the task of transforming a company may be arduous. Just throwing an innovation tool into the mix or asking the chief technology officer to launch yet another innovation challenge probably isn't going to get meaningful results. The effort is a systemic undertaking, akin to growing up, quitting smoking, or losing a lot of weight. It requires a serious level of commitment and a comprehensive and systematic approach to ensure success.

Questions to Reflect Upon

Each of these eight Cs of transformational change raises questions about how to implement them. In other words, principles are great as a framework, but how can we make them work for us?

(*continued*)

(*continued*)

Customer insight must be expanded to discover unarticulated customer needs:

- What kinds of unarticulated needs might our customers have?
- How can we engage our customers so that we can gain the insights we need?

Creativity must be amplified through continuous brainstorming:

- Because our experience with brainstorming hasn't been very positive, how can we make this technique work for us?
- After brainstorming, how do we figure out which ideas are worth pursuing?
- What kinds of creativity might be most important for our organization?
- Will we need new kinds of people to make this brainstorming more effective?
- How can we leverage external resources to help with this?

Constructive leadership takes appropriate risks by adopting incremental business cases to enable faster product cycles:

- In the early stages of exploration, how can we see what might constitute an incremental business case?
- How can an innovation team present these cases to senior management effectively?
- How might these product cycles be integrated with longer-term corporate growth strategies?
- How can we determine what appropriate risks are? What metrics of risk should be considered?

Collaboration happens more effectively in smaller Agile teams and stand-up meetings than monolithic projects and traditional death march meetings.

- How can we structure and conduct such meetings effectively?
- How can we integrate and coordinate the small teams to form the larger innovation group?

Continuous learning must be implemented through retrospectives:

- Are we doing them frequently enough?
- How do we rethink the implementation of continuous learning?
- What are the shared visions at our organization?
- Does learning happen faster individually or in teams?
- How do we turn ourselves and our colleagues into systems thinkers?
- How long does it take to learn something? How can we accelerate this?
- Because one of the best opportunities to implement continuous learning is during retrospectives and innospectives, how can we design them for maximum benefit?

Compensation models need to be modified to incentivize business creativity and accountability:

- When the focus is on learning and long-term goals, how can we design metrics for compensation models?
- How can compensation be tied to explorations where the short-term outcome would be considered a failure, yet the long-term benefit, for example in terms of learning, was significant?

(continued)

(*continued*)

- What happens when compensation models result in certain exceptional individuals receiving much higher pay than their supervisors, perhaps even a couple of levels higher?
- How can we find the appropriate balance of compensation and rewards for the entire team and for exceptional individuals?

Comprehensive software tools and systems that provide measurement and management of both ideation and execution must be deployed:

- What metrics will be most useful for our organization?
- How can the performance of one company be compared with that of another in the same industry?

Cultural norms must encourage leaders to inspire new behaviors and new competencies:

- How can we inspire our leaders to change their behaviors?
- If cultural change is a necessary prerequisite for innovation, how do we raise that as a priority within our organization?

4

THRIVING IN CHANGE

Capitalism is by nature a form or method of economic change and not only never is but never can be stationary.

—Joseph Schumpeter[1]

Strengthening your organization's innovative capacity directly affects its viability and sustainability. In fact, it may be the key to the very survival of your business, and it's so important that management guru Peter Drucker once said, "Every organization needs one core competence: innovation."

> Mastering innovation is a strategic imperative.

Strengthening innovation capacity also leads to higher performance, as common sense tells us that innovative firms outperform their competitors. But is this really true?

In 1999, the consulting firm Arthur D. Little conducted a comprehensive study of 338 of the Fortune 500 and found that the firms rated as highly innovative produced returns to shareholders that were nearly *four times greater* than those produced by the least innovative firms over the period from 1987 to 1996. That bears repeating:

> Highly innovative Fortune 500 companies return four times more value to their shareholders.

Hence, if investors could know in advance which firms will be most innovative, they would buy those stocks, creating an upward spiral of value creation. Those going up will accumulate more resources to leverage. At the same time, investors would dump the laggards, and a downward spiral would then enter into play for the noninnovators. Those heading down would have progressively fewer opportunities, and they'd then slip further behind, regressing down the slippery slope from which escape becomes almost impossible. At the bottom of the slope is only acquisition, bankruptcy, or a miracle.

So what do you do if you're not an innovator?

Start studying, start experimenting, and learn super fast—because the future of your firm, like every firm, is determined largely by its ability to innovate effectively. Is innovation an absolute requirement for survival? You must decide what future you want, and what means you'll use to get there.

DEFINING THE INNOVATION PROCESS

Let's step back for a moment and start with a definition: What exactly is the innovation process?

> Innovation is the art of creating new products, services, and business models that address needs that either are not well articulated or do not yet exist. (Thus, they are generally hard to envision.)

How do we get there?

As we discovered in the previous chapter, the search for hidden knowledge about what's necessary and what's not working is a very early stage requirement of innovation effort, and this process is inherently one of trial and error, question and experimentation, uncertainty and discovery. It's also a bit messy, squishy, mushy, chaotic, unruly, disruptive, provocative, tumultuous, wild, and nonlinear.

This is what's necessary.

Consequently some executives look at the amazing new ideas and products coming from companies such as Apple, Google, or Procter & Gamble, and see only sorcery. Noninnovators often think to themselves, "We could never do that. We don't have the talent or the resources like those companies. We could never do that kind of magic."

However, the truth is that innovation successes don't come from proficiency with arcane magical arts. They are direct outcomes of a disciplined innovation process, a process so familiar to leading companies that it eventually becomes embedded into the core of the organization. These companies are quite willing to engage in the messy, squishy, mushy exploration of possibilities, and they do so in a way that is systematic.

This is the essential paradox of innovation management: The system and the mess are not mutually exclusive; they're entirely compatible! And further, success at innovation depends on *both*.

The systematic approach applies the best tools, including the very best ways to create and manage the inevitable mess, and it addresses the bigger patterns and issues of change in the external environment, thus enabling you to manage the large-scale risks and opportunities facing your organization.

Such a system elevates innovation to what it really should be, a strategic asset.

The results will be evident and powerful: dramatic improvement in your innovation practice all the way from the initial strategic perspective to the heart of the process in the creative endeavor, then to the marketing and sales processes at the end, where you reap the rewards for your efforts in the form of competitive advantage, brand enhancement, revenue growth, and profits.

Another outcome will be the culture of innovative thinking that pervades your entire organization, leading to a virtuous cycle of better skills leading to improved outcomes, leading then to more resources and skill enhancement, etc. Hence, our point is that a systematic approach to innovation requires that change flows simultaneously top down *and* bottom up.

Orchestration from top down addresses large-scale risks in a way that does not hamper innovation capacity, and diffusion from bottom up motivates and trains to yield a significantly enhanced innovation skill set. However, both sides also have to give up something—leaders give up micro-managing innovation and relying too much on process, and everyone agrees to greater visibility and accountability in their workflow. In essence, this approach is like "gene therapy" that reprograms the organizational culture by taking root in everyday behavior and work processes.

CHANGE AND MIND-SET

There are two primary challenges confronting companies that are slow to adapt.

The first is the accelerating rate of change in today's globalized, real-time marketplace, which enforces a brutal pace that has put many organizations on the defensive as they struggle to cope. The second is the mind-set of their top managers.

About the first—change is occurring differently today than it did in the past. Most large companies 20 or 30 years ago were buffered from external impacts by their size, and they could withstand many challenges just by using their sheer bulk to block new entrants from accessing the market. They could easily outspend newcomers on marketing, follow competitors' successful innovations with clones and copies, tie up distributors with exclusive agreements, slash prices below cost, and use economies of scale to outflank and outmuscle competitors. These were very successful tactics.

But today, many of these tactics simply don't work anymore, and consequently the strategic vulnerability of all firms, large and small, is increasing. Nimble newcomers have learned to use speed as an advantage, and they can use the Internet to make a tiny start-up look as big and competent as IBM or Wal-Mart. They can outsource any function, from finance to human resources to manufacturing and distribution, so miniature firms can suddenly have a global presence.

Because they can communicate with anyone, anywhere, start-ups can also leverage interconnections between organizations in business ecosystems, resulting in complexity that is also unprecedented.

Big companies do all that, too. They usually just do it much more slowly.

The second point is about mind-set. When the role of management is understood to be managing the business, then 99 percent (or more) of the effort goes to daily operations, sustaining profitability, and maintaining market share. This is a significant task, and it's enormously difficult.

Unfortunately, the day-to-day mind-set of managers still causes them to look backward to the past for guidance into the future, and in this era of accelerating change, this approach cannot succeed. Instead, successful leaders are now forward-looking agents of transformation for their companies. Reflecting this awareness, a recent McKinsey report opens with this line: "Anyone who pulls the organization in new directions must look inward as well as outward," which makes the point excellently. By "inward" they mean their own ideas, attitudes, and values, their mind-set in other words, and authors Nate Boaz and Erica Ariel Fox go on to note that "McKinsey research and client experience suggest that half of all efforts to transform organizational performance fail either because senior managers don't act as role models for change or because people in the organization defend the status quo."[2]

Seventy years ago the economist Joseph Schumpeter described the overall capitalist system as "creative destruction" and he pointed out that the natural behavior of capitalist systems brings revolution not as the result of undefined external factors, but from within, because of the very nature of competition. We began this chapter with the following quote, which bears repeating: "Capitalism is by nature a form or method of economic change and not only never is but never can be stationary."[3]

A focus on managing the business is a focus on the need and desire for stability, and if 99 percent of everyone is worrying about that, then who's getting ready for tomorrow? In the context of the accelerating change in today's global economy, the relevance and significance of this observation is much greater now than in Schumpeter's own era.

Thus, the mind-set problem is largely a matter of focusing on the wrong things.

> Military leaders are familiar with this tendency; they call it "preparing to fight the last war." Such strategies, even when fully implemented with rigor and discipline, consistently fail.

Examples are everywhere in military history: armored knights slaughtered by the longbow, Napoleon's mobile armies that overwhelmed Europe's static approaches to warfare, France's own Maginot Line (a twentieth-century monument to nineteenth-century thinking), the Polish horse cavalry that rode out to face the Nazi Panzer tank divisions, or civilian aircraft hijacked and turned into guided missiles. The histories of warfare and of business are essentially tales of innovations that rendered past strategies ineffective, ineffectiveness that occurs largely because leaders are seeking stability and profitability and failing to assess the rate of change adequately or to foresee the devastating impact that innovation could have on their own organizations.

Heavyweight champion Mike Tyson said it this way: "Everyone has a plan till they get punched in the mouth."

Regrettably, the faulty misdirection of focus is usually evident only in hindsight—when nations, wars, lives, fortunes, market share, jobs, or stock value have already been lost. For managers as for generals, perfect clarity about the past may be a great lesson, but how does that advise us to deal with future challenges? We need to have an effective way to look forward into the future, and to create it.

This is the goal of innovation and the focus of the Agile process.

Transforming IBM

When Louis Gerstner was CEO of IBM and charged with turning it around from its near-death experience of 1991–1992, he was confronted with a collapsing market and a company that had been so tremendously successful in the past that it

(continued)

(*continued*)

suffered from a mind-set of entitlement. In discussing the enormous strategic decisions required to transform IBM's business model and return to profitability, he remarked, "The hardest part of these decisions was neither the technological nor economic transformations required. It was changing the culture—the mindset and instincts of hundreds of thousands of people."[4]

Given the unpredictable nature of technology-driven competition and the resulting accelerated change, the focus on profitability of existing operations inevitably leads to a dangerous trap. Organizations will be vulnerable to fundamental change—disruptive innovation—introduced by competitors willing to take big risks, who occasionally win big.

A study by Richard Foster and Sarah Kaplan calculated the historical death rate for S&P 500 companies and found that, at the current prevailing rate of mortality, a full 75 percent of those on the list for 2010 will disappear by 2020.[5] That's 375 out of 500 companies that will disappear through merger, bankruptcy, acquisition, or being broken up and sold in pieces. In other words, if your company is currently listed in the S&P 500, the chances are about three in four that it will disappear before 2020.

Does this statistic alarm you?

We hope it does. It should; we see this as a rousing wake-up call, a call to action.

Unfortunately, the vast majority of those at risk will fail because they are not able to adapt with agility, resulting in the slow but inexorable decline in value of their products or services. In other words, within a decade, more innovative firms will dispatch the walking dead.

This is, of course, not really news. For example, a recent McKinsey survey revealed that more than 70 percent of respondents believe that innovation will be one of the top three growth drivers in the coming three to five years.[6] The report was published more than six years ago, and the only change is that now innovation is the number one driver.

The companies that survive, endure, and thrive will be those whose leaders are flexible, adaptable, foresighted, courageous, and yes, keenly innovative. They will produce more than just short-term, incremental, market share–preserving, new products, because they will be adept at the development and introduction of disruptive breakthroughs that tilt the market in their favor and which will become the basis of future profitability.

The Structure of Revolution

The history of scientific revolutions as described by Thomas S. Kuhn, and mentioned earlier at the beginning of Part 1, illustrates the same dynamics.[7] Kuhn has shown quite convincingly how the field of physics gradually shifted from one organizing paradigm, such as Newtonian physics, to the much different model proposed by Albert Einstein. Such a paradigm shift is often a prolonged and traumatic episode through which generations of specialists gradually come to understand that the flaws in their thinking are more effectively addressed with a new and much different model. Many of them resist and fight tooth and nail against the new paradigm, defensively fixated on their preferred models as if their lives depended on it.

The situation with managers and executives is not so different. When an executive holds on to the current dominant paradigm and resists change, that mind-set becomes a tremendous obstacle to nearly everything that's necessary to build a successfully innovative company. Those who are fixated on the ways of the past feel threatened by change, and sometimes they are unable to confront their fears effectively. The psychological trap becomes a much more wicked market trap for the company.

A FRAMEWORK FOR TRANSFORMATION

So, how shall we now proceed? What principles and practices enable transformation?

Progress in any field requires the development of a framework, a structure that organizes the accumulating knowledge and unifies the key discoveries into a set of principles. Law, government, science, technology, business, and medicine have all developed such frameworks. Each field moves forward as new insights emerge that enhance the depth and effectiveness of the principles, which then translate into improvements in practice.

Broadly speaking, however, humanity's understanding of innovation hasn't progressed nearly as much as our understanding of law, for example. This is largely because the pursuit of innovation as a systematic, manageable discipline has been part of human culture for only the past couple of hundred years. Before that, it appears that we progressed slowly, through random trial and error, and in the course of doing so we generated a great number of myths and mistaken beliefs, such as the belief that innovation is magic, when, in fact, it is the outcome of a rigorous process.

Today we're still separating the myths and magical notions from the hard realities of reliable methodology. But we are making significant progress, and it's evident that a broad innovation framework will be eminently useful to all types of organizations, large and small, public and private. We have developed and documented such a framework in a previous book, *The Innovation Master Plan: The CEO's Guide to Innovation.*

The framework described there addresses and organizes a very broad range of issues, from the 30,000-foot perspective of strategy to the nuanced techniques of creative thought and everything in between.

> We are learning how to create and manage a rigorous innovation effort and how to nurture the internal culture and bring forth the creative spirit from the people in our organization. We are also developing tools that greatly facilitate these efforts.

THE INNOVATION MASTER PLAN

Our purpose here is not to repeat the detailed argument of that book, but to provide you with a quick overview, because elements of the same

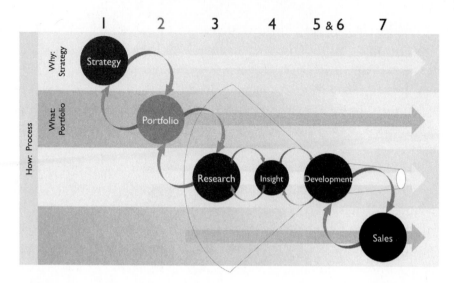

Figure 4.1 The innovation master plan, a comprehensive approach to innovation management

Source: Reproduced by permission from Langdon Morris, *The Innovation Master Plan: The CEO's Guide to Innovation* (Walnut Creek, CA: Innovation Academy, 2011).

framework, particularly the pursuit of speed, will appear shortly in our detailed description of the Agile Innovation process.

The purpose of an Innovation Master Plan (see Figure 4.1) is to guide you, your team, and your entire organization through the complexities of the innovation process during the journey from ideas created through sales, revenues, and profits achieved. Your plan is likely to follow the simple structure based on five critically important questions about innovation in your organization:

- Why innovate?
- What to innovate?
- How to innovate?
- Who innovates?
- Where to innovate?

The question of "Why innovate?" is really a question about strategy and about the linkages among your strategy, the innovation process, and the innovative results you intend to achieve.

The question of "What to innovate?" is about designing and developing your innovation portfolio, which we will explore in detail in Part 2, Chapter 6.

The question of "How to innovate?" will engage you in designing the innovation process that you're going to use to identify, create, and develop the ideas that will become precisely the future innovations that you're setting out to transform into reality. We describe this from the Agile perspective in Chapter 5.

The question of "Who innovates?" is a matter of identifying who's going to do the work of research and development that is the deep core of the innovation process. More broadly, it also concerns your organization's culture and the process of developing and adopting the habits and practices that continually favor and support innovation in all its wonderful manifestations, from the simplest incremental ideas, to the most complex potential breakthroughs, to the new business models and new ventures, which together will compose the innovation portfolio that you'll be working on tomorrow, next year, etc. Culture and the engagement of everyone is the topic of Chapter 7.

The last question, "Where to innovate?", deals with the infrastructure, support systems, and tools that will be used to enable everyone in your organization, and many people outside of it, to participate effectively in your innovation process. Chapters 12 and 13 of Part 3 explore this in detail.

So we're now ready to get into the nuts-and-bolts details of the Agile Innovation framework with the intent of giving you the insights to design your own innovation revolution in your own organization, all to accelerate the process, reduce risk, and expand engagement.

Questions to Reflect Upon

- How well do we understand the implications and the applications of new technologies?
- How well have we been doing at anticipating change?

- How does our research work help us target the right innovation opportunities?

- Are we using a systematic innovation framework to guide our work?

- How are we finding fruitful directions, opportunities that we had not recognized before?

PART II

MANAGING
INNOVATION FOR
TOMORROW

Agile Innovation is both a rigorous discipline and a pervasive and empowering mind-set. It also proactively addresses twin uncertainties: those inherent in the changing external world, and those inherent in the innovation process itself.

As a pathway that leads to mastery of a new philosophy of innovation in business, Agile Innovation fulfills the three essential performance dimensions that are central to all innovation efforts:

1. It significantly *accelerates the innovation process,* bringing positive results more quickly than would otherwise occur. Speed matters, and Agile Innovation provides a significant speed advantage.

2. It *decreases risks of the innovation effort.* Risk is a huge issue and obstacle, and Agile Innovation reduces it.

3. It *engages the entire organization,* tapping into the very best ideas and evoking the creative spirit that is present in people serving in every role and every corner, thus *building the innovation culture* in a deep and enduring way. Innovation thrives best when there's strong input from many people not just for the sake of quantity, but more importantly because they do create high-quality and

meaningful ideas, and they share them. Agile Innovation inspires, enables, and empowers creativity and sharing.

These are ambitious objectives, and they're enormously challenging. Any organization that achieves them rapidly ascends to the highest levels in innovation rankings.

This is the type of leadership to which you and your organization should aspire.

The discussion in the next chapter focuses on the first of these three imperatives, speeding up the process of innovation, because this is where the Agile Software development approach has the most to offer to the innovation effort. We then address the second and third imperatives in the subsequent chapters.

5

ACCELERATING SUCCESS

I feel the need. The need for speed!
—Maverick (played by Tom Cruise) in the movie *Top Gun*

THE NEED FOR SPEED

Because we pursue innovation in a competitive marketplace, speed matters. The faster that great ideas get to market, the faster we earn money, build our brand, and extend our reach into the future.

Weeks or months of delay can be hugely costly; longer delays can even be fatal, for the firm that gets the right product to market quickest is in the best position to gain significant advantage.

There may be little or no market share left for the laggards.

Technology Markets Are Winner Take All

In many markets, particularly those that have a significant technology component, market structures tend toward a winner-take-all dynamic. Many business strategists believe that the number of winner-take-all markets is increasing because technology advantages can create massive barriers to competition. In the past, for example, a wide variety of local stores existed within a given geographic region, but today because of better transportation, logistics, telecommunications, and information technology systems, leading firms can extend their lead, effectively locking local players out. Hence, selling books has transitioned from local bookshops to Amazon.com and its Kindle, the clear winner in digital book readers.

Another example of a winner-take-all market is in the rise of large multinational firms, such as Wal-Mart. These firms leverage their massive scale to gain many advantages over local competitors, thus capturing a large share in almost every market they enter. With their volume purchasing they can negotiate better prices from suppliers, and put in place even better technology that smaller firms simply cannot afford. This becomes a self-reinforcing spiral, and only a fundamental shift will dislodge them.

However, being first is not a guarantee of success. When the first mover doesn't quite get it right, and is not able to capitalize on its advantage, it leaves an opportunity for later entrants to compete effectively. These firms then may gain what is called a second-mover advantage by learning from the mistakes and omissions of the pioneers. So, if you're the second mover, you're desperately hoping that the first makes an error, while the first is working furiously to patch every gap and occupy every niche to prevent second movers from encroaching.

Whether a given firm comes first or second, eventually consolidation in the industry is likely to occur, and then the strongest and deepest firm generally wins. Technology has shifted many market structures to winner take all, and in the biting words of journalist Dana Blankenhorn, when that occurs "there is one winner and everyone else needs to find something else to do."[1]

Until a new generation of technology is invented, that is, and we start all over again.

In the past, firms including IBM and Microsoft were well known for coming second to the market (see the sidebar "Technology Markets Are Winner Take All"), practicing an innovation strategy known as fast follower, wherein they would pay close attention to innovations coming from their competitors and then use their vast capital and market power to copy the winning innovations quickly and overwhelm the pioneers. However, the risks of following are now much greater simply because the market is evolving so much more quickly, and the likelihood of being entirely left out is far greater. Just as hobos don't try to hop on fast-moving trains but they can easily catch a ride on the slow ones, faster markets are hard to catch up with.

Therefore, the first of the three principles we'll explore in Part 2 is the need for speed. We'll discuss how Agile accelerates software development and then extend this thinking to the broader process of innovation management. Because while you may have assumed that Agile is only about technology and software programming, as we noted earlier, Agile is really a *social* system, a way of organizing people to accomplish complex work fast and effectively. Hence, it's an ideal model for the broader innovation effort.

THE SCRUM AND THE SPRINT

The essential work process of Agile Software development takes place in a teaming work activity that's called a *scrum.* This is a core element, an approach to organizing people to achieve goals that require highly coordinated teamwork.

Agile borrows the notion of the scrum from rugby, where it refers to an ordered formation of players who lock arms, put their heads down, and push forward against players from the other team who are doing the same thing. Scrums occur frequently during a rugby game. Superior teams are those that show great strength in the scrum, pushing forward against enormous obstacles, that is, the other team that's pushing back nearly as hard.

Figure 5.1   A rugby scrum showing eight players from each side pushing against one another for control of the ball

Figure 5.1 shows two teams engaged in a scrum, and the power and rigor are entirely evident. Exactly the same eight players are in exactly the same positions for both the white and the dark uniformed teams, pushing as hard as they can. We see both the structure, because the formation is regular and fixed, and the sheer physical force of 16 large men engaged in full exertion.

Similarly, the word *scrimmage,* derived from the word *scrum,* describes a basic concept of American football, where the meaning is the same. In American football the starting point of every play is the line of scrimmage, where players from both teams line up, and upon the start of the play they crash into each other with full force (and a great deal of protective equipment, including helmets and shoulder pads).

Hence, a scrum is a useful metaphor for software development when a team of programmers put their heads down, so to speak, and blast their way through composing a given module or section of code, all the while striving toward a final product that may be larger and much more complex.

One of the key features that distinguishes Agile Software scrums from traditional, long-cycle, large-scale software development projects is that scrum teams organize their work into short segments that generally last two to four weeks. The scrum is thus one short element of a much longer process, a single play in the midst of a longer contest. This is long enough to make meaningful progress, but short enough to sustain clear accountability, maintain focus, and identify specific deliverables that are already meaningful.

Each short segment is termed a *sprint*, a short footrace that's a contest of speed, compared with a longer race, such as a 10,000-kilometer (10K) run or a marathon (26.2 miles), which is a test of endurance.

Although mega-software projects are very much like marathons, or even 100-mile-long ultramarathons, Agile sprints consist of small, digestible portions.

Because Agile projects are broken into these two- to four-week sprint increments, a typical large project may require dozens of sprints to reach completion. Hence, instead of running the marathon in one continuous race, it's like a marathon composed of 26 one-mile-long races or 104 quarter-mile sprints.

What are the advantages of that?

First, because a given chunk of work is expected to be completed in a series of sprints, the work process can more readily be controlled. At the end of each week, progress is assessed and plans are adjusted based on whether the scrum team got to its goal for that period.

This ensures constant feedback, which allows the opportunity to fine-tune the process from sprint to sprint:

Is someone on the team doing exceptionally great work? What are secrets that the rest of us can learn from that person?

Conversely, is one team member lagging consistently behind? In that case, what do we need to do to improve his or her proficiency?

When the results of each sprint are there for the entire scrum team to see, fully evident, fully documented, and fully transparent, procrastination will be intolerable, and peer pressure becomes more objective.

Second, teams can track their progress sprint by sprint and readily assess incremental progress toward the final goal. This is important because, in classic (and failed) software projects, programming teams often fall into the trap of telling themselves that they'll "make up the lost time later in the year (or next year)." In reality, these projects tend to fall further and further behind. Ironically, the underlying complexity and massive project management overhead obscure these realities, reducing accountability.

Third, each unit of completed work is done in collaboration with clients or customers, so the scrum team receives valuable feedback directly from actual end users while working collaboratively with them. The Agile Innovation process optimizes learning, and unpleasant surprises are reduced or eliminated altogether. No client of an Agile project was ever shocked and dismayed by the results because he or she was right there with the team, step by step.

Doesn't this sound like the way innovation projects should be pursued?

Although the variety of activities in a typical innovation project will be far greater than in an Agile programming effort, the principles and the practices are entirely consistent.

Hence, Agile Innovation projects can also be broken into multiweek sprints, during which specific deliverables are planned and expected to be accomplished, and the work is managed accordingly.

We'll get into more detail about the variety of roles and functions in an innovation project below, but first let's take a look at the overall picture of the sprint.

THE AGILE SOFTWARE SPRINT

Every Agile Software developer is familiar with Figure 5.2, the basic diagram that depicts the two- to four-week sprint process.

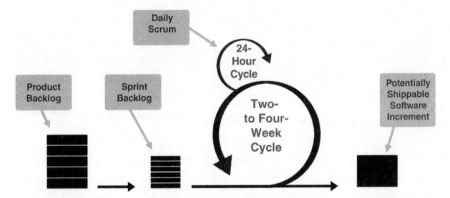

Figure 5.2   The Agile sprint is generally a two- to four-week cycle of work by a programming team, represented by the big looping arrow. The entire cycle is then divided into 24-hour work segments. From the left, the product backlog consists of the stories that need to be implemented in software code. A number of these are selected and placed in the current sprint backlog, which is the work that will be completed during the current two- to four-week sprint. The result of each sprint is usable software, shown as a potentially shippable software increment, meaning that it is completed working code. The cycle is iterated until complete, which is when the product backlog is empty.

The six elements are:

1. The *product backlog*, which is the master list of all the work to do. This list is developed at the very outset of a project.

2. The *sprint backlog*, which is the targeted list of our immediate work. The project management team carefully selects it.

3. The *two- to four-week sprint cycle* itself, where the team accomplishes work.

4. The *24-hour scrum cycle*, where work is done and accounted for daily.

5. The *daily scrum meeting*, where the team maintains alignment throughout the sprint.

6. The *potentially shippable products*, incremental results that are assessed against goals, and of course, assessed from the

(continued)

(*continued*)
customer's perspective, to determine the degree to which they meet or exceed expectations. After the assessment, the product backlog is then revised as needed, and a new sprint is initiated.

This approach is designed to optimize demonstrable progress in software development projects, and because the product backlog can be revised at any time based on new information or because of changing external factors, this system also responds to change with agility.

INNOVATION AND EXTREME SPORTS AT WELLS FARGO

We met Steve Ellis of Wells Fargo a few pages ago. He manages the bank's wholesale banking technology, is also an avid heliboarder, and consequently likes to describe innovation in terms of extreme sports. When we asked him about Wells Fargo's secret sauce for extreme innovation, he said:

There are three basic tenets that we operate from:

First, innovation takes the belief that there is *something* in the idea that will add value for customers, even when a traditional ROI model would tell you to not pursue the idea.

Second, innovation is more about hard work than thinking up the idea; it's more about execution than inspiration.

And third, it's important to get active and rapid feedback during the process. It's also important to remember this: innovation is a bit like snowboarding or riding a motorcycle in that it's safer when you do it just a *little* faster than your comfort zone. A little speed reduces the chances of falling off.

You actually have a much lower probability of falling off than if you go as slow as your fear tells you to. Just a little faster, and you'll also find that you'll learn faster as well.[2]

Active and rapid feedback throughout the process enables us to get past the hype that often surrounds a new idea and learn to see how it really works. This begins, inevitably, with a significant amount of uncertainty, and how you handle that phase of the work sets the stage for the profound learning that can follow.

UNCERTAINTY

A key principle embedded in the Agile Software sprint that is entirely relevant to innovation is that the programming problem being addressed may not be fully understood or defined at the beginning. Innovation projects constantly deal with this sort of uncertainty, and the more ambitious and far-reaching the goal, the more likely it is that the problem itself may remain undefined, and sometimes *undefinable*, even as progress is being made.

By learning more and more about a problem through multiple iterations and progressive levels of detail, innovation teams create a learning system like the Agile sprint.

Technically, in fact, the problem is not being *defined,* but rather it evolves into creation. Thus, the first major act of any significant creative process is precisely *the creation of the problem.*

The process of solving problems through the act of design begins with vision,

A compelling vision, well expressed, is one of the most powerful of forces in human society. It sets up the contrast between what is and what could be, and in this contrast emerges a driving force, a compelling motive. This contrast is the source of creative tension, the energy that drives visionaries, whether they are artists or scientists or entrepreneurs or educators; missionaries or presidents or revolutionaries or parents . . . If you do not somehow take action to fulfill the vision, it will remain in the vague and distant future, inconsequential. But once the quest for fulfillment is begun, this vague future is given distinct shape and form in the present and offers possibilities that once were only dreamed of. In this regard
(continued)

(*continued*)

the fulfillment of a vision transcends time. The vision and its contrast with the current condition has, in effect, created a problem.[3]

Because customers are essential participants in both the Agile Software and the Agile Innovation processes, the results of sprint efforts are tested rigorously and repeatedly in real-world environments where customers experience what we offer, evaluate, and give feedback. Hence, awareness and knowledge of what works, as well as what does not work, gradually replaces uncertainty. Both types of knowledge are highly valuable.

With this in mind, let's now look at the comparable Agile Innovation scrum, the IdeaScrum.

THE AGILE INNOVATION IDEASCRUM

Figure 5.3, shows the Agile Innovation approach, which is nearly the same as that for the Agile Software process described above. Here we'll highlight a few key differences.

Agile Innovation accelerates and transforms the process of moving from ideas to working prototypes and associated business cases. For this part of the discussion, we're assuming that there is already a large collection of great ideas to work on in the organization's Idea Backlog.

Later in this chapter we'll describe where those ideas came from and how they got into the idea repository, through both a structured, proactive ideation process and through spontaneous innovation whereby we capture the best ideas of people as they arise.

The point to be made now is that at this stage of the process, given the high degree of uncertainty inherent in innovation projects, three possible outcomes could result from our development work:

1. We will bring the completed ideas-become-innovations to market if the feedback we gather shows that they constitute useful value propositions for customers.

2. We will discover some ideas to be lacking in some fundamental aspect, such as insufficient market need or demand, or insufficient functionality. These we will set aside and archive, and we'll

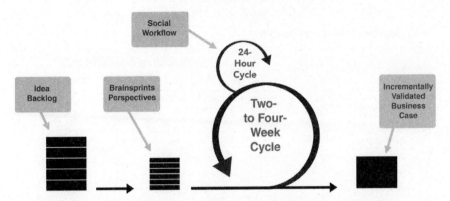

Figure 5.3 The Agile Innovation IdeaScrum is visualized as a two- to four-week cycle of work by an innovation team, represented by the big looping arrow. The entire cycle is then divided into 24-hour work segments. From the left, the idea backlog is the full set of ideas from which one is selected as the topic for the IdeaScrum. The brainsprint perspectives comprise the bulk of the work that will be completed during the current two- to four-week scrum. Each brainsprint could take as little as a day or as long as a week via online collaboration, or from less than an hour to a few hours in a physical brainstorming session. The result of the IdeaScrum is an incrementally validated business case, meaning that our understanding of the idea and its supporting business case have advanced significantly because of the scrum process. The process can be iterated if the business case needs to be more fully defined, and could apply different perspectives in subsequent iterations for depth and completeness.

move on to other ideas, having learned all we can from this experience.

3. Some ideas will remain promising, but the timing for their introduction seems to be poor. These we will set aside for consideration another day.

> There are only three possible outcomes: success, abandonment, or postponement.

The problem, of course, is that at the outset, we don't know what the fate of a given idea will be. Those we consider at the outset to be best

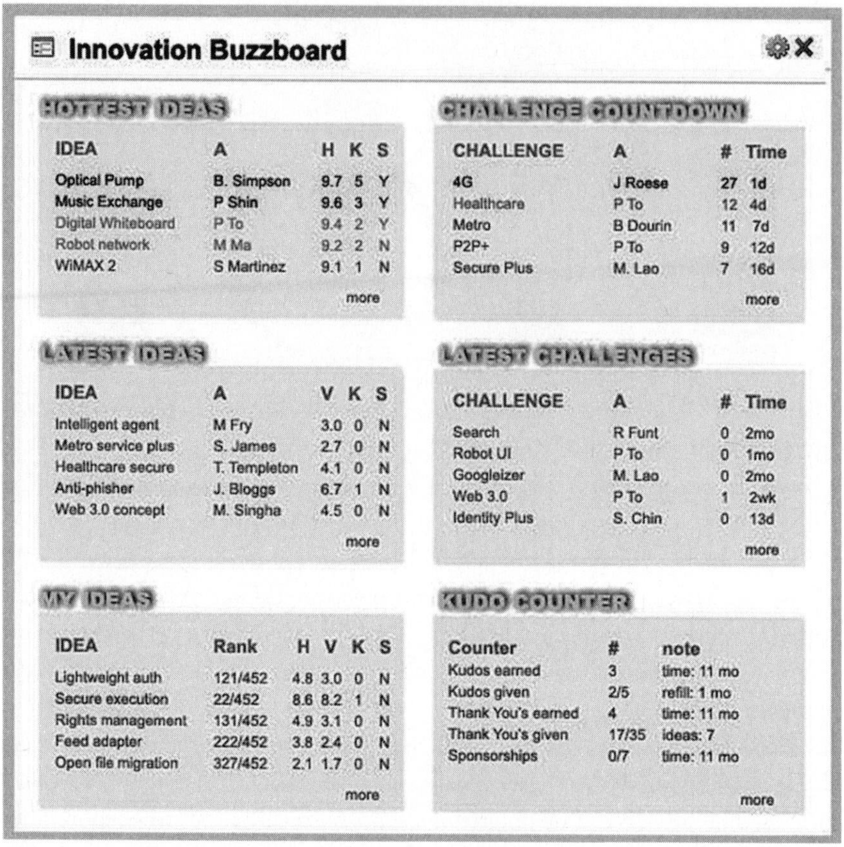

Figure 5.4 Users can maintain a dashboard showing various categories of ideas that have been suggested or are under development. The top four lists reflect the entire organization, whereas the bottom two lists are specific to each individual, and show the ideas he or she has suggested (*My Ideas*), and his or her personal statistics regarding participation in the overall innovation effort. *Kudos* is a form of praise or appreciation received or given, and the CTO can see a special version of this, showing those who are most collaborative or most prolific with ideas.

Source: © 2014 FutureLabConsulting.com

Automating Agile Innovation

Computer systems can support the implementation of Agile Innovation in a variety of ways that can yield enormous performance benefits. Throughout the book we'll use sidebars like this to highlight some of the key activities that can be automated or augmented.

Here's an example: There was once a large telecom company that followed a research model based on academic scientific research, and consequently members of the technical staff were required to make proposals and compete for funding. At one point management noticed that there wasn't much collaboration going on between teams, as research cliques naturally formed with tribal allegiances in the competitive environment that resulted from the funding approach. The vision had been to replicate the feel of an institute of transdisciplinary studies, but what management got instead were knowledge silos that inhibited bigger thinking; they had unintentionally created a battleground.

Desperate for better results and willing to try a radical fix, they asked a consulting firm to install a customized ideation management system configured to address the anti-collaborative nature of the culture. The system applied *gamification* and awarded points not only for idea contributions, but also for sharing comments and ideas to improve upon ideas that had originated with others.

A virtual economy based on these points was created, and the leaderboard that showed the most collaborative team members was proudly displayed on the CTO's innovation dashboard (shown in Figure 5.4). Given a chance to be noticed by the CTO, middle-level R&D managers were motivated to become significantly more collaborative, and a process of cross-disciplinary idea germination began to emerge.

will get resources, time, and effort precisely to figure out what we do, in fact, have.

In this respect, Agile Innovation differs from Agile Software projects, because software projects are assumed from the outset to be valid and feasible and are planned and managed accordingly, whereas innovation projects can and often do retain vast swaths of uncertainty for quite some time. This issue, the uncertainty and the need to reduce the associated risk, is the topic of the next chapter. Here, our concern is on accelerating progress to move projects along as fast as possible, for two reasons.

First, as noted at the beginning of this chapter, the faster we get great ideas to market, the faster we move the market, and earn money. Weeks or months of delay can be hugely costly, and the firm that gets the right products to market quickest generally gains a significant advantage.

Second, the faster we find out which ideas are not great, the faster we can stop wasting resources on them.

Welcome to Medical School!

There is an oft-quoted story about the welcoming speech delivered by the dean of a medical school to all the incoming students at the very first assembly in the fall. "Ladies and gentlemen," he says grandly, "welcome to our esteemed institution of medical education!" He parades around the podium happily. "In four years' time, those of you who complete your studies with us will graduate and go on to brilliant practices in your chosen fields of medicine, and using your vast accumulation of knowledge, you will heal and comfort thousands upon thousands of people throughout the course of your distinguished careers." The young students sit proudly, imagining that great day.

The dean continues, but now in a more somber tone, "However, I do have one bit of bad news for you." He pauses for effect, and gains the rapt attention of the students. "About half of what you will learn during your four years with us is not true."

The students look stunned, thinking, "Why will they be teaching us material that isn't correct?"

The dean explains: "The problem is that, as of today, we just don't know which half is true, and which half is not true."

So it is with innovation. Roughly half of all innovation projects will come to naught, and far fewer than half will go on to brilliant success. At the outset, however, we just don't know which half is which, and we won't until we've been working for a while.

Hence, the Agile Innovation sprint proceeds with the possibility of a null outcome, that is, the death of the project. This is a given—and is one of the main reasons that the very idea of innovation is so difficult for executives in most corporations to grasp or to accept. Especially in a six sigma world of 99.999 percent reliability, how can you possibly allow half of what you do to fail? Clearly, adopting the innovation mind-set requires many adjustments both to expectations, as well as to core processes.

It's also worth noting here that, for a typical corporate executive, the death of *my* project is often seen as bad for *my* career. Consequently, people will do almost anything to avoid killing a project, even when it fully deserves to die, and when prolonging its life is a gigantic waste of precious resources.

In the truly Agile Innovation organization, however, such a death is recognized as a valuable learning experience that moves the overall process along most efficiently. Although we know in advance that 50 percent of all our projects are doomed, we also know that 95 percent of our people are absolutely brilliant.

> So the smart people (everyone) can help us kill off bad projects faster, just as they can help us make the winners into even bigger successes.

It's important to note that profound learning of inestimable value can come from a failed project. Our attitude is that we intend to learn everything we can from failures *and* from successes, and then move on as fast we can.

Tasking People to Join an IdeaScrum

Promising ideas are collected in an Idea Backlog, and people either volunteer or are assigned to participate in the IdeaScrum that develops each one. People are tasked to put their entire focus on either improving ideas—or killing them off quickly. The result is a much more efficient and effective validation process for the good ideas.

(continued)

(continued)

Hence, instead of relying on conventional practice and hoping that people will interact and comment on ideas, a team is specifically charged with this task, thus avoiding the common problem that when everybody is responsible, nobody is responsible.

An effective team consists of those with the skills necessary to analyze the idea, design usage vignettes, develop early prototypes,

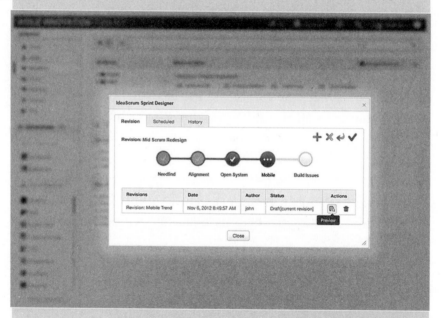

Figure 5.5 Workflow in an IdeaScrum is managed through a combination of project management, team dialog, the daily stand-up meeting, and automated workflow tracking, which is shown here. This screenshot shows the configuration of perspectives for an online IdeaScrum system. Need finding, alignment, and open system are complete; mobile is in process, and build issues will be addressed next. The names of the tasks are, of course, specific to each project and each organization, so these are just representative of the principle that work is broken into discrete elements that can be readily tracked. This is a critical element of both success and speed, particularly for large and complex innovation projects.

Source: © 2014 FutureLabConsulting.com

interact with the client participants to solicit their input, and promote the idea across the organization to solicit interest, feedback, and participation. These tasks are accomplished through iterative sprints, each of which advances the idea from its initial state of fuzziness through progressive levels of refinement.

Figure 5.5 shows how this can be automated.

The simple flow diagram shows where the idea is in its development, with the stages identified as *need finding*, or early-stage research; *alignment*, gaining consensus on what the research reveals; *open system*, gathering input from many stakeholders; *mobile*, the current stage of development; and finally *build issues*, identifying the pluses and minuses that enable final assessment.

SOCIAL WORKFLOW

As we've noted, the Agile Software development process is a social innovation, meaning that it defines a different and much more effective set of working relationships for the members of a project team, and it employs a different way of coordinating and accomplishing large-scale programming tasks.

As we also mentioned, Agile exists because traditional approaches to the development of large and complex software systems have such a consistent record of failure, and the inventors of Agile realized that a fundamental flaw in conventional thinking was precisely how the work was organized. So Agile is simply a redesign—and a brilliantly successful one—that pioneers a better way.

One of the key elements of Agile is its approach to work assignment and tracking to manage the flow of tasks that must be accomplished. Although Agile doesn't use this term, the notion of *social workflow* concisely captures the essence of this simple yet powerful approach.

> To coordinate and drive progress, we present the concept of "social workflow," a way to coordinate and drive progress through lightweight, social network–based co-accountability.

Broadly speaking, social workflow includes two key functions. First, the social aspect of work and its coordination is based on the assignment and acceptance of tasks. This is managed through feedback loops that report when tasks have or have not been completed. Automating this role creates enormous advantages in terms of effectiveness, transparency, reminders, and coordination across multiple tasks that may also be involved in different projects.

The second function expands on automated tracking to enable tracking of large sets of projects over time. This is enormously valuable in helping improve the ability to estimate and therefore to manage a team's capacity to get meaningful work done.

Automating Social Workflow

During a typical Agile project, each day begins with the daily scrum meeting, 10 minutes for coordination and checking in, after which the programmers are generally left alone to work for the rest of the day without interruption.

In Agile Innovation, the organization and coordination may be a bit more complex because there is likely to be a significant variety of tasks across many disciplines, and because people are likely to be working in multiple locations. In addition, some team members may be fulfilling other roles or jobs in parallel, and they have to manage operational responsibilities along with their innovation tasks.

Consequently, the organization and coordination burden for a typical Agile Innovation project is likely to be significantly more demanding, and automation will bring great benefits.

Social workflow systems communicate progress, trigger deadlines, and manage communication efforts, so, for example, when we wish to delegate a task, we can initiate an *action request*. Upon acceptance, the system tracks progress and issues the appropriate notifications. Because a typical project may have hundreds of associated tasks and may generate thousands of requests, automating all this prevents key deliverables from being forgotten, and no one wastes time repeating status updates.

People can be gently reminded a day or two in advance regarding deadlines on tasks that they have accepted, whereas the multitude of actions that are going on that people don't need to know about can be maintained quietly in the background until people wish to know, and then they can easily check the system for a status update without having to bother anyone else. See Figure 5.6.

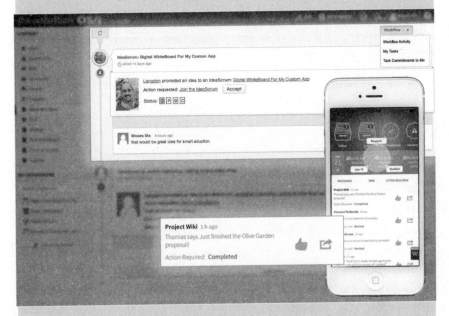

Figure 5.6   This composite image shows the desktop notation for a new idea, *Digital WhiteBoard for My Custom App,* as well as a screenshot of the workflow tracker on the iPhone, highlighting a message that a project has been completed. Syncing the desktop and mobile versions supports dynamic data capture and updating regardless of location, and enables each individual to track all tasks and commitments more easily. Hence, no more missed deadlines or unpleasant surprises because of the *I forgot* excuse, which is simply no longer valid. By automating this aspect of workflow management, team members no longer need to be nagged, enabling communication to focus on activities that add value.

Source: © 2014 FutureLabConsulting.com

A major benefit of social workflow is that it simplifies and clarifies how messages are routed to those who really need to know, and tasks are routed to people who are ready to do them. In addition, artificial intelligence filters can aggregate large data sets into manageable chunks to support more complex analytical functions and data aggregation across multiple projects, thus promoting broader organizational learning.

Real-time progress tracking and metrics are fed into the same system that's used for virtual collaboration, so everyone has ready access to status updates. As with Agile Software work, there is full transparency, which greatly simplifies the project management role. Problems become readily evident, and therefore procrastination is nearly impossible.

THE RESEARCH CYCLE: NEED FINDING, MODELING, IDEATION, AND PROTOTYPING

Where do great ideas come from? Obviously they come from many sources, which means that any systematic innovation process must support and sustain multiple efforts at ideation in parallel.

In large organizations, exploratory work is happening all the time through the development of new technology in the R&D lab as well as through the evaluation of new technology coming from external sources. There are ongoing efforts to develop new practices, methods, and approaches that may also lead to new ideas. The evolution of the innovation spirit throughout the organization, and in its broader eco-system of partners, customers, and suppliers, constitute two vastly rich sources of ideas, so insiders and outsiders will be providing a steady flow of interesting and worthwhile possibilities.

Ideas, constantly emerging from all these sources and perhaps other ones, are shared in various forums, both face to face and technology assisted, and it therefore requires an ongoing effort to manage this process. Together, all this could be characterized as an activity of harvesting, of deliberately and carefully gathering lots of ideas from lots of sources.

However, the sheer volume of input can be overwhelming, and thus the next steps require assessing and choosing the best ideas; developing them into valuable and implementable new products, services, business models, and ventures; and bringing them successfully to market.

Typically it is the chief innovation officer's role to manage this at a high level and perhaps an innovation champion's role to manage day-to-day tasks and activities.

But still it is not nearly enough.

It's also important—mandatory, even—for the organization to pursue and create great ideas proactively.

> To do so systematically requires a formal research process, and we refer to this as the *research cycle,* a rigorous approach to generating critically important information about the future.

Based on this information new insights will come, and many lead to new ideas for products, services, business models, processes, procedures, etc., an endless stream of potential value to explore and develop.

As we have noted, throughout the Agile Innovation process we are focusing particularly on understanding the real and often hidden needs of customers, knowledge that we expect to use to create new products and services that yield competitive advantage.

Within the work cycles described by IdeaScrums and sprints (see Figure 5.7), we are moving through a specific process of learning,

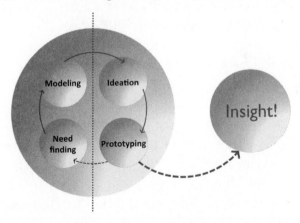

Figure 5.7   Research consists of four major subactivities: need finding, modeling, ideation, and prototyping. The result is insight, which is clarity about needs, about opportunities, and about how to create value for customers (see Figure 5.8). *Source:* Reproduced by permission from Langdon Morris, *The Innovation Master Plan: The CEO's Guide to Innovation* (Walnut Creek, CA: Innovation Academy, 2011).

progressing through iterations of work toward greater specificity of needs and opportunities, emerging eventually (which could be quite soon) with validated concepts that are ready for implementation.

This is broadly thought of as the research stage of the innovation process and generally occurs in four steps: need finding, modeling, ideation, and prototyping, which together lead to insight. This framework was developed by professors Michael Barry of Stanford University and Sara Beckman of the University of California, Berkeley, and is documented in their award-winning paper, "Innovation as a Learning Process: Embedding Design Thinking." They have both been very generous and helpful mentors to us for many years.[4]

NEED FINDING

We have already discussed many elements of need finding, which is the search to identify hidden needs, behaviors, motivations, and attitudes that customers have but may not be aware of, and are therefore unable to describe even when we ask them directly.

One of the most useful research methods is ethnography, the study of human culture and human behavior.

In Agile Software projects, knowledge of customer needs is recognized as critical to success, and it's represented on project teams by actual customers, who are expected to work side by side with programmers to define the user stories, the use cases, and ultimately the working software that will become the finished product. This is a long-term partnership and working relationship that lasts from the outset of a project through its completion, possibly many months later.

The presence of customers who intimately know and can articulate their own needs is intended to assure that the programming team addresses real requirements and does not engage in feature creep or in eliminating required functionality.

In Agile Innovation projects, the situation is a bit more complex, both because the range of projects that may be undertaken is much broader given that the targets can include incremental improvements, breakthroughs, new business models, pure technology plays, internally directed operational improvements, etc., and because the degree of uncertainty is likely to be considerably higher.

Nevertheless, intimate customer knowledge remains critical to success. However, we have found consistently that customers (or potential customers) often *may not be able to provide the depth of input necessary* to be particularly useful across a broad range of innovation topics related to functionality, technology, branding, etc.

> Therefore, it's essential to gain insight into the many hidden dimensions of the customer experience, and the technique of ethnographic research has proved to be particularly effective.

This method of uncovering hidden knowledge about customer behaviors, needs, attitudes, and values is very reliable, and possible even in the sales department, as we discovered in the short case study about Wells Fargo that was mentioned in Chapter 3.

Ethnography works so well precisely because it enables us to uncover important knowledge that most people are unable to describe concerning their own deep feelings and attitudes, or why they believe what they believe. For example, your very liberal brother-in-law and your very conservative uncle can each be entirely confident of his own political views, yet each may not understand why the other believes such obvious nonsense. These patterns persist in society precisely because of our own lack of self-awareness, for a great many things about ourselves are well hidden from us.

However, trained observers can and do discover them by employing ethnographic techniques in a careful process of discussion and observation, revealing these hidden essentials by looking behind what people say to expose the deeper roots of beliefs and attitudes.

This often leads to profound insights.

Hence, the early stages of the research process frequently include a heavy dose of ethnographic observations to identify needs that take many forms: psychological, functional, and aesthetic. Our knowledge of all these various forms provides insights that define innovation opportunities and deeply inform the process of developing new ideas as well as the subsequent process of transforming ideas into innovations.

Need finding through the ethnographic methodology is one of the areas in which Agile Innovation distinguishes itself from traditional approaches, as it's not a matter of waiting around for people to come up with good ideas; it is instead a proactive process of going out and uncovering needs that may expose powerful innovation opportunities.

PROACTIVE INNOVATION

What needs are we looking for? We start perhaps by investigating areas where we've already defined strategic intent and strategic necessity, thereby creating a strong connection between our organization's strategy and the innovation process. In this way Agile Innovation is a tightly focused endeavor, a proactive one guided specifically by strategic priorities, and conversely it's therefore most definitely *not* a miscellaneous collection of random ideas.

Hence, as we saw in the Wells Fargo example, the successes of the sales teams didn't depend on customers coming to them with requests or problems. On the contrary, by actively going to customer locations, observing them at work, noticing the communication patterns, evaluating the methods and tools they used, and their interactions, Wells Fargo teams were able to make genuinely helpful suggestions to improve the clients' performance in treasury and finance. Precisely because the observations and suggestions were grounded in the everyday reality of the clients' actual experiences, and were obviously provided for their benefit, clients readily recognized these ideas as practical, workable solutions that did indeed add value, not as self-serving sales pitches.

This approach transformed the relationship between salesperson and customer because the salesperson was no longer pushing a solution but instead became a trusted partner helping solve a real business problem. And as we have learned in the technology markets, when the customer *pulls* the solution in this way, it grows virally, which is hugely more effective than when a company tries to *push* technology out to the market.

Ethnography and need finding thus represent fundamental shifts in the processes of learning, innovating, *and* selling by transforming push into pull, sales into service.

Note also that the Wells Fargo innovators we met earlier are not innovation consultants, nor are they R&D people. They're the sales force. Thus, Wells Fargo achieved another important strategic goal, distributing the process of and responsibility for innovation throughout the organization, thus helping create a genuine innovation culture.

> Developing a culture of innovation is a major objective in Agile Innovation.

At the same time, we also recognize that there is a limit to what salespeople can do. While they can and do identify current, hidden needs, figure out how to meet current needs with current offers, and may even glimpse future needs and communicate those insights back to the organization, they are not generally technologists. They probably won't invent breakthrough tools, nor do hard-core programming, develop base technology, design strategic architectures, design apps, or gain regulatory approval for future products. For that, we need focused innovation teams, with diverse talents and skills that we cannot expect salespeople to have.

These are Agile Innovation scrum teams, on which salespeople may be valued team members, along with many others whose varied forms of expertise are all essential to innovation success. Thus, the objective of merging Agile with innovation is to bring the insights gained from Agile Software methodology about speed and accountability to the work of creating innovation more generally.

Okay, so following a thorough process of collecting the hidden needs, what do we do next?

MODELING

Need finding provides the raw material for the development of conceptual models that describe both the tacit and explicit needs and behaviors of customers, and explain how particular products and services may be able to meet those needs.

These tacit needs may be shaped by new technologies that become available in the marketplace, and will thus become essential ingredients of the new products and services that we wish to bring to that very marketplace. Who knew, for example, that it would one day be necessary for every consumer products company to have a Facebook strategy, and yet here we are today with precisely that requirement, and teams of people working in every organization to orchestrate the social media strategy.

The modeling process is a meticulous activity of thinking through all the information that need finding has gathered and then identifying the most compelling explanations that show how decisions are made, models that tell us how and why customers make the choices that they do.

IDEATION

We then use our discoveries from need finding and modeling to explore many other possibilities for products and services through the ideation stage. How many new ways can we find to meet the needs that we've identified?

What new events, trends, and patterns occurred that we didn't expect, and that caused us to rethink the way we organize our business, or the products and services that we may want to offer our customers?

In the ideation stage we also learn about our own innovation process. In what ways is our process efficient and inefficient? What ideas can we come up with to improve it?

A very useful methodology to explore the emerging marketplace is called idealized design, an application of systems thinking that can be used in a workshop setting to explore ideal solutions to specific customer problems.

Trend analysis, self-diagnosis, and idealized design are just a few of the many approaches to ideation that you can apply as you transform concepts that you've identified in the modeling process into ideas for specific product and service offerings.

For the purposes of this discussion, let's assume that there is an idea which is the focus of our work. We are a scrum team tasked to transform the idea from the raw concept to a finished state.

As noted earlier, *finished* means one of three possible outcomes:

1. Finished product (ready to market as a brilliant customer value proposition)
2. Killed (valuable learning experience)
3. Shelved (temporarily, due to timing)

All three are valid and valuable, and our immediate goal is to get to the right outcome in the least amount of time. Our larger objective, undertaken in parallel, is to get the very best ideas to market as fast as possible, which is accomplished by having multiple teams working through a wide variety and massive quantity of ideas, identifying and further defining the best ones, and advancing those relentlessly to completion.

We organize a great deal of this work in IdeaScrum teams, whose members represent all the pertinent and critical domains of knowledge. Salespeople and customers participate directly, and the specific focus of a team's work is to develop prototypes and the related business case, which will be based on the technical description of the idea and its underlying value proposition.

By organizing the work in one- to four-week-long idea sprints, ideas are developed and refined in iterative cycles of work, and thus the business case is progressively refined from an initial, rough concept into one that is very specific. The intermediate goal is to understand each idea's potential fully and completely and to identify those in which the customer value proposition is magnificent, utterly compelling, and entirely irresistible.

But how do we know what constitutes a great value proposition?

THE CUSTOMER VALUE PROPOSITION

One way to think about this is to recognize that customers have options, and when they're buying just about any product or service there are choices that may solve their problem at a variety of price levels. If we're talking about cars, there's basic transportation at one extreme, as simple and inexpensive as possible, and complete luxury at the other end. For basic transportation you may choose to buy your friend's 20-year-old clunker because he'll take $500 for it and it still runs, or if things have been going really well, perhaps you'll choose a high-end Lexus, Tesla, or Mercedes.

At both ends of the spectrum you'll be driving (as long as the clunker keeps running), but your experience will be quite different from one to the other.

Just about everything you can buy comes in more or less the same range, so we can generalize this to say that at one extreme you have basic commodities, no frills, and at the other you have such magnificent experiences that you become a dedicated customer, loyal for life, and in fact a friend. You proudly wear the Tesla T-shirt, and you gladly take your friends for a ride and tell them how great the car is.

This is what Figure 5.8 shows—from basic value as a customer at one end to differentiated value as a loyal partner at the other.

In your innovation projects, you'll target whichever level of value is right for your customer and your market, and you'll design the entire delivery and support process to sustain the appropriate type of relationship.

Note also that a very inexpensive product or service can still command huge loyalty and trust. Starbucks has done this brilliantly, and although a coffee from Starbucks is more expensive than the 50-cent cup available at the local diner, it's not costing a fortune. Consequently, millions are bought every day.

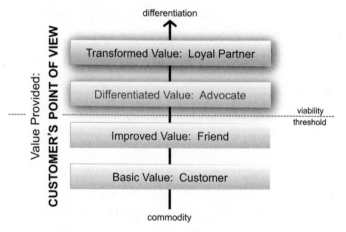

Figure 5.8   The customer value proposition model shows that the customer may perceive a product or service as a commodity value at the bottom, with three progressive stages of increased value above. The dashed line represents the threshold, below which we probably do not want to go. That is, unless our proposed product or service offers at least differentiated value, it's not likely to be worthy of our effort and investment. Furthermore, the model is a test for us, because if we cannot clearly describe why we think our proposed offer fits into any of these four categories, then our idea is not sufficiently developed, and we have further work to do.

PROTOTYPING

The goal of each Agile Software sprint cycle is to develop, validate, refine, and finalize one specific chunk of code. The measurement of achieved value in Agile Software projects is clear: Working software is the tangible goal because properly running code is an indisputable form of validation.

Achieving this requires a defined end goal, input from customers that is relevant to the code, clarity on the specific dimensions of the business case that are to be addressed, and the focused efforts of the programming team.

In Agile Innovation, the comparable effort focuses on rapid prototyping of both the idea and the business case that supports it. The ultimate goal is a fully articulated working model of the idea, and a fully validated business case with a complete implementation plan.

Hence, the best ideas exposed in the ideation process certainly should become prototypes, physical or conceptual versions that you will use to test your ideas and examine them in operational detail to gain tangible experiences. Through that testing you'll discover at a much deeper level what works and what doesn't work, which will then direct you toward the additional research that's necessary to transform good concepts into great workable products.

For many products and services, you may create tens or dozens of prototypes and may then further test the best of these in additional research cycles, beginning again with need finding. You may go through many cycles of the research process with your most promising ideas, leading to subsequent research that may then focus on finding technological solutions, new materials, or better product design solutions. Often you'll do this not only within your firm's design and engineering teams, but in conjunction with one or more partners, as the following case study about the implementation of Apple's CarPlay dashboard interface into Volvo's product line shows quite clearly.

VOLVO + APPLE + SYMBIO + AGILE = CREATING A NEW IN-CAR INTERFACE IN RECORD TIME

The most interesting innovations in today's high-tech world often come about when multiple firms work together, with each bringing its unique expertise to a process in which they co-create new solutions. When Apple released its CarPlay Interface in 2013, a set of design tools that enable carmakers to integrate iPhone and iPad technology into their dashboard display systems, automakers immediately knew that they had a great opportunity to extend Apple's renowned innovations into new uses. Many manufacturers, including Mercedes, Ferrari, and Volvo, immediately launched design efforts to integrate CarPlay.

Of course, the challenge for the automakers was to deal with an entirely new set of design and engineering factors. How much new hardware technology was actually needed in the car to make CarPlay work? What interface would be the safest? What screen displays worked most intuitively? What were the software issues? And how would smartphones and tablets connect to a car's screens to provide the optimal user experience?

At the same time, the team also needed to figure out how the new interface would work in concert with existing touch screen systems that already controlled in-car audio entertainment, GPS, climate, maintenance information, backup cameras, and the growing list of other functions that connect through the dashboard display.

In the past, it generally took more than a year to sort out the complex design issues relating to dashboard design, primarily due to safety requirements, the difficulties of embedded systems programming, and frequently the need for specially designed hardware. The development process was long and cumbersome—designs were made on paper or wireframes in graphic design software, and then passed to embedded systems programmers for implementation in software, whereupon they would then be returned to designers and testers for feedback and review, etc. Back and forth they would go until everyone was satisfied, an exhaustive process that ate up a lot of time.

However, Volvo wanted to be first to market with the best solution that would provide the best possible experience to their customers, so they sought a better and faster way to work. Volvo's leaders realized that in addition to their existing innovation and ideation talent they needed to augment their team with engineers who could rapidly determine which approaches would work technically and which wouldn't, and who had the Agile expertise to handle rapid cycle design, prototyping, and testing. For this they turned to Symbio, a Silicon Valley–based software and engineering firm with deep expertise in embedded systems, rapid cycle, design thinking, and Agile.

To maximize execution speed a Symbio design team co-located with the Volvo team, and worked hand in hand to validate new ideas, while remote engineering teams in Scandinavia and China supported the ideation process as well as the subsequent productization.

At the outset of the design process they found that while other automakers were implementing CarPlay through an either/or, full screen approach, meaning that users could launch CarPlay from the car's system and it would take over the display screen, or the reverse, the car's system could exist as an icon on CarPlay. But the Volvo–Symbio team's early design tests revealed that this solution was not ideal because switching between the two interfaces was jarring and non-intuitive to users.

So what was a better alternative, and how could the design be completed quickly? Symbio's expertise with Agile and embedded prototyping tools would enable the team to quickly brainstorm, build, and test sample interfaces, but these tools had not been widely used at Volvo, and initially there was resistance. After experiencing the power of the rapid development to generate dynamic prototypes, the Volvo team became fully convinced, and working together this way they completed many design iterations until a potential solution emerged which would enable CarPlay to run either in a window or on the entire screen. This required a larger screen, but by using the rapid prototyping process again they built and tested various combinations and locations of controls until they arrived at an intuitive interface that took advantage of CarPlay's unique capabilities.

The Volvo CarPlay solution was first presented in New York at the International Auto Show in March 2014, and early reports from the automotive press praised it as the most user friendly of the implementations from any automaker. Adario Strange of Mashable offered these comments in his review:[5]

The first thing we noticed was that touchscreen and application-launch actions were as snappy and smooth as they are on the iPhone, so if you're already familiar with iOS, CarPlay will be a breeze to use. But it's when you ask for directions that you see the true mobile power of CarPlay. After requesting directions to a location in Manhattan, Siri presented several options on the CarPlay interface. Select one, and you are presented with a detailed, turn-by-turn routing map, complete with the 3D-buildings option in Apple's iPhone Maps app. Making a call was just a matter of pushing the Siri button (which will be accessible via the steering wheel), and saying, "Call John Doe."

While using CarPlay, I noticed that although I didn't need to look at the screen, I was nevertheless compelled to, simply because it's an attractive display with amazing graphics. Both Volvo and Apple said distracted driving is something they're both actively working to prevent. Stephen Chick, a member of Apple's CarPlay team, said, "The whole point of CarPlay is to have a safe environment in the car for your iPhone. That's the experience we want to bring because we realize that using your iPhone itself is not the way that we want to go in the car."

By engaging in a rigorous process of co-creation, which included locating Volvo and Symbio team members together, using Agile methods and rapid prototyping software and expertise, quick iterations that enabled them to evaluate multiple design options, focusing on usability and the customer's experience, leveraging Symbio's global talent base, and using a design centered approach, the result was a great solution in less than 50 percent of the usual time.

In the words of Jonas Söderqvist, Volvo's Director of User Experience and Connectivity, "It's been great to collaborate with Symbio. They formed a perfect partnership with our competences to focus on what our customers want and making the experience come alive."

● ● ●

This journey through multiple iterations of design, prototyping, and testing may also lead you to redefine your understanding of the opportunities in the market that you're pursuing. Hence, you may continue to explore the design possibilities iteratively through additional cycles of need finding, modeling, ideation, and prototyping until at last you reach conclusions that you feel are solid, robust, demonstrably backed by evidence, and which generate great enthusiasm: Because of dedicated and concentrated work, a great product or service is about to be born!

Extensive experimentation and testing have given you tremendous confidence that customers will, in fact, embrace the product or service enthusiastically, and when this occurs, you will transition from the research process to the welcome moment of clarity that signifies *insight*.

INSIGHT

When insight emerges and you see with great confidence how a new product or service will be configured to genuinely meet significant customer needs, you will know exactly how it will work in the marketplace, how it will add value for the customer's experience, and how it will add value for your company as well.

Hence, insight is not so much a stage or a process in the innovation activity as it is a moment of precision and vision, a moment when you see and understand with great depth of understanding how a potential innovation will be used and valued in the market. It is at this point that you can fully express a validated customer value proposition.

THE AGILE INNOVATION PROCESS

When we put all the steps together, Figures 5.9, 5.10, and 5.11 show what the process looks like.

FACILITATING THE WORKFLOW

An IdeaScrum is likely to be facilitated by an experienced innovation coach who's responsible for stimulating group ideation, guiding the overall process, training the team in innovation techniques, scheduling

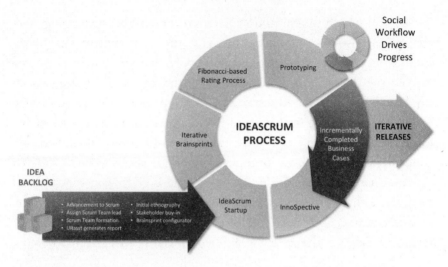

Figure 5.9   The idea backlog is a repository of ideas that we wish to develop. Based on our assessment of market and strategic factors, we advance the most important or promising ideas into the IdeaScrum, assign a team lead, form the team, and commence work. The six elements of the large wheel represent six major types of activities that will occur iteratively throughout the process: start-up, leading to iterative brainsprints for ideation and brainstorming, Fibonacci-based rating process to rank the various ideas (explained later in this chapter), prototyping selected ideas, and progressive development of the business case. The smaller wheel represents the use of social workflow tools to help manage tasks and progress. Portions of work are released for review and assessment as completed.

face-to-face brainstorming sessions when necessary, and completing all the other tasks necessary to removing impediments to the team's ability to deliver truly great ideas, great business cases, and fast progress.

Scrum Master and Innovation Champion

In Agile Software methodology the person performing the project leadership role is sometimes called the *scrum master*. The role is doubtless a critical one, but because we're not so comfortable with the implied master-slave concept, we prefer *champion, coach, leader*, or *facilitator*.

Like scrum masters, innovation champions focus on these four key functions:

- Defining and prioritizing the tasks to be done.
- Leading the short, daily team meetings that enable real-time coordination, tracking, and collection of metrics.
- Continuously identifying and assessing potential project risks and managing those risks upward (i.e., managing the relationship between the scrum team and the rest of the organization so that the scrum team is protected from interference—or in scientist Dr. W. Edwards Deming's word, *tampering*).
- Leading the execution of projects through a series of brief high-intensity iterative work sprints.

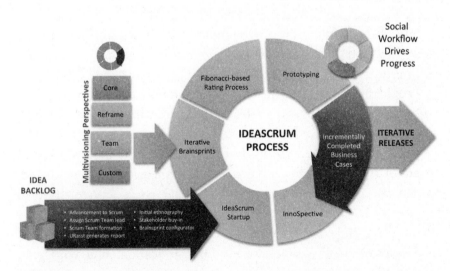

Figure 5.10 The addition of multivisioning perspectives as a key element of brainsprints. Multivisioning is a technique to improve the quality of brainstorming by helping individuals and groups see the problem or situation differently, and is an essential technique for improving overall idea quality. (Multivisioning is described in more detail in Chapter 10.)

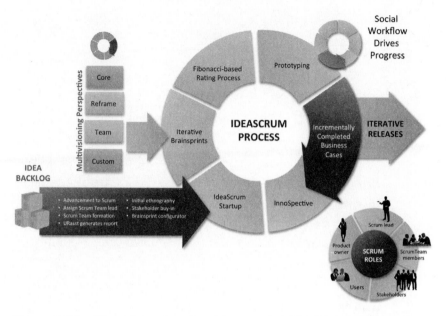

Figure 5.11   The roles to be played in a typical IdeaScrum.

SPONTANEOUS INNOVATION

While all this work at proactive innovation is going on, the ongoing and parallel process of *spontaneous innovation* continues uninterrupted.

People throughout the organization are coming up with and sharing ideas, both in response to strategically targeted innovation initiatives and because of their own unplanned and spontaneous inspirations.

Many of these ideas are likely to be brilliant, certainly worthy of attention. They therefore need to be developed, sorted, and shared, which we often do by creating a virtual space in which ideas appear as an innovation activity feed, where others can then *like* them just as they do on Facebook. People can also suggest variations and improvements, ask questions for clarification, and engage in dialog, all of which are positive instances of engagement in the innovation process.

The more likes and dialog an idea accumulates, the higher it rises in the stack, and the more frequently people will notice it. This is an organic, market-driven process that helps differentiate the better or more popular ideas, which can point to ideas that focused IdeaScrums should further explore.

Eventually innovation managers will decide which ideas should progress to the next level, the IdeaScrum, but in any case the ongoing dialog constitutes a valuable learning forum in which the firm's future products and services are the primary topic of conversation, thereby reinforcing the prevalence of innovation as a key means by which change and adaptation take place organically throughout the organization.

Sketching the Maquette

Steve Blank, that brilliant guy who started the Lean Start-up movement, notes that, "No one besides venture capitalists and the late Soviet Union requires five-year plans to forecast complete unknowns. These plans are generally fiction, and dreaming them up is almost always a waste of time."[6]

Instead, Agile Innovation Adopts Lao Tzu's Advice That "A Journey of a Thousand Miles Begins with a Single Step."

Hence, Agile Innovators break down big ideas into steps that compose *visually demonstrable innovations.* Each step contributes valuable information to the overall business case that lays out the rationale and opportunity, thus avoiding the paralysis-by-analysis approach, which holds that we have to work out the whole thing in utterly meticulous detail before we start.

The Agile approach is to start with small, useful steps that could include, for example, creating mock-ups (of whatever the idea is) and collecting customer input on them, completing a first-iteration, bottom-up market size analysis, or identifying suitable pilot sites for a new product and gathering expressions of interest from potential clients.

Each of these steps should be relatively modest, requiring little financial investment and posing minimal risk to the company's

(continued)

(*continued*)

brand. The idea is to build value, test, and pivot rapidly, which is the very clear and brilliant thesis of the lean start-up movement.

In this way the business case is built iteratively, with each subsequent version constituting the next payment on the ultimate requirement for a complete and comprehensive business case or business plan.

Sometimes this incremental business case is referred to as a *business case canvas* or a *business panorama*™. Using sculpture as an analogy, we could call the first pass at this incremental business plan a gesture, a rapidly executed rendering of the work that captures the essence of what is expected to be beautiful eventually.

Drawn gestures usually take only a few minutes to complete, but a sculpture might take 20 to 30 minutes and require that you consider the work from every angle. The goal of gesture sketching and rough sculpting is to experiment, to identify that which is truly worth executing in totality, and this is precisely the goal for the incrementally developed business case as well.

If each iteration of the sketch retains its own alluring beauty, as layer upon layer of detailed information is added, then the likelihood is quite good that the finished work is going to be beautiful—that is, successful in the market.

Eventually you go so far as to build a *maquette*, the French word for a scale model, which is useful for visualizing ideas without incurring the cost and effort of producing the full-scale product in the actual materials. Auto companies are famous for their clay maquettes, the best of which eventually become real cars made of steel.

Perhaps most important, a maquette is necessary before your patron—in Agile, this is probably senior management—will commission the work, that is, provide the funding required to fully develop your validated prototype.

GATHERING FEEDBACK

During the course of working on an idea, an IdeaScrum development team may want to gather feedback from a broader group of interested and knowledgeable stakeholders. When this occurs, you can post the idea on your online innovation system for comments, and send a blanket invitation out to people to request their review and input, a crowdsourcing function that online innovation management tools should have.

At this point, the IdeaScrum is open for review and suggestions from anyone in the company. Progress tracking records and burn down charts (see Figure 5.12) will be available for everyone to consider as well, so they can see the history of the project.

Reviewers are also asked to rate the project along various performance dimensions, such as technical merit, white space potential, and *cool factor.*

When evaluating a pipeline of prospective ideas, the challenge is to decide which are the best. The numerical rating scale is not a simple 1 to 5 score but rather a Fibonacci series scale of 1, 2, 3, 5, and 8. This rating

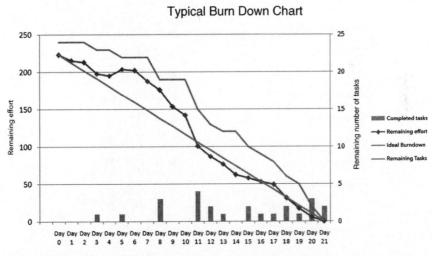

Figure 5.12   A typical burn down chart, with about 225 tasks to complete during a 21-day sprint. By charting progress daily, it's easy to calculate the trajectory and estimate whether the project is on schedule. This provides powerful feedback for the project team and for project managers.

system will push the very best ideas to the top and provide much better clarity and visibility for the standouts.

This is similar to scrum poker, or planning poker, a consensus-based technique for estimating the relative size and scope of a given set of development goals for a software development project that is in the planning stages. In planning poker, members of a group share their estimates by placing numbered cards face down on the table, rather than speaking them aloud. As the cards are revealed, the estimates are discussed. By selecting their own card but hiding it in this way, the group avoids the cognitive biases of anchoring or groupthink, wherein the first number spoken aloud sets a precedent for subsequent estimates. Instead, members must think it through for themselves and then explain their own estimate as the cards are turned up one by one. This is a much more thoughtful and honest dialog, and the resulting estimates are generally much more reliable (see Figures 5.13 and 5.14).

Because a full idea pipeline should consist of hundreds of ideas, helping the best ones stand out more clearly makes the task of portfolio

Criteria	Rating
Development Cost	1 2 3 **5** 8
Uniqueness	1 2 3 5 **8**
Innovation accelerator	1 2 3 5 **8**
Low technical risk	1 2 3 5 **8**
Market Potential	1 2 3 **5** 8
Strategic Alignment	1 **2** 3 5 8
Development Time	1 2 **3** 5 8
Patentability	1 2 3 **5** 8
Competitive durability	1 2 3 **5** 8
Technical Merit	1 2 **3** 5 8

Figure 5.13 Each individual player makes an assessment of a given idea according to the 10 criteria listed. The rating numbers are a Fibonacci series to add more emphasis to high scores and thus more strongly differentiate the criteria that rate high, because the good ideas otherwise clump together.

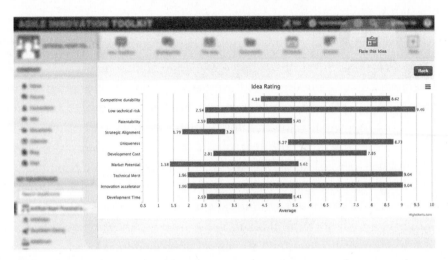

Figure 5.14 By automating the evaluation process, we can readily see the low and high scores and the range for each criterion.

management much easier and the firm as a whole is better able to identify and put resources toward the ideas that are collectively judged to have the most potential.

However, experience also shows that an occasional low-scoring idea might happen to be a great one, just underappreciated. Thus, we're not ceding the decision-making power to a vote, but we certainly are listening closely to the opinions of people whom we trust as knowledgeable.

Over time, the review process will improve as portfolio managers and scrum leaders get better at gathering and interpreting feedback, and thus the organization as a whole gets better at assessing new ideas, and more efficient at managing innovation.

Agile Innovation begins with lightweight documentation to assure a rapid start, and it proceeds via incremental funding that is released at every step, thereby keeping risk low. If a new product or service includes a software component or some other artifact that can be rapidly generated or prototyped, then the gesture or maquette is prepared as early as possible, along with its incrementally growing business case.

Remember, the reason for creating a working prototype, whether in software code, clay maquette, cardboard, foam, a flow chart, or in any other form, is to help assess its value. The purpose is not to allay the fears of investors, stakeholders, or managers, but to validate with customers that they really do need and want *this* solution, and that they're willing to pay for it too.

Hence, some form of customer validation should accompany each incremental component of the business case. This enables progressive achievement of fully validated ideas, and provides for early and frequent customer input that leads to implementable designs.

With the benefit of all this feedback you may find out quickly that the original idea lacks that essential quality of beauty, or the potential or intended value, and that customers don't warmly embrace it. Here, honesty plays a critical role, and the team needs to be brutally open to reality. Cancelling a project before substantial investment takes place is a valid outcome, a win, and worthy of appreciation.

Hence, unlike other operational aspects of the business, failing faster in the innovation effort is a good thing as long as we extract the maximum learning and then apply that learning to our subsequent work. In fact, that focus on learning is a key aspect of how we reduce the risks inherent in the innovation process, which is exactly the topic of the next chapter.

Questions to Reflect Upon

- Although the Agile approach can work in software development, how effective could it be in the much more complex environment of innovating complicated technology products?
- Because teamwork is so important in Agile, how can we find the right people to join Agile teams?
- How can we engage our customers in the Agile process?
- Adopting and implementing Agile might be very challenging to our organization. How can we change our habits to enable this?
- What kind of corporate culture facilitates Agile?
- How will top management monitor progress and resource allocation in Agile processes?

6

REDUCING
INNOVATION RISK

It concerns us that, in the wake of the financial crisis, many companies have shied away from investing in the future growth of their companies.

— Laurence Fink, chair and CEO, BlackRock[1]

The most common reason that companies fail to innovate is because they're afraid of the risks. But what they do not take into account is the risk inherent in *not* innovating.

This view is nicely expressed by Facebook CEO Mark Zuckerberg: "The biggest risk is not taking any risk. In a world that changing really quickly, the only strategy that is guaranteed to fail is not taking risks."[2] In far too many cases, the lack of innovation puts companies into a downward spiral, and they ultimately succumb to their own incapacity.

But it is a learned incapacity, not an inborn one, a limitation that comes about largely because of how firms are managed, because of choices that their leaders make. Hence, it can be overcome, unlearned with the proper combination of a new mind-set and a different approach.

The approach, however, has to de-risk the overall innovation effort while enabling investment in projects that are indeed inherently high in risk. This is a neat trick for sure, but it is one that can be accomplished; it is our topic in this chapter.

A System for Innovation

The mind-set part, from the perspective of senior leadership, is straightforward. Innovation is essential to survival, so it is mandatory. Given that perspective, the task is to devise and adopt the right methods, the *how* that enables effective investment. The mind-set shift that the rest of the organization must embrace, including the processes and communications that make it real, is a bit more involved, and it's the subject of the next chapter.

Before we get to that, though, let's discuss the necessary approach, which is a comprehensive innovation system.

To begin, we must first address the strategic perspective, or as we labeled it in a previous book, *The Innovation Master Plan*, the *why* of innovation.

The *why*, of course, is that the competitive marketplace puts a premium on innovation, which means that the noninnovative firms that fall behind are highly susceptible to early mortality. Hence, organizations must plan for innovation, align planning with action, and make it happen. This is of course not so simple to do, or everyone would already be doing it.

The difference between them is highlighted in a comment by General Dwight Eisenhower, supreme allied commander in Europe and eventual U.S. president. It was he who decided on the strategy that led to the D-Day crossing of the English Channel in 1944, the single largest military engagement in history. The movements of tens of thousands of troops, thousands of ships, plus all the necessary aircraft, tanks, trucks, jeeps, and many tons of food and supplies necessary to get the massive D-Day invasion force to the beaches, across them, and forward into

France were all planned in advance, step by step, by the commander's meticulous planning team.

As an act of military planning, D-Day was probably the most complicated endeavor that had ever been attempted, so it's perhaps more than a bit ironic that Eisenhower subsequently commented that, "In preparing for battle, I have always found that plans are useless but planning is indispensable."[3]

The relative worthlessness of the plan reflects the utter unpredictability of battle and the very high likelihood that from the first sighting of the beach onward, things would not go as planned. Unexpected events did indeed occur throughout D-Day, although the overall result was remarkably close to what the Allies intended because of the extreme dedication and commitment of all involved.

The value of the careful planning, meanwhile, relates to the great importance of clearly defining goals, establishing effective lines of communication, predefining alternative courses of action in the (likely) event that the first plan isn't working out (move on to plan B, plan C, etc.), and having some clarity about what the other units in the force may be doing so that our unit can make the best use of its firepower to achieve the shared objective when things start to go differently than the plan led us to expect.

Indeed, it was the entirely dedicated pursuit of the goal through amazing self-sacrifice that enabled the D-Day forces to overcome the aspects of the plan that did not work as intended: 6,900 allied ships effectively delivered 150,000 troops and nearly 30,000 vehicles in an astonishingly short time.

This is smart planning, which not only defines the goals to achieve but also anticipates likely and possible course changes and contingencies that may be necessary.

In today's business world, planning takes place against the backdrop of accelerating change, which demands the rapid and continuous preparation and delivery of new products and services to the market. This creates an unprecedented requirement for a constant and highly productive effort at innovation.

The point, of course, is that the critical connection between the huge importance of planning and the relative uselessness of the plan is the exact connection between strategy and action. In strategy development we must clearly define our goals and the pathway we intend to traverse to achieve them while recognizing that we are likely—even certain—to have to adapt, adjust, revise, or even abandon our plans as we encounter the unexpected along the way.

The underlying threads are strategic intent and the alignment of the team or organization in that direction. This why strategy and planning are so important and are as essential for business innovation as for large (and small) military actions.

STRATEGY FOR AGILE INNOVATION

The strategic planning process for Agile Innovation consists of five steps:

1. Inward and outward awareness
2. Differential diagnosis
3. Articulation of the corporate utility function
4. Chartering of self-optimizing innovation teams
5. Development of a pivotable portfolio

INWARD AND OUTWARD AWARENESS

In the military this is referred to as *situational awareness*; in innovation, the focus is on learning how to see in a new way.

Product designers know the value of design ethnography and observational fieldwork for detecting unarticulated needs on which to build products. Agile Strategy extends this to include internal capabilities and disruptive business models as well as market opportunities.

Hence, this is both inwardly and outwardly directed.

To be successful, you not only need to see into the future to anticipate where the market and technology are headed, you also must look deeply into the heart of your customers to grasp their innermost aspirations. Perhaps even more important, is to see through your own internal blind spots and identify what may be holding you back so you can stop doing the things that aren't working anymore.

As we mentioned, what's needed is the ability to look at something that everyone else around you thinks isn't broken—but actually is broken—to expose innovation opportunities that are hidden in plain sight. Like the emperor's new clothes, once you invent something innovative, everyone else will suddenly see it too, remarking, "Of course, why didn't I see something so obvious and simple that was staring me in the face?" Mastering this ability will keep you ahead of your competition.

> The secret of innovation is the ability to look at something that everyone else around you thinks isn't broken—and see that it actually is. This enables you to discover opportunities that are hidden in plain sight.

Differential Diagnosis

Differential diagnosis is a term popularized by the superlative diagnostician Gregory House, MD, who is, sadly, fictitious. The TV show features a team of stunningly attractive doctors who work under a brilliant but cantankerous diagnostician in a metropolitan hospital. Each week the team convenes in the hospital situation room to brainstorm the possible causes of a rare and perplexing set of life-threatening medical symptoms. The patient's condition worsens as Dr. House and team try repeatedly to figure out the mystery. Failed treatments provide additional clues, enabling them to solve the puzzle and cure the disease at about page 30 of the 35-page script, or in the fifty-fifth minute.

The way it works as a method is that each of the doctors on House's team is a specialist, so each sees the symptoms from the perspective of his or her specialty training. The endocrinologist interprets the symptoms from endocrinology, the neurologist from neurology, the cardiologist from cardiology, etc. By coming together as a team with medical knowledge spanning diverse specialties they cross-fertilize their knowledge to come up with better diagnoses. And when all else fails, House breaks into the patient's home to see what's hidden there, knowing that the patient's environment can reveal causes that nobody noticed or thought were important enough to mention.

The traps that Dr. House overcomes are also waiting for the Agile Innovator, including various forms of bias, as well as motivational gaps. Thus, a pain point presented to your CTO will likely be perceived as a technology problem, while your CFO will see a request for funding. Your industrial design team will see the design flaws, the marketing group will see a lack of effective communication with customers, etc. They all may be right, but you won't make real progress unless you bring greater diversity and operate as a differential diagnosis *team*. Agile Innovation strategy follows the same principle, meaning that you need a team diverse enough to avoid thinking too narrowly and being trapped in any of these biases.

ARTICULATION OF THE CORPORATE UTILITY FUNCTION

Utility is a concept in economics and game theory, a measure of the ability of a product or service to satisfy needs or wants. Whereas consumer utility is difficult to measure because you'll have difficulty measuring benefit, satisfaction, or happiness, corporate utility is measurable in terms of business metrics, such as ROI, customer satisfaction, patents filed, or social return.

Our approach to corporate utility involves something called an "additive von Neumann utility function," but if you're not an economist or game theorist think of corporate utility as a way of combining profitability, cost, return horizon, competitive durability, impact to intellectual property strategy, impact to internal learning and processes, etc. For example, if your CFO tells you that all projects must make significant profits within two quarters, these cash flow concerns mean that the return horizon becomes the dominant factor in the utility function. If the budget is limited, then cost is the major factor. By articulating the corporate utility function clearly, it becomes possible for the entire organization to align with corporate strategy holistically.

The details of how to do this optimally are beyond the scope of this book, but we strongly recommend that innovation leaders study and master the concept and the principles, as they are central to an effective innovation portfolio process.

CHARTERING OF SELF-OPTIMIZING
INNOVATION TEAMS

Once you articulate the corporate utility function effectively, it becomes a compass telling you in which direction to proceed. Agile Innovation teams can then use the feedback it provides to align their efforts for maximum utility, that is, maximum benefit to the organization.

Teams should therefore tune their IdeaScrum process to reflect the corporate utility function, which is effectively a process of self-optimization. The IdeaScrum system is composed of iterative brainsprints, each adopting various perspectives, or ideation lenses related to the core corporate value drivers. For example, if improving a company's IP portfolio is important, then a brainsprint could be dedicated to increasing the patentability of an idea. If time to monetization is vital, then a brainsprint focused on how to generate revenues faster is a key driver. In this way, individual innovation teams will act in alignment with the corporate strategy to a much more profound level than was possible heretofore.

Note, however, that the perspectives derived from the corporate utility analysis are not the be-all and end-all for an IdeaScrum. In addition to utility optimization, every IdeaScrum should include an early stage sprint to harvest preexisting ideas and reflections. (We call this emptying the teacup, after the parable of the Zen master who kept filling the teacup for a new student until the tea flowed over the edge and pooled on the table, which was the master's way of explaining why it's necessary to let go of whatever you're holding on to and allow your mind to think freely and allow new insights to enter.)

It's also important to consider reframing questions that stimulate radical thinking (favorites include "How can we invert this idea?" and "How do we billion-ify this idea?") A more detailed discussion of reframing is presented in Chapter 10.

Questions are essential tools that both inspire useful new perspectives, and also enable the inquiry process to be shaped and directed. Identifying the most compelling questions is a major progress milestone:

Jonas Salk, inventor of the polio vaccine, once said, "What people think of as the moment of discovery is really the discovery of the question."

He was right, of course: It's the questions that drive innovation. And if a new question arises, a strategically significant one, then the practice of self-optimization means that individual projects and indeed the entire portfolio must pivot to align optimally with a changing utility function.

DEVELOPMENT OF A PIVOTABLE PORTFOLIO

Defining the corporate utility function enables a significant transformation by providing the basis for what we call a *pivotable portfolio,* meaning a portfolio that can be tuned to account for changes in investment priorities.

This becomes relevant when there is a change in the external environment that necessitates a change in the innovation portfolio. Because we anticipate that this may happen with some frequency, pivots need to occur rapidly and with as little pain as possible.

We'll describe the mechanics of the pivot below, but what's especially relevant here is that by aligning their work with the corporate utility function, we have brought new levels of rigor to the innovation effort by blending clear and focused definition of our goals with alert and systematic learning and exploration to overcome the inherent uncertainties in the process of reaching those very goals.

In essence, there are three ways to reduce innovation risk without unduly hampering agility: (1) by using portfolio thinking to reduce the risk of overall failure by diversification across various dimensions of innovation, which is explained in the following section; (2) by systematically applying metrics to tighten the uncertainty over time for all projects in the pipeline; and (3) by "rating the raters," which we examine more closely later in this chapter in the section titled "Evaluating the Reviewers."

Further, given the importance of this innovation journey to the future of the organization, everyone must be engaged, and hence invoking the innovation culture is a critical priority. We will discuss the culture in the next chapter, but first we need to understand how strategic intent at the leadership level can be transformed into the Agile Innovation social workflow at the implementation level. The *innovation portfolio* concept is our essential method of making this happen.

PORTFOLIO THINKING

Strategic planning efforts have made your goal or goals clear. How will you achieve them? Because the purpose of your strategy is to prepare your organization for a highly uncertain future, you must in fact create not only one single future, but also a suite of compelling future *options,* or scenarios, that describe the products and services that you expect your organization will have to create to be successful in a variety of possible future market conditions.

In some of these scenarios a given set of products and services will be essential to your success, whereas in other conceivable futures an entirely different set will be required; the rub is that as of today you simply do not and indeed cannot know which future will emerge.

Consequently, you will prepare many potential innovations and then allow time to unfold and history to reveal which (if any) is the right set.

The downside of this, of course, is that you will end up preparing new products and services that never make it to market. Indeed, this is one of the inevitable risks of dealing with and preparing for an uncertain future, a situation that is entirely unavoidable. And this is one of the main reasons that the logic of innovation is often deeply resisted by those who embrace the operations mentality: "Oh, the waste!" they will lament.

They will, in one sense, be entirely correct, and yet the history of business shows conclusively that every attempt to eliminate the waste results in the death of innovation.

> How, then, can you optimize your innovation investment and minimize your innovation risk?

This is precisely why you will apply innovation portfolio logic.

Such logic, practiced by professional stock portfolio managers and venture capitalists, is designed to counteract the danger of concentration risk, the danger of putting all the eggs in a single basket and then dropping the basket and ending up with only broken eggs.

If you select a single prediction of the future and align all your innovation investments to that singular expectation, this is equivalent to a single basket. If your chosen future emerges you will be a hero, but the odds of that are triflingly small. The more likely outcome is that you'll guess wrong, and the eggs will all shatter, leaving you with nothing but shell pieces and a gooey mess.

Think about your retirement portfolio. If you invest only in energy companies, for example, then the value of your portfolio will plummet when the energy sector as a whole goes down. An even worse strategy is to invest in a single company, a strategy that no sober investor would dare consider no matter how attractive the company may be today. Those who kept their entire retirement savings in Enron, Kodak, Lehman Brothers, or any of the former giants that collapsed suffered greatly when these companies collapsed.

That's why you have only some of your savings invested in energy and some in bonds, technology companies, consumer goods, and transportation. The goal to keep in mind is that you are seeking *an overall return* on the portfolio, knowing that at any given time some investments will inevitably fall or lag behind.

The trap that many managers fall into is that they so dislike the prospect of wasting precious capital, an aversion to waste that is in general a positive quality, that they insist that every innovation investment has to perform well. This is in fact an impossibility, and striving for it will kill innovation because it will drive the innovation team toward only sure things and *prevent* them from taking appropriate and necessary risks.

The reality is that you cannot innovate your way to greatness in small increments, and as big leaps are necessary to achieve big rewards, this means that it's necessary to take risks that may be uncomfortably ambitious.

Thus, the only suitable way to measure the performance of the innovation management team is on the performance of their portfolio *as a whole*. It is for this exact reason that we admire Warren Buffet for the overall performance of Berkshire Hathaway and do not lose faith in him although his very first investment was a complete bust. It is the total, annualized return that matters, particularly given the enormous uncertainties of this pesky, uncertain future thing.

The mind-set of portfolio thinking is the basis for a rational and optimal approach to managing risk.

The Venture Model

The same concept of the innovation portfolio is also used to structure the venture capitalist's collection of high-promise, high-risk start-up companies, and provides a very good model for the Agile Innovation portfolio.

Venture portfolios typically consist of investments in 20 or more companies selected in the expectation (and hope) that a least a couple of them will break through to produce gigantic returns (10- to 20-fold) within a few years. The underlying premise of this type of investing is that the investor must anticipate the future direction and needs of the market and find investment opportunities that will prosper.

Because the market and the future are both highly unpredictable, however, venture capitalists don't choose a single future solution into which they put all their capital. Instead, they avoid concentration risk by having many eggs in many baskets and by pursuing a variety of innovation projects that address multiple marketplaces in diverse ways.

> Applying this principle to your company means that you must achieve appropriate variety by investing in different types of innovations.

Four Types of Innovation

Different types of innovations address different aspects of the future, different types of risk, and different business needs, ranging from short-term, immediate-term, or market share–oriented requirements, to those that are long term, strategic, and intended to bring fundamental change to the market and the organization.

Incremental innovations are small changes to existing products and services. Every organization pursues these in the normal course of managing its products and services, largely because customers simply expect things to get better on a more or less constant basis. When Wal-Mart advertises "new, lower prices," which it does continually, this is the overt proclamation of incremental improvement. Similarly, when Starbucks introduces a new beverage, Toyota improves the brakes on its cars, Nestlé creates a new flavor of yogurt, or T-Mobile introduces a new subscription offer for its mobile phone customers, these are examples of incremental innovation.

Incremental innovations are regularly created in the normal flow of work, because every product manager keeps an ongoing list of possible improvements and upgrades. The most important of these are periodically selected for implementation and the changes are made, all with the intent of maintaining or slightly improving market share.

Incremental innovations are often highlighted in advertising in an attempt to convince customers that a given company is always making things better. In this respect, innovation is not only an inward-facing business function but also an important part of the company's public image.

Breakthrough innovations are higher-risk and generally longer-term projects. When they're successful, much higher rewards can be obtained, such as significant competitive advantage resulting from a change in the structure of the marketplace. The work of creating breakthroughs requires a different process from the pursuit of incremental innovations since more significant investments, fundamental strategic choices, and new competences are necessary.

Breakthroughs that succeed—such as Apple's iPod, iPhone, and iPad or Toyota's Prius—significantly enhance the brand and the market position of the companies that produce them. But intended breakthroughs can also fail, and when they do, they often do so spectacularly. For example, Coca-Cola introduced "new Coke" with great fanfare, but the market roundly rejected the product. The company was deeply embarrassed and soon withdrew the product. Boeing introduced its 787 jetliner, made largely of carbon fiber composite materials rather than aluminum, but technical problems delayed completion of the project, and subsequent technical problems caused further delays, costing Boeing billions of dollars and enormous public relations problems.

Of course, it's also true that these types of failures should be avoided in the first place, and one could argue that a more rigorous innovation process would have prevented these errors from making it to the marketplace. We would agree with that criticism, and indeed one of the main arguments for an innovation system that uses Agile Innovation is to avoid such outcomes, to catch these types of problems in the lab, perhaps during an IdeaScrum or in testing prototypes with actual customers.

Business model innovations are those that provide better customer experiences. A perfect example is the Apple App Store, which was a new approach to software distribution, a different type of business for Apple, and a disruption that changed the market in Apple's favor (and definitely a breakthrough). As with all breakthroughs, the pursuit of new business models is an intentional investment process that lies outside the normal flow of incremental improvements. Specialized teams can also explore and develop business model innovations, and it is advisable, for instance, to have a team focused entirely on how new technology is altering the marketplace, in that one of the most prominent features of the technological advances that are currently driving change is that they regularly become the basis upon which compelling new business models are being developed, as we see with eBay, Uber, Amazon.com, Google, and so many more.

The successful ones, and there are many examples, are highly disruptive to the established competitors, highly advantageous to many customers, and often lead to important new enterprises.

New venture innovations come about when a company recognizes that an entirely new market needs to be explored and developed. A perfect example is Nokia's entry into the mobile phone business, which occurred long after it had started in the paper and then the rubber industries. A more recent example is Toyota's creation of the Lexus brand to compete in the luxury car market.

In most cases, a new venture takes a company into a significantly new business area, doing so by means either of the creation of a business from scratch, or by an acquisition. In both cases new competences, new infrastructure, and new branding are required, and these fundamental changes are made with the expectation of significant long-term benefits.

The business design and initial staffing for new ventures is often done through a SWAT team approach, whereby a group of highly experienced team members is assembled to represent each of the major departments or disciplines that are required, and they dedicate their time for months to the development and (ideally) perfection of the venture. For most of the staff this is a full-time commitment, but it's often equivalent to having two full-time jobs. It's also a huge opportunity that may arise only once in a career—innovation at full speed, and with intense pressure to get it perfect in the shortest time possible.

Because speed is a critically important factor in all four types of innovation pursuits, Agile methods can make an enormous contribution. As a set of social and managerial conventions that are designed to eliminate unnecessary work, optimize the completion of essential work, and do so in the minimum time, Agile can provide significant competitive advantage.

But as we noted above, organizations that fear the risks associated with innovation gradually migrate their efforts toward an incremental-only approach, which itself creates higher risk for the long term. As our colleague Bill Miller often said, "If you focus only on incremental innovation, you will never find the future," and that is indeed a high-risk strategy, because the future will certainly find, and punish, you.

Consequently, the logic of portfolio design and management should become a core competence, one followed with exceptional rigor. The specific steps we recommend are described in the next section.

INNOVATION PORTFOLIO DESIGN

The Agile Innovation approach to portfolio management is structured in these major steps. We will look at each of them in turn.[4]

Step 1: Define the strategic terrain.

Step 2: Determine the performance requirements for the innovation effort.

Step 3: Design the innovation selection process.

Step 4: Build the portfolio.

Step 5: Make ongoing portfolio improvements.

STEP 1: DEFINE THE STRATEGIC TERRAIN

The strategic terrain, your company's competitive market landscape, is central to the design of your innovation portfolio because the innovation projects and ideas that you'll eventually have under development must align with the major strategic themes that are occurring outside. Similarly, you should also consider projects that are already under way in light of the same themes so that you can prioritize your efforts, and perhaps pivot the emphasis as needed. As we noted above, killing projects that deserve to die is a virtue in this world where speed is so important and you need to concentrate your talented people on the most promising and pertinent opportunities.

Hence, we recommend that you write a detailed statement that articulates the overall strategic direction for the innovation effort. This document is important because it will become a reference point that many people will use to channel their own thinking and decision making. It will help everyone understand your organization's strategic intentions so that they can align their own work and thinking with those key principles and concepts.

This is not to say that such choices and priorities will be permanent. In fact, we know that the opposite is true, because something will probably happen later today, next week, or next month that could radically change the situation, possibly forcing a significant change of direction. You should expect that to happen, although you probably won't know in advance when it will.

For each of the major strategic themes that are important for your organization's future, you should then consider developing specific projects that might have incremental value, as well as looking for potential breakthroughs and new business models. You may even want to consider new ventures that address the major strategic themes that are long-term drivers of change in your markets. Of course, technology will almost certainly play a critical role in all types of innovations.

Once you choose the themes, the next question will relate to the quantity.

> What is the right number of projects to address for each strategic theme?

The answer will be specific to your organization. No one but you can decide whether to develop 5, 10, or more projects per topic. With time and experience you will adjust your thinking and your portfolio to reflect the learning that you accomplish along the way, but you'll probably start with a guess.

Indeed, this is an important aspect of the overall Agile Innovation portfolio management process: It will require patience and time to develop and fine-tune your portfolio. The time we're talking about is at least two to three years, because that's how long it may take for projects to be completed, get to market, and start generating feedback.

STEP 2: DETERMINE THE PERFORMANCE REQUIREMENTS FOR THE INNOVATION EFFORT

What results do we want our innovation investments to achieve?

One part of the answer to this question is determined by the rate at which your existing products and services are aging and becoming obsolete in the marketplace. How fast, in other words, are existing revenue and profit streams declining? This rate foretells the future and reflects not only the future marketability of your existing products and services, but also the pace of competition in the marketplace, and thus how your competitors are evolving.

The rate of decline, sometimes called the *burn down rate*, is important for the Agile Innovator to know with some precision, because it tells you exactly how much revenue has to be achieved or made up through the innovation process to maintain the current level of revenue and profit. (Note that this is a slightly different concept of burn down than the one mentioned earlier in relation to project management; here we're talking about declining revenue, not a declining to-do list.)

For some products, such as cell phones, the revenue burn down rate is very fast. Most handsets are marketable for six months or less, so a steady stream of new ones is constantly in the development pipeline. In other industries, such as heavy equipment and commercial aircraft, the rate of change is much slower. But regardless of the industry in which your company competes, the decline rate is a factor that you must understand clearly.

You also need to be tracking the strategic factors that could abruptly accelerate the decline rate, and modeling how such changes might actually occur. Typically, again, faster decline comes about through technology innovation, and there is a lot of new technology emerging into the market that will certainly have major impact—nanotechnology, biotechnology, sensors, effectors, robots, etc., will all play a role in making today's new products obsolete by tomorrow, or perhaps even by this evening.

In addition, you have to factor in your organization's growth goals, generally expressed in terms of revenues and profits. These goals have been set, or will be set, by the CEO or the board, and they will likely reflect the organization's cost of capital, plus a risk premium for the character of the innovation process.

Taken together, the decline or burn down rate plus the growth goal tells you something of great importance:

> The analysis will show exactly how much the innovation process must achieve both in terms of revenues and profits going into the future, year by year.

Therefore, the overall mix of your portfolio must be carefully designed to achieve these goals, all the while avoiding concentration risk, preparing for and leveraging new technologies, anticipating major moves by competitors, understanding and accounting for evolving needs and preferences of your customers, and addressing the various time frames associated with the four types of innovation. Yes, it's a lot. But it's all entirely necessary.

Putting all these factors into a single model is by no means a simple exercise, but it's a critically important one, and if yours is a large organization then this must be worked out in detail across multiple markets, multiple product and services lines, and probably multiple business units.

STEP 3: DESIGN THE INNOVATION SELECTION PROCESS

To meet the innovation requirements that will become clear through the efforts in step 2 you'll need a lot of ideas. Hence, a key goal of the effective innovation effort is to gather hundreds or possibly even thousands of new ideas, based on the awareness that any of them may become vitally important to new innovation projects and the rounding out of a robust portfolio. The challenge, of course, is to select the right ones without becoming completely confused, to avoid overlap while avoiding gaps, and even to simply recognize which are the best.

For all these reasons, you need a systematic and orderly method of evaluating ideas and deciding which ones you're going to invest in, and of expressing why.

So now that you've modeled the strategic environment, you know what your strategic goals are, and you've identified the revenue targets that are expected to come from innovation investments in the coming years, you must next define the specific criteria that you're going to use to evaluate innovation ideas and projects. This evaluation will apply to ongoing projects as well as to newly suggested ideas. (As noted earlier, existing projects need to be reevaluated because when they were initiated and funds committed the decision criteria may have been different from the criteria that are most appropriate today.)

Developing the criteria is the basis for a systematic approach to evaluating the ideas, and for each of the four types of innovation, the specific criteria will likely be different.

The criteria will include assessment of risk, which could be financial risk, risk of not succeeding (i.e., that the idea really doesn't work out), technology risk, distribution risk, external system risk, and market risk.

Other suitable criteria may include these: fit with existing products and services, fit with existing organizational capabilities, how well the product addresses key customer pain points, how well it accomplishes important jobs for customers, how well it helps the company adapt to accelerating change, etc.

We generally categorize the criteria into two or three groups. *Market-facing criteria* include external factors, such as evolving customer need and technological change, whereas *internal criteria* cover factors such as existing competences, fit with existing brand, and development cost. A third section listing risk factors is also useful.

Figure 6.1 is a sample form that is typical, but of course each set of criteria is specific to a given organization. It's never a good idea to use someone else's list to evaluate potential innovations for your organization.

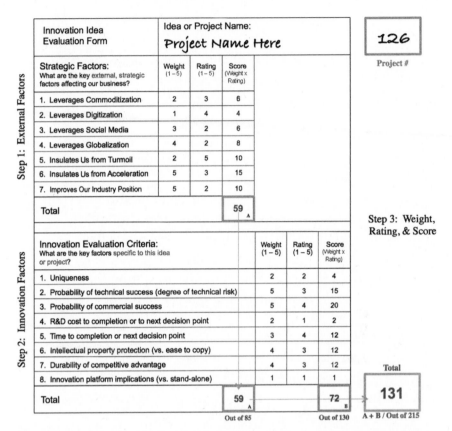

Figure 6.1 It's common that ideas need to be evaluated for external, strategic factors as well as internal factors, as shown here. Because not all criteria are of equal importance, the weighting column allows us to place emphasis as needed.

Technology-Enabled Idea Evaluation

Technology can provide very helpful support for this process, particularly when a large number of ideas are being considered. For example, if you install an idea-gathering system at your company, you'll find that a lot of idea submissions are duplications and similarities. Approaches such as computational linguistics and semantic analysis can prune similar ideas, or better yet,

(continued)

(continued)

cluster ideas with related themes or intents, and then alert the individual people whose interests are aligned so that they can connect and learn from one another.

Technology is critical for managing large databases of ideas-in-progress, tracking the existing idea portfolio, and mapping the new ideas onto the existing ones to help identify areas where new efforts are necessary or unnecessary.

We already discussed the idea of pivoting the innovation portfolio, that is, using systematic idea evaluation and dynamic weighting of evaluation criteria to facilitate more rapid adaptation (hello, Darwin?) when there is a change in the external environment. By shifting the weighting for a set of criteria, we can immediately find out which projects are most relevant to a new set of strategic conditions. This is strategic what-if analysis.

It can also help us learn who among our colleagues is best at the various stages and processes of innovation, by looking carefully at individual contributions across the stages (see the following sidebar, "Evaluating the Reviewers"). This is, of course, very valuable for coaching and training, and in composing teams that have the right mix of skills and strengths.

In summary, the right technology will keep an enormous store of data, which when properly analyzed and presented, provides invaluable support to the complex thinking, planning, decision making, and coordination tasks that constitute a systemic approach to innovation management.

Some of the evaluation criteria will be more important than others, so you'll also weight each of them. As we noted above, we use the Fibonacci scale, 1, 2, 3, 5, 8, which helps the higher-scoring factors stand out. Criteria that are more important will also have a higher-weighting score, whereas the less critical factors will of course be lower.

For a given cycle of the evaluation process, where you may be considering 10 or 20 new ideas, the weighting should be the same across all the ideas. But depending on the type of innovation and the specific internal and external context at the time you do the evaluation, you may choose to adjust the weighting in the future. Significant external changes, competitors' initiatives, new technologies, or regulatory changes could alter the overall context, and lead you to alter the weighting on your list of criteria, or even to change some or all of the criteria.

Evaluating the Reviewers

When you post an idea on the innovation system to gather input, you'll probably be interested in feedback from just about anyone who has relevant knowledge or experience. Over time, however, by tracking the accumulated feedback and correlating it with

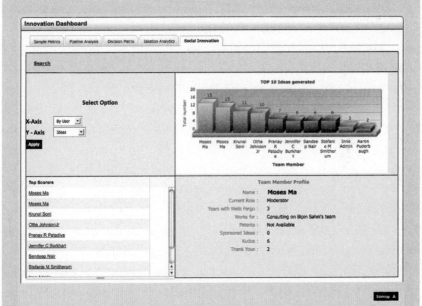

Figure 6.2 It's useful to track who is producing the most ideas.

(*continued*)

(*continued*)

subsequent innovation project results, you'll be able to identify the individuals who consistently offer the most valuable inputs.

That is, by reviewing the data showing how people voted in their evaluation assessments, you can also *weight the performance of the people* by looking at their track record in picking winners. This is of course similar to what portfolio managers do with their own portfolios; they increase the investments in those funds that are performing well, and reduce or eliminate those funds that are doing poorly.

It's also what services such as Morningstar do by rating the risk and performance of individual funds and categories of funds, all with the intent to help investors find the best match for their investment goals *and* their tolerance for risk.

Hence, the reviewers themselves can be weighted according to how successful they have been at recognizing successful projects in previous voting cycles. The weighted voting system is thus adaptive, because weights are adjusted on a continual basis.

Those with the best earned reputations in giving feedback get a higher rating, meaning that their feedback is weighted more heavily in aggregating the results during subsequent review periods. This means that technology is playing a role in making your organization smarter by helping identify the superior contributors.

Step 4: Build the Portfolio

Now we'll describe the actual process for assessment of risk and reward so that you can decide which ideas are worth pursuing.

The scenario here is that we have a set of 20 ideas to evaluate, and a group of 10 people is participating in the idea evaluation session. Note that only substantive and well-developed ideas should be evaluated, because these conversations will be detailed and highly influential, and it's not worth this depth of time investment for ideas that are in the rough, early stages of formulation.

First, there is a short discussion of the evaluation criteria so that everyone understands the criteria and what they mean. Next, each idea is presented by an *idea owner*, who is fully familiar with the idea and its development to date. After 10 to 15 minutes of presentation, questions, and answers, each of the 10 people scores his or her own evaluation form, without discussion. It's important not to discuss until everyone is finished so that there is no possibility of groupthink or undue influence.

Once everyone has scored the idea, a tally is made. Whenever the scores have more than two digits' difference, the people with these varying scores discuss their assessment. These discussions are good learning opportunities and often lead to agreement about the right score.

Once the conversations are complete the scores are recorded, and the group moves on to the next idea. It probably takes 2 to 3 hours to complete evaluation of 10 ideas. For each idea, average the scores from all evaluators, and plot the average scores on a risk-reward matrix (see Figure 6.3). Based on this evaluation process, the ideas that score highest in reward and lowest in risk will be found to the upper right.

However, ideas that score lower in reward or higher in risk may still be important or necessary investments. The evaluation process does not make the decision for us; it simply enables us to compare ideas that may be quite different from one another, giving us an apples-to-apples assessment. We choose to invest according to our judgment, possibly incorporating other decision-making factors that the list of criteria may not reflect. (Although it would take a very strong argument to overcome a very low ranking, and the discussion might cause us to reconsider our evaluation criteria.)

This standard portfolio management technique enables the organization to manage risk strategically and structure investments for an optimal level of return.

STEP 5: MAKE ONGOING PORTFOLIO IMPROVEMENTS

The final step to consider is an ongoing process, not really a step, because the selected projects will now enter the Agile Innovation development process, which could be a long one. Scrum teams will

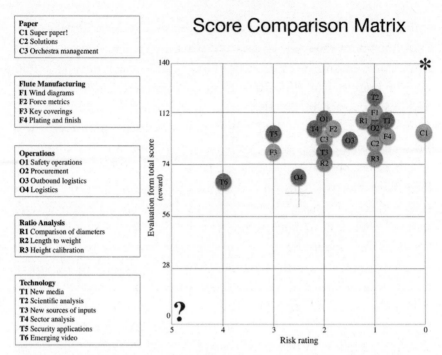

Paper
C1 Super paper!
C2 Solutions
C3 Orchestra management

Flute Manufacturing
F1 Wind diagrams
F2 Force metrics
F3 Key coverings
F4 Plating and finish

Operations
O1 Safety operations
O2 Procurement
O3 Outbound logistics
O4 Logistics

Ratio Analysis
R1 Comparison of diameters
R2 Length to weight
R3 Height calibration

Technology
T1 New media
T2 Scientific analysis
T3 New sources of inputs
T4 Sector analysis
T5 Security applications
T6 Emerging video

Figure 6.3 The 5 × 5 matrix enables us to compare the ratings on a set of 20 ideas, based on the idea evaluation form (Figure 6.1). The upper right is the sweet spot, whereas the lower left is the lowest ranking. Those ideas that are plotted to the upper right are therefore *probably* better, but we do not use this matrix to make the decision for us. *Instead, this plot is an input to the decision process.* Hence, although T6 may be the lowest-ranking idea in the set, it may nevertheless be developed further for any number of strategic or market reasons, whereas conversely T2 may not be selected. Note that the risk scale at the bottom is reversed, because high risk (to the left) generally indicates less desirability. (The project names, listed to the left, are hypothetical, although the base data were taken from an actual assessment activity.)

be assigned to work on them in sprints, and the portfolio as a whole will begin to emerge.

Each project team will develop the business case, which will evolve through rapid prototyping, customer interactions, and focused design work across many essential disciplines, which may include product or service design, marketing, operations, supply chain, manufacturing, finance, etc.

Multidisciplinary teams will be moving forward quickly, and you'll see which projects come to fruition over time and what impact they have both in the market and in terms of revenues and profits.

The overall goal is to balance greater freedom for autonomous Agile Innovation teams to do great work more efficiently, while automating the control infrastructure so that managers have improved visibility over the entire process. Similar to the management of Agile Software projects, Agile Innovation requires that every team member participate in the social workflow system to provide visibility into collaborative performance, accountability, creativity, and the collection of metrics. This is the promise of the real-time enterprise of the twenty-first century. And clearly, such an ambitious goal is too complex to undertake manually and thus requires carefully designed software support.

PORTFOLIO SUCCESS FACTORS

Some projects in your innovation portfolio, just as in any other portfolio, will inevitably be more successful than others. Some will fail, and you may need to remind yourself, or others, that in the right context this is both inevitable and even positive.

> Unlike most other parts of your business, where failure is considered entirely negative and is to be resolutely avoided, failing as a way to learn must become a central tenet in your innovation culture.

Even with this intellectual awareness, managers, even innovation managers, are sometimes reluctant to acknowledge that the logic of innovation portfolio management calls for the possibility of, and indeed the likelihood of failure.

Therefore, the Agile Innovator must be a persistent advocate for portfolio thinking from the outset, and must help (and occasionally remind) the rest of the executive team to understand the valuable role that failure plays in the overall process of innovation development.

To put it as concisely as possible, careful research has shown that attempts to eliminate the failures have the unintended and entirely undesirable consequence of also eliminating the big successes. Doing so pushes the overall innovation effort into a narrow band of mediocre middle ground, and although it can succeed in limiting the losses, the cost of doing so is far too high.[5]

Another critical success factor is obtaining the right level of capital investment for the innovation portfolio. Without enough money you'll find yourself constantly doing project triage, which will slow down your progress, frustrate everyone involved, and detract from the successes that might otherwise be achievable. However, to determine the right approach to capital investment and capital management requires that you also put in place the right metrics, which we will discuss now.

MEASURE TO MANAGE

Quite a large number of people will tell you that "If you can't measure it, you can't manage it," a comment that has been variously attributed to Peter Drucker, W. Edwards Deming, and probably quite a few other management gurus. However, unlike most core business processes such as operations, manufacturing, and logistics, the results of the innovation process, with creativity as its source and learning as one of its critical outputs, are somewhat difficult to measure.

Part of the power of the Agile Software approach comes exactly from its ability to measure the cadence and velocity of software development in an unprecedented and detailed way by using the rich data developed and documented every day during each sprint. Managers use this invaluable stream of data to assess how projects are doing, and perhaps best of all, they can do so *without* having to disturb the programmers for progress reports.

Agile Innovation brings meaningful measurement to the art of innovation by using similar performance metrics that analyze and identify strengths and weaknesses. By looking at factors including innovation velocity, the innovation balance sheet, overall ROI across the portfolio, revenues and profits achieved from innovation, and comparative rates of innovation across industry and competitors, we can indeed obtain useful data that inform the multidimensional measurement of innovation success rates and investment efficiency.

We can also, as we noted in an earlier sidebar, gain a great deal of useful knowledge about the involvement of our people in the innovation process, and determine who provides the best inputs across various stages of innovation development, thus enabling us to make the best use of their talents and bringing progressive improvement to our overall effort.

Metrics such as these make it genuinely possible for innovation to become an organizational function that, like the others, is dashboard driven, with the possibility of instant audits and ongoing feedback that you can and must use to fine-tune your innovation processes. This will also help you shift resources to those areas that are most likely to achieve the desired returns, and hence, to make progressive improvement in performance and in results.

Innovation and the Balance Sheet

The ability to quantify innovation performance effectively and accurately and to value a company's innovation portfolio reliably may eventually lead to a small revolution in the form of new financial reporting standards. Because innovation is a critical driver of company value, government regulators eventually could mandate that publicly traded companies regularly report on the key drivers of their innovation performance.

A critical problem with this concept, though, is the inherent and necessary privacy that surrounds the innovation effort. No company would want the contents of its pipeline to be made public, for very good reason.

Therefore, the way these data are compiled and reported will surely matter, and appropriate protections will have to be in place. If this can be done, these metrics would allow investors and companies to analyze their own strengths and weaknesses more effectively and allow management to plan and predict innovation value better.

(continued)

(*continued*)

Someday, perhaps, these reporting metrics could include:

- Innovation balance sheet
- Innovation velocity
- Innovation failure and success rates
- Innovation investment efficiency

One day in the future when a complete set of innovation metrics becomes the accepted standard, business leaders will look back to our time and wonder how anyone ever lived without them. Meanwhile, the challenge for today is that very few companies even know what their own innovation metrics are, and even if they do, they're certainly not ready to report them in public.

Nevertheless, these are probably the most useful forward-looking statistics that any company could muster about itself. Having the software that automates collecting these data, and useful standards for innovation management and measurement, is vital for making the quantum leap to the next level of innovation management.

BROADER INNOVATION PORTFOLIO METRICS

In addition to the four metrics mentioned in the previous sidebar (innovation balance sheet, innovation velocity, innovation failure and success rates, and innovation investment efficiency), there are also others of importance. As with strategy metrics, they are both qualitative and quantitative.

Some key qualitative metrics include:

- How does our innovation portfolio compare with what we think our competitors may be planning? It's important for us to gain as much information as we can using ethical means about what our competitors have in their innovation pipelines, because that will potentially influence our thinking about what should be in our own innovation pipeline as well.

- Do we have the right balance of incremental and breakthrough projects? As we noted earlier, the innovation decision process in many companies drives them to develop innovation portfolios that are entirely incremental, simply because incremental ideas are easier to understand, have a higher success rate, and represent opportunities to sustain or improve market share. Although breakthrough projects are higher risk, they must *not* be neglected, because they offer the potential to effect structural advantage in the market, and thus, they could yield much higher rewards. If we pursue them with rigor then a significant number might lead to future business lines, products, and services. We also need to be investing in business model innovations and considering potential new ventures to explore new markets.

- Are we introducing breakthroughs at a sufficient rate to keep up with change, or even to get ahead? Your thoughts on this question will also influence your decisions about the design of your overall innovation portfolio and the balance between incremental innovation and breakthrough innovations.

As an innovation portfolio manager, you should also consider that some projects and even entire brands can be created and used for experimentation, to explore the nature of consumer preference in the marketplace and push the envelope to track the evolution of tastes in the market. The more rapidly your markets are changing, the more focus you must put on these fundamental experiments, because they will help you avoid falling behind.

As for quantitative metrics, you must measure how your innovation portfolio is performing along these dimensions:

- Do we have a satisfying success rate? (Like Goldilocks, just right: not too high, not too low.)

- What impact did our most cutting-edge ideas and projects have in the marketplace? Did we set the world on fire? If not, why not?

- What sales and profits did they achieve?

- Did we diversify across the innovation types? Is our reach getting broader?

- Did we balance short- and long-term projects?
- Is there sufficient strategic alignment among our projects?

These qualitative and quantitative metrics will provide you with powerful management capabilities that you'll use to improve your results, your pipeline, and the performance of your team progressively. Overall, the development and use of metrics is a very worthwhile investment in and of itself, which should pay off nicely.

AUTOMATING PORTFOLIO MANAGEMENT

Collecting rating and voting data by the user community, criteria weighting, and evaluating the performance of everyone involved in creating, developing, and evaluating ideas become the basis of effective management. Collecting and sorting this information for senior management to use in the portfolio management process can and should be automated. In fact, a comprehensive, company-wide innovation effort in a large organization is probably not possible *without* automation.

Analyzing collaborative innovation metrics should include real-time what-if analysis, drag-and-drop interactivity, and group collaboration functionality to allow the senior management team not only to discuss ideas but also to determine individual weighting preferences for criteria.

REDUX: THE PIVOTABLE PORTFOLIO

But suppose that something happens in the external environment that causes the entire strategic situation to change. Suddenly projects that may have looked great a few months ago become irrelevant, and projects that were on the back burner become essential and come rushing toward the front. In this situation, how do we nimbly shuffle the portfolio to seize the strategic advantage or deflect the impending crisis?

Earlier we referred to this capability as the *pivotable portfolio*, a method of pivoting the entire effort to reflect a reshuffling of the strategic deck. Here we will look at the mechanics and the technology to support it (see Figure 6.4).

The underlying problem generally relates to the criteria that you use to evaluate projects; overnight, a criterion that was hugely important

Figure 6.4 We can pivot the portfolio as needed by adjusting the weighting of criteria. This would be done as follows: In the box on the lower left labeled *Select Option*, the four horizontal sliders can be dragged left or right to reflect a new set of conditions. Locating the slider to the left indicates low importance and thus low weighting, whereas to the right is high importance and high weighting. Adjusting any slider or combination of sliders in either direction will therefore change the idea score, shown on the bar graph to the right. Hence, idea 1 now ranks highest according to the new weighting. Although five ideas are in the *Idea Score* box, the point, of course, is that for organizations that are working on hundreds of ideas, the capacity to adjust, or pivot, the portfolio is nearly impossible without this form of automated approach.
Source: © 2014 FutureLabConsulting.com

dropped off the chart. In more technical language, the *utility function* changed.

Because your entire portfolio has been constructed according to a set of specific evaluation criteria that were weighted from the outset, you can change the weighting and dynamically, on the dashboard in front of you (see the sidebar and Figure 6.5), the entire thing will pivot in front of your eyes: Voila!

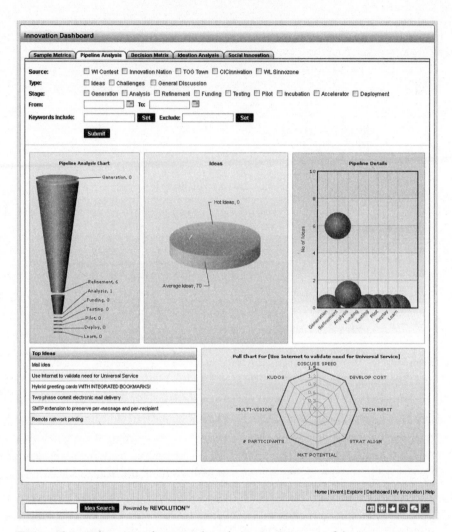

Figure 6.5 It's essential to visualize the innovation portfolio in many ways to get a full understanding of the status of the work in progress, and thus to manage it effectively. For example, in this view, the portfolio can be analyzed in terms of a pipeline and individual ideas viewed on a spider chart.
Source: © 2014 FutureLabConsulting.com

High- and low-priority projects will switch positions, and the newly critical projects will become fully evident.

However, suppose it's not an outright crisis but a need for some fine-tuning. Perhaps the CFO is demanding that the return horizon is next quarter. Then projects that exceed the targeted delivery time will see utility reduced, and may even require exceptional approval to proceed. Conversely, projects with short-term value creation increase utility, and by putting more resources on them, perhaps they can be hyper-accelerated.

Therefore, your dashboard software should map pivot vectors in utility space, that is, should allow you to reassess and reallocate across projects with the simple movement of a slider. Further, these pivots should track and display some sort of incremental value or ROI change.

The Innovation Dashboard

One of the primary reasons that innovation efforts are not well supported in organizations is that senior management's lack of visibility into what's going on inside the innovation effort makes them nervous. The finance department constantly receives requests for funds but is appropriately reluctant to invest in innovation because they can't track innovation progress effectively. To the CFO, money seems to be disappearing into a black hole, and no self-respecting finance officer wishes to be known as the source of this unaccountable largesse.

Therefore, the innovation dashboard is a critical tool to support effective portfolio management and to engage the finance office as the *partner* of innovation rather than its adversary. By providing the needed visibility, finance executives, and indeed all senior managers, gain access to both the overview of the entire innovation effort, as well as the details.

Just as in Agile Software development, the innovation dashboard provides essential functionality, and the exchange of visibility for autonomy is an entirely fair exchange. In many cases, the transaction will also involve visibility in exchange for needed capital.

(continued)

(*continued*)

The innovation dashboard enables managers to get an effective overview, to assess how projects are composed, and to see progress in a highly visible format. It should also indicate how the driving forces that have shaped the organization's strategy are reflected in each of the various projects, in the aggregate of all projects, and in the evaluation process for each one.

In fact, information on each individual project is easily accessible by clicking through, so users can go from the highest level of aggregate trend information to the revealing details of any project and each driving force.

Status updates on each project can simply be colored in green, yellow, or red, and the dashboard also shows, in a simple graphic format, the financial commitment made to each project, the funds committed versus the funds actually spent, and the innovation budget in aggregate.

All this information is essential to managing innovation while mitigating risk, and is a powerful tool for transforming worrisome uncertainty about the future into a dynamically proactive process of creating the future.

SUMMARY

The theme of this chapter is risk, and the full focus is on reducing it so that innovation investments will become an entirely normal activity in your organization. There's no way to escape the fact that innovation is risky, but there are lots of ways to control, manage, and mitigate that risk, and we have discussed many of them in this chapter.

Agile Innovation does this through clever and appropriate use of the portfolio principle, through a carefully structured process of evaluating ideas, by rigorously applying the scrum and sprint processes described in the previous chapter to speed things along, and by using technology to both automate the drudgery and provide unprecedented visibility, all the while enabling everyone—workers, managers, and leaders—to focus on creating and adding value.

Questions to Reflect Upon

- How does our organization define the boundaries of acceptable risk?
- How does our organization respond to potential risks after they become real?
- How do we distribute risk over a portfolio of different types of innovations (incremental versus breakthrough versus business models)?
- How does our innovation strategy align with our strategies for growth of the business?
- What metrics do we use to design our innovation portfolio?
- Do we have the technology necessary to manage innovation as a rigorous business process?

7

ENGAGING WITH COLLABORATIVE TEAMS

Culture isn't just one aspect of the game—it is the game. In the end, an organization is nothing more than the collective capacity of its people to create value.

—Louis Gerstner[1]

TRANSCENDING LIMITATIONS

The possibility of innovation is born when you transcend the beliefs that limit your thinking and engage in the search for new and better ways. When people are doing this consistently and throughout your organization, you will see a pattern begin to emerge which you will recognize as the dawning of the innovation culture.

This will happen when there is a total commitment to the view that everyone in your organization can make a real and meaningful contribution to the innovation process. Everyone can, in fact, be an innovator; part of your leadership task may be to inspire employees to believe this, because, in company after company, it has become conclusively evident that strong and focused leadership is absolutely required to bring forth and develop the innovation culture. Greatness cannot be achieved by indifferent leadership.

However, the notion of culture as a quality that describes an organization emerges out of experience. It is not something that results from a management decision, so although no one can mandate a particular type of culture ("The beatings will continue until morale improves . . ."), the role of leadership is to create the conditions in which it *may* emerge. As Gerstner wrote about the transformation of IBM, "Management doesn't change culture. Management invites the workforce itself to change the culture."[2]

A particular culture thus comes about when the beliefs *and* behaviors of many people, including the leaders as well as a significant percentage of the others, become aligned with respect to intent, values, *and* action. All three matter—and deeply. Without intent, there will certainly not be innovation; without the supporting values there will not be innovation, and of course without the requisite actions there will not be innovation either.

> An innovation culture must be inspired and nurtured. It cannot be ordered on-demand.

You begin by setting the example with your own behavior, by consistently sharing your views on the importance of innovation, by constantly promoting the value of innovation, and especially by making business choices that favor innovation, even when those choices are difficult ones.

Another of the key choices that leaders must make is to set aside their own egos and to adopt instead an attitude of support. Egotism and behaviors that often accompany it, bullying and manipulation, will squash the spirit of innovation and will in fact lead to the opposite kind of culture.

To evoke and develop the culture of innovation we must define what it is, what it is not, and how to achieve it. In the prior two chapters, we explored the Agile Innovation process as social workflow and as a rigorous process of portfolio management, and here we focus specifically on the culture and on your role as a leader in building it.

WHAT IS INNOVATION?

Innovation, we all know, is many things. It is an art, a science, and in many cases, a vision of a better future. For some, for Agile Innovation leaders and champions and creative geniuses in particular, it's also a passion, a set of specific skills, and even a lifestyle.

As an art it's similar to other media of creative expression, a craft you may perfect only after a long period of serious effort. As a science, it's based on learning to see the reality of things as they are instead of through filtered or distorted perceptions, but it also blends facts with elusive visions to identify not only what is, but also what could be, and especially what should be.

The Innovation Path

Some people (many people?) may attempt to innovate because it's expected or try to appear creative and toss in a few half-baked ideas when innovation season comes around, or when the CEO launches yet another ideation contest. But most people don't pursue innovation as though their lives depended on it, so they don't develop the skill or the passion.

Some do, however, live for the pursuit of innovation, and many of these are the ones we admire and emulate as innovation icons.

There is a striking photo of Steve Jobs sitting on the floor of an empty house in the zazen position (the cross-legged position of Zen meditation), and because we know a bit about his life and his accomplishments, the photo suggests that Apple and innovation are his meditation, his koan, and perhaps his path.

With no need for and no time for furniture, he achieved clarity by maintaining an intense focus on creating the future. For Jobs, innovation was his art and his life.

Does anyone in your company pursue innovation with this level of intention and intensity? Are people spending more time vying for praise than inventing, trying to take credit for someone else's ideas, or recycling old concepts over and over? Or are they rising above politics, accessing their inner genius, and innovating like the company's life depends on them?

Awakening people to the rigors of this path may shape, if not define, the future of your organization.

PEOPLE ARE THE CORE

People are naturally at the very core of everything involving innovation.

People (not computers) have ideas and visions about how the future could or should be different. People choose the best ones to invest in. People develop them, transforming rough concepts into precise objects, processes, practices, and ultimately into products and services that other people, as customers, are the ones who buy (or don't).

Most aspects of the Agile Innovation process involve the work of teams of people, and although we must not discount the role of individuals and their creative thoughts and inspirations, the bulk of the work is done in teams because innovation is inherently complex by nature, and multidisciplinary in its realization.

Hence, success at Agile Innovation, like success in Agile Software development, requires that organizations develop very high levels of proficiency in forming and managing teams.

> Self-organizing and self-optimizing teams are essential to Agile Innovation.

Teams are also well suited to the fascinating intellectual challenges of exploration work because self-organized team members are more likely to be self-motivated and willing to take on and do a brilliant job with the many complex and challenging roles that are essential to achieving innovation success.

This is why Jobs said, "My model for business is The Beatles. They were four guys who kept each other's kind of negative tendencies in check. They balanced each other and the total was greater than the sum of the parts. That's how I see business: great things in business are never done by one person, they're done by a team of people."[3]

But even self-organizing Agile Innovation teams are not leaderless. A crew needs the helmsman to steer the ship in the right direction; a symphony, and even a quartet, needs a conductor or a leader; a basketball team needs a point guard, all for the same reason. Hence, self-organizing teams aren't characterized by a lack of leadership but rather by a certain *style* of leadership.

While the right style for you depends on who you are and the way you prefer to express yourself, there are consistent themes that recur across many types of personalities. You can probably make your own list of traits based on your own observations of innovators you've met and worked with in the past; our list includes openness, honesty, and sincerity, of course, as well as curiosity, patience for results to emerge, as well as the impatience that drives the process forward.

No matter which specific qualities you feel are most important, the innovation culture as a whole emerges, again, when people see their company as an innovator, when they identify themselves as innovators, and when they feel that preserving, protecting, and practicing

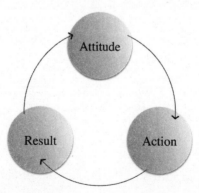

Figure 7.1 The right attitude leads to taking the right actions, which leads to positive results, which reinforces the right attitude, etc. Setting up such a positive or virtuous cycle is an essential aspect of effective innovation management and of the development of the innovation culture.

innovation are essential to their own expectations of themselves. And once achieved, success at innovation is thereby reinforced and becomes a self-sustaining cycle of attitude, action, and result.

THE VIRTUOUS CYCLE: KEY ELEMENTS OF THE INNOVATION CULTURE

Although senior leaders cannot dictate any sort of culture into existence, putting these key elements in place can help significantly to bring forth the innovation culture. These actions should focus on getting the right people, developing the right skills, and implementing the right roles. We'll discuss each of these now.

THE RIGHT PEOPLE

One of the downfalls of the business process reengineering (BPR) movement was the false expectation that good processes could compensate for less capable staff. Therefore, getting the right people wasn't considered as critical to success as getting the right process.

The Agile Innovation philosophy is nearly the opposite. Although some structure and process are certainly necessary, Agile's approach is similar to that of Steve Jobs. In his view, either you were A-team material or you were entirely unqualified. His language was more colorful, including terms such as *complete bozo* to express his disdain for those who were less than excellent, and he had a very clear focus on eliminating the bozos and working only with the A players:

For most things in life, the range between best and average is 30 percent or so. The best airplane flight, the best meal, they may be 30 percent better than your average one. What I saw with Woz was somebody who was 50 times better than the average engineer. He could have meetings in his head. The Mac team was an attempt to build a whole team like that, A players. People said that they wouldn't get along, they'd hate working with each other. But I realized that A players like to work with A players, they just didn't like working with C players. At Pixar, it was a whole company of A players.

(continued)

(*continued*)

When I got back to Apple, that's what I decided to try to do. You need to have a collaborative hiring process. When we hire someone, even if they're going to be in marketing, I will have them talk to the design folks and the engineers. My role model was J. Robert Oppenheimer. I read about the type of people he sought for the atom bomb project. I wasn't nearly as good as he was, but that's what I aspired to do.[4]

Allowing C players into the organization would be like opening a crack in a dam. Soon, the whole place would be flooded with mediocrity, and great work would become marginalized if not utterly impossible.

Hence, Agile Innovation suggests that you focus on recruiting great people, creating great products, and implementing great processes—in that order.

Why?

Because without the right people, nothing great can be built. Without a laser focus on the product, extraneous activities creep in that detract from both quality and speed. And without a useful (but minimal) process framework, you'll inevitably see the inefficiencies balloon, and the level of bureaucracy will soon get out of hand.

Having the right people implies, of course, that you must also get rid of the wrong ones. At a more subtle level, it also means that you need to recruit people with the highly desirable (and therefore elusive) combination of the right technical skills, the innovation mind-set, and an additional set of innovation-specific skills, which are not so widely understood.

THE RIGHT SKILLS

The technical skills are well known: business knowledge, such as finance, marketing, sales, programming, operations, supply chain, etc., plus innovation skills such as interface design, research, product design, all of the engineering disciplines, human factors design, and many others.

However, you can't create effective innovation teams by simply having one person in each of the key roles related to the business and innovation functions. It works much better if each of your team members has some of the requisite technical and business skills plus some of the talents and aptitudes that are particular to the innovation process, including empathy, listening, observing, modeling, ideating, and prototyping. Combining these skill sets leads to people with exceptional depth and all-star capability, just the sort you're looking for.

We think that in the future people will include these aptitudes on their résumés, but since at present these skills fall outside of the business norm, you may have to probe carefully during the recruiting process to find people who are proficient. We already encountered many of these skills in our detailed discussion of the innovation process in Chapter 5, especially in regard to the research process from need finding through modeling, ideation, and prototyping. Because they're outside of the norm, we'll describe the needed skills here in more detail.

Innovation Skills

- *Empathy:* Success at innovation requires people who see and listen more deeply than others, a skill known as empathy. Those with high empathy and great observational skills often lead the need-finding process.

- *Listening and observing:* Observing how people think and interact enables us to recognize the emotional connections that people have with other people, ideas, products, services, and brands.

- *Modeling:* Innovation teams also require people who can take a set of observations and extract the essential learnings, the process we call modeling. These are abstract, conceptual skills.

- *Ideating:* You'll also need people who are prolific in coming up with ideas—creative people, wild thinkers, people who make surprising connections.

(continued)

(continued)

- *Prototyping:* Those who can sketch, build, create maquettes, and quickly create elegant prototypes are essential in helping us transform ideas into possibilities and then into testable artifacts. These are skills of people who like to make things.

- *Risk tolerance:* Exploration and experimentation, the foundations of most innovation activities, entail the risk of making mistakes—of failing—and then learning from those mistakes. Those who are not comfortable in this mode of work will not be a good fit for the innovation effort.[5]

These skills are essential, but because they are not the norm in most organizations, people who can do this work need to be protected so that they can thrive. As Rob Austin and Lee Devin have noted, "Artful managers must also do their part; they must create conditions in which makers can work at risk. Willingness to work at risk is vital in artful making, in part because exploration is uncomfortable."[6]

It's not realistic to expect to find all these skills in one person, but talented innovation team members may possess two or three, and the most successful innovation teams generally have all these skills represented.

Once we recognize the importance of these roles, it's easier to grasp why most large organizations aren't very good at innovation: Most rarely (never?) recruit for these skills, and few compose innovation teams with them in mind.

Not surprisingly, venture capital–backed start-ups that are more sensitized to the critical importance of innovation often *do* recruit for these specific talents, and one of the most prestigious training grounds for these skills is in the heart of Silicon Valley at the Stanford University graduate program called the d.school. The *d* stands for design, and the methodology is called *design thinking*, which emphasizes, naturally enough, empathy, ideation, and prototyping.

The lovely book by Idris Mootee explains this quite eloquently. "Design thinking is the search for a magical balance between business and art; structure and chaos; intuition and logic; concept and execution; playfulness and formality; and control and empowerment."[7]

Program graduates are highly sought after, and generally have no problem finding great positions in outstanding companies throughout Silicon Valley and beyond.

THE RIGHT ROLES IN THE INNOVATION CULTURE

Over the course of many years of focused work we've come to recognize that effective innovation accomplishments (meaning not just a happy one-time accident but consistent performance over the long term) occur in a suitable corporate culture where three specific roles are well defined and executed.

Hence, in addition to the Agile Innovation business processes that define the process and the structure, and in addition to creating teams with the right mix of skills, the way you structure the innovation *organization* is important.

The three critical roles are:

- The creative geniuses, who utilize all the technical and innovation skills
- The innovation managers (or facilitators, coaches, or champions), who keep the innovation effort moving forward from day to day
- The innovation leaders, who bear the senior management responsibility[8]

This absolutely does not mean that each individual can play only one of these roles, and in fact everyone in the organization may be a genius, *and* a manager, *as well as* a leader. However, the three roles are fundamentally different. Although any individual can indeed play all three roles, no one plays all three *at the same time*. While you're actively engaged in the creative process, you may be participating as a creative genius, but at other phases of the process, you may be functioning as an innovation leader or manager. Mixing the three leads to confusion and diminishes the quality of the results.

CREATIVE GENIUS

The essential distinguishing characteristic of a creative genius is the capacity to see what others do not see, to uncover secrets through observation, empathy, and ideation that no one else has found. Examples include iconic geniuses throughout history, such as Leonardo da Vinci and Thomas Edison, who saw the world in new ways and discovered concepts, facts, and principles that others had not seen.

Creative geniuses explore incessantly, ask questions endlessly, and are driven by their curiosity to understand the world more deeply. Their exploration often leads them to envision how the world could be better. The difference thus created between their vision of future possibilities and what they experience in reality is the source of creative tension, which drives them to pursue their visions.

> Creative geniuses commonly ask questions such as "Why?" and "What if?" and take creative risks in the quest for satisfying answers.

Many are fearless and inexhaustible in the pursuit of solutions to the complex problems they're curious about. They may also be quite disciplined about this, gathering research, rigorously developing models that explain complex realities, and endlessly exploring new ideas.

Note how well this process matches with the research process that we described previously; it is, in fact, the same thing. Gathering such research can be called need finding, while developing models leads to new concepts and explanations, resulting in new ideas and solutions at the core of ideation and prototyping.

However, we've also found that some creative geniuses can be difficult to deal with. Perhaps this is because they're so focused on their own curiosity, their own ideas, and the questions that interest them, so they may neglect polite conversation or social convention. This is one of the team dynamics that must be closely managed, for these people can be tremendously valuable but sometimes annoying. It's important to prevent annoyance from ballooning into polarizing anger. Hence, because creative geniuses are so tremendously valuable to an organization they may need to be supported in a unique and specific way so that they can be contributing members while not creating extra frustration for themselves or for others.

Another great characteristic of creative geniuses is that they're quite willing to fail at any given time, as long as they feel that they're on the road to eventual success. We remember Thomas Edison's experience developing the incandescent lightbulb, which required about 10,000 attempts before success was achieved. Edison himself didn't consider those experiments as failures. His own comment was very revealing: "We learned 9,999 ways not to make a lightbulb." (The quote is probably a paraphrase, and the exact number remains a mystery. Various literature searches disclose numbers from hundreds to thousands.)

For Edison, this process of learning was a necessary and satisfying result, where others may have felt ego-damaging failure. Such persistence is characteristic of the creative genius and is a highly desirable attribute in the people on your team when you're grappling with difficult problems.

Hence, you'll want to recruit many creative geniuses to your organization, and you'll have to guide and support them.

AGILE INNOVATION CHAMPIONS

The second key role necessary to the innovation culture is that of innovation manager or champion. We've also called this person the coach or facilitator; all of these titles are valid.

> Champions play the role of conductor, captain, and scrum leader, which they do by opening the way for others, by organizing and supporting the innovation process, and by providing the right tools and infrastructure so that others can be successful.

This is not, however, a champion in the sense of an Olympic record-holder, the one and only best athlete, but the older concept of one who selflessly serves and represents others, such as the way a medieval knight was expected to serve his king.

Champions in contemporary organizations often are middle managers who serve as the bridge between senior managers and people working directly with customers. Their job in the middle is to understand the realities of the marketplace, the specific needs and desires of customers, as well as the organization's overall strategic direction, and to serve as a conduit of information and guidance in both directions.

Innovation champions have the rare ability to know when to push for innovation goals that are so important and valuable that rule breaking in the pursuit of the right goals is justified.

In a project-focused role, innovation champions contribute to success in these essential ways:

- Focusing the team on accountability and delivering results
- Supporting a group of individuals to function well as a team
- Helping all individuals develop their own capabilities
- Providing the team with needed resources while removing roadblocks
- Coaching the team and the customers
- Orchestrating the team's rhythm
- Helping the team connect the work with organizational priorities and strategies.

You can see that the essence of an Agile Innovation champion's role lies not in creating Gantt charts or status reports (although those are still necessary); it is in being focused on creating and facilitating high performance. Hence, after assembling a great team of people with the right combination of experience, talent, and aptitude, you may also have to spend some time managing team alignment. Even if all members of the team are bona fide geniuses, and especially if they are, clashing egos and complex, team-destroying, interpersonal issues can lead to conflict. Acknowledging this possibility is the first and perhaps most important step in avoiding it. Dealing proactively with it is the next. We will discuss this critical role in more detail in the next chapter.

One more very useful skill for the successful Agile Innovation champion to possess is a sophisticated systems thinking perspective. Many successful champions use their systems thinking skills and training to define the critical links between the purpose of innovation and the process of achieving innovation in a comprehensive way. These connections are critical to obtaining support and ultimately to creating value. Hence, the Agile Innovator is often a generalist with experience across many fields and disciplines that enable him or her to see across the boundaries to forge vital connections, rather than a specialist with a deep expertise in only one field.

AGILE INNOVATION LEADERS

The third role that is essential to the Agile Innovation culture is that of innovation leader. This person looks to the future and engages the entire organization in the quest to achieve the vision and its associated strategic objectives.

In the Agile Innovation process, leaders are those who set policies, who determine, for example, how much capital to invest in incremental innovation or in breakthroughs or new business models. They also establish innovation targets, and define many of the specific accomplishments that the organization should achieve. Leaders will articulate their expectations for the innovation process and for the broad participation of people throughout the organization.

One of the most important roles for innovation leaders, if not *the* most important, is to exemplify their commitment, as we mentioned above, and thus set the tone by their own example, demonstrating their commitment to the innovation journey by passionately inspiring and encouraging, and sometimes requiring that other people participate in the process.

Many innovation leaders have found that celebrating notable failures and the learning that results is a very positive message for the organization to receive. For example, Tata Group, one of India's greatest corporations, holds an annual innovation contest that attracts dozens of teams from all the company's many business units worldwide to share their successes and to compete for acknowledgment. In recent years, the company added another category to the innovation awards program, a category called *Dare to Try*, which acknowledges and celebrates notable ideas that were not successful—failures, in other words. When Tata Chairman Mr. Rata Tata stands up in front of the annual ceremony and announces the winners in the Dare to Try category, he sends a powerful message throughout the organization, reaffirming that intelligent failure is necessary, appreciated, and valued. From such actions, and in such a culture, it is quite easy to see the seeds of greatness emerge.

Support for the innovation process thus requires leaders to accept and acknowledge the value of intelligent failure in innovation.

A culture where it's safe to fail, both as a matter of policy and as a reality of daily life and work, allows and encourages people to explore their own ideas and to follow them wherever they may lead. Any outcome, whether initially labeled as success or failure, is recognized as valuable because what is learned from thoughtful efforts contributes to the growth of knowledge that eventually leads to success.

In summary, these three roles comprise an effective organizational framework upon which the right people with the right skills can discover and create the future. In its fullest expression, the innovation culture is a profound accomplishment and the basis upon which future successes can be built.

Cargo Cult Innovation

What happens when managers wrest control of the innovation agenda, even when they're really not very interested in it? We call these people cargo cult managers. During World War II, vast amounts of war materiel were airdropped into Melanesian islands by both the Japanese and later by the American armies that were based there. At the end of the war, of course, the air bases were abandoned and cargo was no longer being delivered. In an attempt to keep the cargo supplies coming, cargo cult rituals were developed by islanders who adopted a whole slew of cult-like behaviors, including the construction of mock airstrips, mock airports, and radios made out of coconuts and straw, in the belief that these structures would then attract more aircraft full of actual cargo. Believers staged parade drills and marched with twigs for rifles and *USA* painted on their bodies.

Cargo cult innovation is pointless, ritualistic behavior that is only a hollow show, one without substance. Cargo cult managers are the ones who use all the right buzzwords . . . but in reality, their personal agendas are the single biggest threat to true innovation in your organization. These people can only pursue their agenda of politics, top-down control, empire-building, and gatekeeping.

Cargo cult managers are often the ones who put the *no* in in*no*vation, because you hear them say no far more often than you hear them say anything positive.

Perhaps it's obvious, but we're rather insistent on this point because we've seen how damaging it can be. In one company we worked with, a brilliant team came up with a brilliant idea, but when singled out for praise, they humbly deferred, insisting the idea was a team effort. "In that case," a senior manager announced, "I'll take the credit, since the team works for me." It was the last great idea they ever had.

Hence, perhaps the greatest dangers to innovation aren't posed by the laggards or the ones who openly resist innovation. It's the cargo cult manipulators who jump on the bandwagon when it's fashionable but have neither the interest nor the talent for the hard work that brings innovation about. Learn the difference between authentic innovation and cargo cult innovation, and you're well on your way to neutralizing their threat.

PROMOTING COMPREHENSIVE TRANSFORMATION AT WELLS FARGO

Wells Fargo is a good example of how a systematic approach to applying the three roles can help transform an organization that really is committed to innovation. A recent project focused on a loan-processing center that consists of about 400 employees operating in four locations, who handle commercial loan applications for the entire bank. When the project started, this group was considered one of the least innovative in the company. Key stakeholders often referred to this division in an unflattering way, as one that was "trapped in the bowels of the company." There was no expectation that things would change in any substantive way. Once trapped, they would always be trapped.

The group was quite efficient and well managed, but it had been unable to achieve improvements in throughput—as measured by documents processed per person—and it was assumed that most of the possible innovations had already been wrung out of the organization. The system that collected ideas for process improvements had received fewer than a dozen ideas from this group during the previous year. Margot Golding, an executive vice president at the bank, explains:

> I was 20 years and eight positions into a cross-functional Wells Fargo career, mostly on the institutional banking front lines. This group was an interesting challenge in that it felt like a "stuck" culture of people wedded to 8 hours of daily routine. The innovation project was an effort to change the culture from a "phoning it in" to "engaged, with a personal stake in achieving productivity increases." Everyone was assuming that we didn't have what it took to contribute to the innovation process. What we wanted to do was to prove everyone wrong and to "move the needle" by achieving an order-of-magnitude change that would definitively prove that innovation can come from anywhere within the organization.

Hence, Golding commissioned an aggressive pilot program with the intent to demonstrate the value of a systematic and comprehensive approach to change. Actions included a detailed ethnography-based innovation assessment, an intensive six-week innovation training for team leaders, the installation and configuration of a new ideation software tool, the installation of *thinkspot* brainstorming rooms that included videoconferencing to support greater collaboration between the distributed office locations, and incentives for those who contributed innovative ideas. In addition, a key factor was the establishment of a strong *iTeam* led by Wynn Roberts, who was a creative thinker and excited by the idea of bringing innovation to loan processing.

The ethnographic research led to a key discovery. The group had a culture of people who had ritualized the processes and encouraged a no-complaining culture that did not inspire change. This unintentionally suppressed discovery of pain points where innovation could make a difference.

It became evident that Wells Fargo embodied a stoic and heroic culture. Consequently, people avoided complaining and instead worked extra hard to get their work done even if their systems weren't working correctly. People just came in early, worked late, and found work-arounds, and the few process innovations that were generated came from senior managers who observed inconsistencies that had come about because of ritualized behaviors instituted by previous managers.

During the training program that followed the ethnographic analysis, it was made explicitly clear that it would be okay to complain—as long as you accompanied the complaint with a solution—and people would be rewarded for innovativeness and solutions. About a third of the staff in this operations environment viewed their job as boring and routine and were planning to be there only long enough to step to something more challenging and engaging. This subset of the group had the potential to outperform, but simply didn't. However, this program produced positive momentum, as people realized that their ideas were valued and that things could get better. As they started to see that this could be a rewarding place to work, the mood and attitudes of the staff greatly improved.

These changes made it acceptable for people to suggest process innovations without appearing that they were complaining, and it resulted in a massive surge in innovativeness. Twenty years of pent-up frustration and stoic work-arounds exploded in a flood of more than 700 ideas submitted in the first six months of the pilot, reflecting a better than 50-fold increase in the baseline rate of innovation. In addition, the system outperformed every other division in terms of ideas per employee by a factor of 10.

Were any of these ideas actually any good? After all, the quantity of ideas may be a nice metric, but if none of the ideas are helpful, then that's not meaningful.

In the final tally, nearly 100 ideas, or about 15 percent of the total, were judged *significant*. Some of the ideas inspired important process innovations, including the development of a new credit applications platform website, an enterprise fax solution, and significant enhancements to an imaging system that reduced the time required to locate documents.

In addition, this project led to more benefits across the organization, including these:

- By making the innovation system open and transparent, people learned that not all the ideas could or would be funded, and consequently team members didn't take it personally when their pet idea didn't get implemented.

- The increased focus on innovation helped the company restart its core intellectual property strategy, which had languished. Although it had only a dozen patents before this era of innovation began, it is now aggressively developing a complete portfolio.

- This operations group simply did not consider itself innovative, which led it not even to *try* to be innovative. During the course of the project, many team members realized that they actually were quite innovative, and subsequently they innovated more than the rest of the company. This has improved the organization's attitudes and increased a sense of being part of a winning team, yielding better employee retention.

- Explicit documentation of ideas improved corporate memory, which helped the group stop reinventing the wheel every few years.

After rating and refinement, the portfolio of 700 ideas produced 40 good ones and 5 excellent ones. Management believed that activity levels increased around 5 percent per year, even though staffing was essentially flat. However, Golding adds, "It wasn't the ideas or process innovations that had the greatest impact. It was the effect that the innovation program had on the attitude and culture of the staff. Being listened to and valued increased the motivational level of the group, and you could see a subtle but immediate impact on processing throughput and also in the quality of customer service."

SUMMARY: INNOVATION CULTURE METRICS

As you work to develop the innovation culture in your organization and evaluate your performance, one of the most important metrics to consider is speed. Applying the principles and practices of Agile Innovation should lead to a significant acceleration of innovation project completion, steadily increasing year after year.

> Your organization can get faster and better at turning ideas into completed innovations that deliver value in the marketplace.

Over time, you can expect to see an increasing number of people who are participating in the innovation process across all phases, from research to idea gathering and throughout development. Innovation is the cool, exciting place to be, the hope and expectation for the future, so eventually everyone will want to join. That spirit will contribute enormously to achieving your end goal, which, of course, is generating stunning revenues and handsome profits with innovations.

You should also expect the quality of the innovation contributions of each person to rise. The capability of individuals, teams, departments, and entire business units will improve, and as the ongoing performance of the organization and its innovation efforts thrive at the same time, the much sought-after virtuous cycle will result.

The quality of the ideas being shared should also improve. As people learn, they naturally recognize business opportunities that are less obvious, and they can propose better opportunities for both incremental and breakthrough innovation possibilities.

Overall, the goal is constant improvement, continuous and valuable learning that is applied and transformed into positive business outcomes. Although the focus is on the actions needed to meet the challenges of external change, the larger goal is to perceive change as an ally, to embrace new mind-sets that will yield increasing value for the company.

This is the ultimate benefit of developing an innovation culture in your organization, achieving a potentially massive return on the significant investment of time and effort.

Questions to Reflect Upon

- How do we define *innovation* in terms of people and corporate culture?
- What are key roles in our innovation organization?
- How is the Agile process different from the ones we use?
- What does our innovation pipeline look like, and how has it been created?

8

BUILDING AGILE
INNOVATION AS A
CORE
COMPETENCE

Define the right outcomes and then let each person find his own route towards those outcomes.
                    —Marcus Buckingham and Curt Coffman, 1999

One aspect of the Agile Software development process that works so well is the explicit social contract between the programmers and the managers, one that's quite different from what's considered normal in traditional software development organizations. The resulting behavioral change is enormous, and it's a huge part of the reason that Agile is so successful.

In this chapter we'll explore some additional management practices that will support the development and maturation of Agile Innovation in your organization.

AGILE COACHING

The purpose of coaching and team development is to unleash the capabilities of each member of the team and of the team as whole. One of the most effective forces that coaches use is the motivation that comes when people understand what is needed and expected of them in terms of outcomes, because this defines targets, scope, and ambition.

With this useful context in mind, each individual can then be guided on his or her own route, continuously improving domain knowledge (both technical and business), self-discipline, and teaming skills. Because we're dealing with A-team players, as long as the ways of working and the chosen routes are compatible, autonomy will inevitably lead to better results since A-team players are by definition self-motivated, competent, and share the same aspiration to produce great work. The right people want the opportunity to figure out for themselves how to deliver the desired results, so the best managers and leaders manage to outcomes, not activities, because this engages internal drive rather than imposing external carrots and sticks.

Achieving the product vision requires an understanding of the project's boundary conditions, so team leaders need to help all team members grasp not only the actual schedule, but also the reasons *why* the dates are critical. The better the team members comprehend a project's constraints, the more able they will be to work within those boundary conditions and make sound trade-off decisions in their day-to-day work.

Nevertheless, from time to time it's likely that every team member or even the entire team will become mired in the details and perhaps lose sight of the goal. When this happens, a project manager must provide some coaching by refocusing the team, and there are many ways to do this. One way is by engaging members in an assessment of the project to date to reset at the task level, which will essentially recalibrate the sprint and reassess the backlog. It can also reinvigorate a group by reminding members of their ultimate purpose, and reiterating the role that their output will play in the broader organization's goals.

Visual management is an effective and painless way that coaches can reinforce project goals. Putting up signs, graphics, or posters in locations where they'll be seen frequently can be a subtle but effective reminder of project parameters and objectives. It's important, though, that these visual reminders not convey hype or platitudes, because that will have the unintended effect of turning people off.

FACILITATING AND MANAGING COLLABORATION

Self-organizing teams are, by definition, proficient at collaboration. The factors that support effective collaboration include choice, trust and respect, an open flow of information, honest debate, active participation in decision making, interaction, and accountability.

CHOICE

People are most effective when they have choice about the work they do. Most of us do not expect or require total control or autonomy, but we also don't work well when we lack structure. Consequently, proficient leaders collaborate with their colleagues to identify the right projects, roles, and responsibilities that meet the needs of the organization and the individual. During times of crisis, of course, we all pitch in and do whatever's needed, as we saw in the short case study on Southwest Airlines' 10-minute turn, but during less intense periods we like to have some say in what's expected of us.

TRUST AND RESPECT

Trust and respect are, of course, very closely linked, and people are simply not inclined to respect those they don't trust, and vice versa. (This is another reason that having the wrong people on a team can have such a detrimental effect—lack of respect degrades trust, and a downward spiral ensues.)

"Trust is the confidence among team members that their peers' intentions are good, and that there is no reason to be protective or careful around the group," says Patrick Lencioni in his very interesting study of team dynamics.[1] Trust enables team members to share their half-baked ideas without fear of ridicule, and because they're innovation pros, they also know that the greatest ideas often began as half-baked ones.

Respect comes from understanding other people's roles in a project and recognizing their competence to fulfill those roles. Engineers who understand how product marketing contributes to project success, and product marketing people who acknowledge engineering's essential contribution to product design and manufacturing (to take two engineering roles) will be more effective team contributors because they will naturally be inclined to rely on the expertise of their teammates.

OPEN FLOW

Complex systems, such as large project organizations, are characterized by interaction and information flow. Too little coordination and information can result in teams that diverge too far, making integration a nightmare. Too much coordination and information flow, on the other hand, can mire teams in constant meetings and lead quickly to information overload.

In our experience, it's much better to create project systems based on information pull rather than information push. There should be an abundance of information available to each individual and to the team as a whole, but most of it should reside in a well-organized repository that people can browse, search as they require, and retrieve from as needed. The amount that is pushed out in the form of instructions, requirements, and announcements should be minimized.

Another dimension of openness is a key factor in the success of the idea collection process. As described earlier, the development of a widespread innovation culture means that people throughout the organization are encouraged to share their ideas whenever they arise. Sharing ideas frequently occurs via an idea portal of some kind, an online submission tool. Many tools do this, and it's not too difficult to accumulate a very large collection of ideas rapidly. But what happens next is actually the critical step that often determines success or failure.

Why is this?

Our ideas, it seems, are a lot like our children. People feel deeply attached to the ideas that they come up with, and because of their sense of attachment they want to know what's happening to their ideas throughout the innovation process. Did my idea get past the first screening? Is it moving forward to the project stage? Who's in charge of it now? These are all common and logical concerns.

However, if an idea is submitted and then it just disappears, never to be seen or heard from again, the result is generally discouragement, demotivation, and thus a very short useful life for the idea collection system. When people lose confidence and interest in the process, they will simply refrain from participating.

Conversely, keeping people informed maintains engagement. While people are smart enough to know that not every idea is a good one, and not every idea will advance to the development stage, honest feedback about the assessment and the outcome, plus a strong dose of honest encouragement and appreciation, are all necessary and valuable. Simple thoughtfulness as well as open disclosure will do a lot to sustain the system and make it an integral and productive aspect of the company's culture over the long term.

For the innovation team, however, this may require a considerable investment of time. An automatically generated e-mail acknowledging the submission of an idea is fine, but it's not sufficient. Someone on the innovation team has to take the time to respond to people, to update them, and to acknowledge them.

> When you build your staffing model for the innovation team, allow a considerable amount of staff effort for maintenance of the idea submission system and for ongoing dialog with the growing pool of people who will become enthusiastic about sharing their best ideas.

HONESTY

There is more to successful interactions than just talking. From time to time in any project team's development, it will happen that widely divergent opinions and high stakes characterize crucial conversations, which usually leads to emotional intensity. These are make-or-break conversations, ones in which the character of a team is forged.

Do these conversations degenerate into personal attacks and finger-pointing, or do these conflicts help the team align? A couple of factors seem to determine whether the team has the self-discipline and character to engage successfully and move beyond their differences, or becomes stuck and degenerates into a clash of personalities.

The first factor is a commitment to honesty. Each and every member must take the initiative to raise the issue when others are not performing or behaving according to team rules. No one should be exempt, because ignoring problems and letting them fester isn't acceptable behavior and it doesn't lead to success. Thus, even an administrative assistant may need to point out a project manager's omission if the situation dictates.

The second critical factor is that conversations must be directed toward getting all the relevant information out on the table for the group's consideration. Keeping secrets does not serve a project team.

DECISION MAKING

Decision making is central to effective collaboration. Anyone can chat about the design of a product, but genuine collaboration to find brilliant solutions to complex challenges means working together in a focused way to define the necessary features, figure out how to build them, document the design, and build the business case.

Literally thousands of decisions, both large and small, must be made over the life of a complex project, and how a team handles those decisions determines whether effective collaboration is occurring. Some teams arrive at quick decisions by deferring to the technical lead, and others are driven by those with the loudest voices, but neither of those situations is conducive to true collaboration, nor are they conducive to achieving the best results.

When a team is developing genuinely innovative ideas, however, the information available to those who must make decisions generally remains fuzzy for quite some time. Customer preferences and unarticulated needs may not be clear, new technologies may be untried, and the best designs may not be at all apparent. In Agile Innovation, therefore, fuzzy logic usually is the necessity rather than the exception, and teams can sometimes become frozen by the lack of clarity and drift into analysis paralysis.

When all the discussion, debate, and dialog have reached an impasse, or when the ambiguity of the situation overwhelms the decision making capability of the team, it is then that a leader must step in and give the team direction. The effective leader absorbs the ambiguity, takes responsibility for the decision, and enables the team to get on with the work.

INTERACTION

One of the principles of adaptive organizations is that innovative results emerge from interactions among diverse individuals. Each person brings different ideas, information, and insights to the development process, and often the integration of these various perspectives results in breakthroughs.

As we have noted, innovation teams may require the technical expertise of engineers, product specialists, and scientists from diverse domains, and the best solutions often emerge when they work together to consolidate their expertise into consistently high-quality designs.

To accomplish this, individuals balance the time they need to spend alone to develop their particular piece of the product puzzle with face-to-face time interacting with others to fit the pieces together. Frequent interactions help generate understanding, leading to greater mutual respect and trust.

> Without enough interaction among team members, synergy of ideas won't happen, and innovation suffers.

Interaction can take many forms, from brainstorming sessions to spontaneous hallway chats, from formal technical design reviews to online group discussions, and, in the software world, pair programming. Regardless of the method, the objectives are the same: to share information, to co-create a product feature or development artifact, or to make a joint decision based on a shared understanding of what is best.

Innovation champions and project managers must encourage and enable this peer-to-peer interaction, particularly as pressure mounts and individuals have a tendency to "go dark" when they're self-absorbed in intense production mode.

ACCOUNTABILITY

Accountability is the secret sauce necessary for creating self-organizing teams that work well. When a software developer commits to delivering a particular feature, he or she accepts accountability for that delivery. Similarly, when a team commits to delivering a set of features by the end of the second project milestone, all members of the team are accountable.

The same is true for Agile Innovation teams. For example, when an idea owner helps prioritize a sequence of design iterations and features, she agrees to be accountable for providing all the necessary information on the project's requirements. Facilitators, likewise, agree to be accountable for resolving impediments to team progress. When a team member commits to providing market size estimates within a week, he has agreed to be accountable.

When any team member commits to a deliverable, when the team as a whole makes commitments to the customer, and when the project manager commits to provide the team with particular resources, they are all agreeing to be held accountable, and being able to trust that your teammates will deliver is the glue that holds the team together.

> It is crucial that each and every member of an IdeaScrum team hold the others to their commitments, because co-accountability is critical in Agile Innovation.

REMOVING ROADBLOCKS

When individuals are waiting for resources such as computers, lab equipment, or staff assistance, they lose productivity, and worse, they lose precious and irreplaceable time. Project managers contribute directly to the achievement of results by ensuring team members have the resources they need. This style of project management is based on the commitment to serve the needs of a team, an approach Robert Greenleaf aptly called "servant leadership."[2] In this model, the leader works for the team rather than the other way around.

Impediments may include lack of resources, lack of information, or lack of decisions; whatever they are, it is the project manager or champion's role to address and overcome them.

ORCHESTRATING TEAM RHYTHM

At times, a project manager's job mirrors that of an orchestra conductor, keeping all the instruments in rhythm while bringing each section into the music precisely at the right time. In other situations, the team operates more like a jazz band, with each player improvising around a common structure.

Agile projects are rhythmic and iterative, alternating between intensity and reflection, as teams work to deliver features and then pause to learn from the results. There is the rhythm of daily integration meetings and interactions with customers on feature details, and the rhythm of peer-to-peer interactions as designers, engineers, customers, and business specialists meet at whiteboards to thrash through a design before shifting to more private reflection and work. In total, this reveals itself as an underlying rhythm of thinking, designing, building, testing, and then reflecting on increments of work.

There is also likely to be a parallel emotional rhythm of anxiety and euphoria as people struggle to understand and solve, and ultimately succeed in solving problems that once seemed intractable.

Project managers provide tremendous value by orchestrating this beat, guiding team members to make time to reflect after high-pressure delivery work, helping them find the right balance of working alone and working collaboratively, and helping them deal with anxiety and ambiguity.

However, this way of working doesn't work for everyone, and those who are unable to overcome their discomfort with these varying rhythms may experience difficulty transitioning to this kind of team, and in the end it may not be for them. Although some people have a strong preference for linearity, the execution of Agile Innovation is rarely linear.

The Innovation Audit

How do you determine what your own organization's innovation strengths and weaknesses are so that you know where to focus your improvements?

To measure your organization's capacity for innovation, a comprehensive and honest audit is essential. It will identify what's working well, what's not working, and how to design and implement the needed corrections. The audit should focus on evaluating the critical factors that enable innovation to thrive and should examine a broad range of issues from the human and cultural to the structure and process, to the strategy and investment.

Over the course of many years we've identified seven technical factors that are critical to innovation performance and seven others that are cultural.

The technical factors are:

1. Alignment of strategy and innovation
2. Contents of the current innovation portfolio or pipeline and the ideal portfolio
3. Research capabilities in the sciences as well as in need finding and human interaction
4. Innovation management capabilities and roles
5. Alignment of innovation with sales
6. Innovation metrics and rewards
7. Infrastructure, including methods and tools

The cultural factors are generally more subjective, but are also crucial in ensuring the effectiveness of your organization's innovation performance. These factors are:

1. Innovation culture
2. Creativity capacity

3. Level of trust

4. Quality of leadership

5. Mind-set

6. Attitude

7. Tone

It works well to conduct the audit by holding conversations with people throughout the organization, not just senior managers. You should also interview outsiders, including customers, suppliers, and partners, to learn their views on your firm's innovation performance, strengths, and weaknesses. Interviews often last 30 to 60 minutes, although they could also be longer. After conducting perhaps 50 of them, you should have a very good understanding of the innovation capacity at your company, its strengths, and its weaknesses.

The goal of the audit is, of course, to identify major improvement areas, and it's not unusual to find as many as a dozen or more key action items that the enterprise could focus on. These will become the primary drivers of an innovation action plan.[3]

INNOVATION IS A TEAM SPORT

Over the years we've identified these key factors that have proven particularly important to the success of innovation managers. The first of those is simply helping people manage their time well, particularly for team members who are not dedicated to an innovation initiative, for there is a strong danger that they will become absorbed or overwhelmed with day-to-day work and won't have sufficient time to explore new ideas or fulfill their scrum responsibilities. Part of the innovation manager's role is therefore to help people find the time, or make the time, to participate effectively in the innovation effort.

Some organizations, such as Google and 3M, are well known for encouraging their staff to spend up to 10 or 20 percent of their time working on their own ideas, an institutional policy designed to foster creativity and exploration. However, when we talk to people at these companies, they sometimes tell us that these programs don't work quite as advertised. At one company that ostensibly had such a policy, the 10 or 20 percent was expected to be *in addition* to the 100 percent of their time that was already committed. Another employee told us that so few people actually had that arrangement that it had become irrelevant. Hence, we are reminded that if something sounds too good to be true, it's probably not true.

Despite these issues, the underlying problem of time management is one that absolutely must be addressed, both as a strategic matter of getting the innovation work done and as a cultural matter of promoting values that are important to long-term sustainability and success.

A second critical factor that enables innovation managers and champions to be effective is networking actively to find the people who are exploring new ideas and then figuring out how to support them in their work. In other words, it's the manager's job to find the creative geniuses throughout the organization, not the other way around.

Because innovation champions are most effective when they develop large networks, a deeply shy or introspective person might not be the best choice for the innovation champion role, while an outgoing personality can make a big impact by generating enthusiasm and a high volume of outputs from the many stakeholders who will participate in the innovation process. This doesn't mean that an introvert cannot be successful, but it does mean that a shy person may need to push him or herself hard to get out and engage with others, encouraging and challenging them in ways that might have previously been uncomfortable, even when sitting quietly and doing research is the attractive option.

A third factor is to develop the skill of visual modeling, which we've briefly mentioned above. The ability to turn ideas into visuals, diagrams, and stories can help people understand and more easily communicate about emerging, complex, or underlying ideas, projects, and external realities. Innovation champions may develop the skills at drawing or modeling themselves, and they may need to recruit people who have those skills to their teams.

The Innovation SWAT Team

Innovation SWAT teams are created for the express purpose of solving specific problems or developing particular ideas. Scion, the American subsidiary of Toyota, was created by just such an innovation SWAT team, which worked for about 18 months to create the new brand and its products, leading up to the very successful launch in 2002.

Because these teams are typically composed of people from a variety of disciplines, part of the work to be done is cross-disciplinary learning, discovering which aspects of each member's expertise are relevant to the issues at hand.

Choosing who participates on a SWAT team is obviously critical to success. Former Scion leader Jim Farley once commented that the key principles he followed when recruiting a team were that members had to be great talents in their fields (A-team talents, in fact), and they had to be the sort of people who would be honest in a meeting, even if it meant telling the boss (which was Jim) that he was wrong. Without honesty, he realized, great work was nearly impossible.

This naturally led to passionate arguments about key design topics, but Farley was convinced that the arguments were a positive and necessary part of the process.

For its first few years after launch Scion's sales results were so far above the initial projections that he was proven correct in his assessment. His leadership skills were also strongly admired in the industry, and he was subsequently recruited to join Ford.

Around the same time that Scion was being developed, work at the movie studio Pixar on the film *Toy Story 2* was moving forward. By 1998 after three years of hard work, expectations were high. However, when CTO Oren Jacob and his production team reviewed the results they were so disappointed that they told Pixar senior executives that the movie was horrible, and might even ruin the company if released as it was.

(continued)

(*continued*)

After watching the film, Steve Jobs, chief creative officer John Lasseter, and president Ed Catmull agreed, and a major rework effort was launched. Within eight months the film was completely rewritten and went on to become one of the most critically acclaimed animated movies of all time.

The moral is clear: Be honest. Stand up for what you believe in. And have the courage to insist on reworking whatever does not meet your standards of quality.[4]

A different type of SWAT team can convene for a very short time, perhaps only a day or two, specifically to bring together a group of innovative thinkers to stimulate new ideas. This is an excellent way to generate a lot of great ideas to fill up a pipeline when a new innovation initiative is being launched. We often convene these teams by bringing together extremely talented and accomplished people who come from quite diverse backgrounds and fields. Dancers, musicians, accountants, health care professionals, truck drivers, all have points of view, experiences, and especially their own that, when tapped appropriately, can add depth, flavor, and ultimately insight to the ideation process.

To achieve sustainable high performance quickly, both types of SWAT teams require a lot of facilitation, a topic we will discuss in detail in Chapter 12.

SUMMARY: COURAGE IS A CORE COMPETENCE

There is no way to learn how to walk without having the experience of falling, and children at that young age are so completely focused on the intense desire to walk that they hardly notice the frequent falls because their sense of purpose is so overwhelming. The occasional crash into a solid object may provoke howls of pain, but within moments they're back on their feet and staggering around again, learning balance and muscle control. They are simply compelled to explore despite any and all obstacles.

However, if the fear of falling down overpowers their need or desire, then this natural developmental step is delayed.

> Courage is a core competence. Someone who is afraid to fail simply will not learn or innovate effectively, because creativity, experimentation, and the possibility of failure are inextricably linked.

With most children, the falls are merely a brief transitional stage that occur for a few months, and they move on to mastering other challenges day by day, including running, reading, writing, and riding bicycles.

Chances are, their parents have been hovering nearby through many of these milestones, steering them clear of obstacles or hurriedly moving things out of the way when they were first learning to walk, and providing them with the materials and experiences needed for learning to take place. The children, however, are often unaware of this because they're so focused on their inner drives.

Success at innovation follows a similar course, for falling down is the essential modality in which would-be innovators work. The process *requires* that people explore new ideas, and they must be willing to take risks and fall. The likelihood of eventual success is greatly enhanced if someone is actively removing obstacles for them, although the innovators need not know that they're being supported in this way.

Unfortunately, this attitude is not the norm in the corporate world. Most people don't realize how substantial the obstacles might be, and even fewer take on the role of removing them. However, this is one of the most important factors that contributes to innovation success. Hence, innovation champions and leaders can do a great deal to enhance the innovation efforts of those throughout their organizations by adopting the attitude and taking the actions to support and protect their innovation teams from unwelcome interference, and by removing any and all distractions. These practices, along with everything else we've mentioned in this chapter, are essential elements of the Agile Innovation core competence.

Questions to Reflect Upon

- How do we manage innovation?
- How mature is our expression of innovation as a core competence?
- In what areas do we most need to improve?
- How are decisions made at critical points in our innovation process?
- In our organization, what are the major innovation roadblocks, and how are they dealt with?
- How do we assess progress in our innovation projects?
- How do our innovation team members interact with each other and with management?
- Are we giving people the right support?

PART III

LEADING THE REVOLUTION

FROM PLANS TO ACTIONS

During times of universal deceit, telling the truth becomes a revolutionary act.

—George Orwell

INNOVATE AS IF YOUR LIFE DEPENDS ON IT

There's a great scene in the movie *Walk the Line* in which the young Johnny Cash is auditioning for record producer Sam Phillips. Cash is singing an old gospel song, but Phillips cuts him off well before he's done. Of course, Cash protests. "Hey," Cash demands, "why you didn't let us bring it home?"

To which Phillips responds:

> Bring . . . bring it home? All right, let's bring it home. If you was hit by a truck and you was lying out there in that gutter dying, and you had time to sing one song. Huh? One song that people would remember before you're dirt. One song that would let God know how you felt about your time here
> *(continued)*

(*continued*)

on Earth. One song that would sum you up. You tellin' me that's the song you'd sing? That same Jimmy Davis tune we hear on the radio all day, about your peace within, and how it's real, and how you're gonna shout it? Or . . . would you sing somethin' different. Somethin' real. Somethin' you felt. Cause I'm telling you right now, that's the kind of song people want to hear. That's the kind of song that truly saves people. It ain't got nothin' to do with believin' in God, Mr. Cash. It has to do with believin' in yourself.[1]

Making innovation successful demands the same mind-set. You've got to bring it home like you believe it!

In this part of the book, we'll explore the many critical elements that transform your own commitment and passion for innovation into organizational performance and value creation.

So we'll start with a question:

Do you believe in yourself?

9

DEVELOPING
AGILE LEADERSHIP

Failure is not an option.

—Gene Kranz, NASA

A classic story of innovating as if someone's life depended on it
(because three lives did) occurred during the flight of Apollo 13,
when an accident in the spacecraft sparked the rather large understate-
ment, "Houston, we have a problem." Indeed, the lives of the astronauts
really did depend on solving the multiple problems that the oxygen tank
explosion caused. The propulsion system, the oxygen-scrubbing system,
the navigation system, and the power generation all failed, and the
astronauts faced the real likelihood that they would not survive.

The story of the race to solve all these problems and bring the
astronauts home alive is a compelling demonstration of the capacity to
do the impossible. In the 1995 movie version, flight director Gene
Kranz (impeccably portrayed by Ed Harris) captured the moment
perfectly when he gravely intoned, "Failure is not an option."

Through an epic process of brilliant creativity, innovation, and engineering, the astronauts did make it back alive.

And actually there's a lot more to the story of Apollo 13 than is told in the movie. About 20 years ago Langdon had the good fortune to meet Dr. Ken Cox, a NASA scientist who, as Langdon subsequently learned, played a critical role in the drama. In Langdon and William L. Miller's book, *Fourth Generation R&D,* Cox's story was included as a case study, and because the story is so relevant and thoroughly embodies the spirit of Agile Innovation, we are including it here.

Ken Cox is a brilliant man, and as you read his story, as told from his own perspective, you will appreciate his deep insight, total commitment, and profoundly innovative spirit.

How Apollo 13 Was Able to Return to Earth[1]

When the explosion occurred onboard Apollo 13 in April of 1970, I got a call at my home across from the Manned Spacecraft Center (now it is called the Johnson Space Center) at about 1:00 in the morning and I was told to get to Mission Control right away. So I went there and I listened to the whole drama unfold, and I was part of the process of figuring out what to do to bring the spacecraft and the astronauts safely back to Earth. I was part of that activity on the ground, listening as the life support system began to drain out of the command service module, as we realized that we must use the lunar module as a lifeboat.

When I saw the movie *Apollo 13,* the emotions, my experience, how people felt . . . *Apollo 13* was a very emotional film for me to watch. It depicted, in my judgment, with very great credibility, the spirit of everyone trying to save that mission and bring the astronauts back.

To do this required us to use the Apollo spacecraft in a way that it was not designed to be used, and I'm going to tell part of the story of how this was done.

Most of the fundamental decisions about how to design the Apollo spacecraft were made in the early 1960s. The Apollo system consisted of three spacecraft: the command module, the attached command service module, and the lunar module (see Figure 9.1).

The Apollo command and command service modules were built by North American (later Rockwell), while the lunar module was built by Grumman.

One of the main design issues was that if you launched a rocket toward the moon, you would swing around the moon and come back toward the Earth, but you wouldn't make it to the Earth and get a good entry. So Apollo was designed to inject into lunar orbit by firing the big engine of the command service module, a major Delta V propulsion burn, and then to achieve a good Earth reentry trajectory with another engine firing.

The original designs for the engines' control systems called for analog controls, because the spacecraft prior to Apollo, the Mercury and Gemini systems, were analog. They were built like airplanes had always been built. Digital computers as we know them today, digital systems, had never been built for an aircraft or a spacecraft.

A major decision made in approximately 1964, after the original designs were essentially completed, because someone realized, "Wait a minute, computers are coming and they give us a lot more capability." So NASA made the very fundamental decision to go to digital primary control systems for all three modules, with backup analog systems which would be built as planned by the spacecraft contractors.

The primary system, though, was the beginning of the new digital avionics, digital flight control systems for Apollo. There was no precedent with regard to previous spacecraft that had ever had digital systems before. Because of my prior background in digital systems, I was given the responsibility to develop the primary control systems for all of the Apollo vehicles from scratch.

Since the primary contractors did not have experience in digital control, the MIT Instrumentation Lab (later the name was changed to Charles Stark Draper Lab) was given responsibility for the primary control systems software, computer, and digital computer implementation that was used for all three modules, and my role was to manage the project.

Right from the beginning, I had one heck of an integration job, and I did it from scratch. There was no precedent. There were no reports

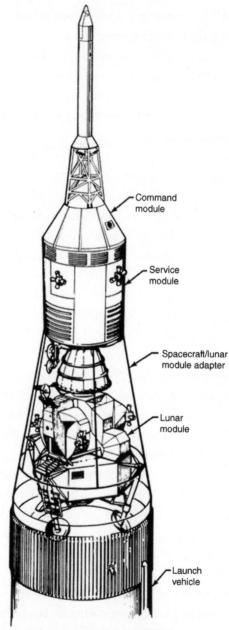

**APOLLO LAUNCH CONFIGURATION FOR
LUNAR LANDING MISSION**

saying, "Here's the way we have built these systems in the past," and so it was a brand-new, open ball game.

I had gotten advice from Grumman and from North American, but they both wanted to use the digital capability, the new capability with exactly the same filters, exactly the same gains, exactly the same feedback loops as an analog system. They both advised me that the only way to do it was to stick to the tried and true, the analog design techniques, and just digitize it.

I did not want to do that. I realized that there were inherent properties of digital systems that were not available in analog systems. There were some good properties and some bad properties, but if you used the digital systems right you got some capabilities that are not at all equivalent, positive capabilities. So there was a big, roaring debate which I was right in the middle of, on this whole question of the philosophy of how do you develop digital systems.

The great advantage of going digital was flexibility. You could make your control systems independent of the hardware sensors and effectors. You could change your control parameters after receiving actual flight test data. For example, we found out later that we didn't model all of the atmospheric properties correctly at the initial edge of the atmosphere. No airplanes had ever gotten up to that altitude, so we didn't have any real flight data. For all of the spacecraft, the mass properties were constantly changing, but once you built an analog control system you had no flexibility to make adjustments. You would find out when you got up in flight that the basic modeling was different than what you designed to.

Figure 9.1 The Apollo spacecraft configuration, shown at launch. The command module and the lunar module were separate spacecraft, and the oxygen tank explosion on the service module rendered the command module systems inoperative. Only by using the lunar module systems to operate the command module were the astronauts able to return to Earth. The technical capability to link the two spacecraft and operate them as one system was the essential innovation pioneered by Cox and described in this story.

With analog control systems, you would have had to physically remove the hardware and build new hardware. But because we had a digital system, we immediately changed the programming after the first Apollo flight and adjusted for extra firings and extra activity on the flight control system. In a digital system, it's a snap. You just go in there and adjust a few figures. So it was definitely the right thing to do because it gave Apollo mission flexibility with extremely low impact on the overall program.

I should mention that the computers that we were dealing with were very primitive by today's standards. The total memory of the onboard computers was about 16 K, and flight control only took about 35 percent to 40 percent of that. The rest of the code was concerned with navigation, guidance, targeting, and communication between Earth and the spacecraft. It was programmed in HAL [high-order assembly language], which was developed at MIT.

So now we are in late 1967, about 21 months before the first moon landing with Apollo 11, and 30 months before Apollo 13. We were working on the digital control system, and the people at MIT and I discussed the idea that we really ought to have a contingency mode for coming back from the moon if something happened and you could not fire the big command service module engine. What happens if there is a problem, and you cannot use the big engine? That was the drama of Apollo 13. Do we have contingency flight control, or contingency capabilities if something happened and we could not use the big engine? If you had the lunar module and command service module docked, the main engine on the lunar module could provide the incremental burn that was required so that we could get on the right trajectory to come back to Earth.

We said, "Look, we think we have the time to add this capability to the digital control system, and we don't think it's that big a deal." It wasn't like we were running hell-bent for leather and we were up against schedule constraints, and so I pushed real hard to say, "Well, let's put it in, damn it. This is an enhanced capability if something happens."

Now mind you, we could not define with any credibility or any predictability what the probability was that something would go wrong with the big engine, but it was obvious to us that if anything happened to the command service module and the big engine was not available to make this required burn in order to loop around the moon and come back, the spacecraft just should have the capability to use the engine in the lunar module.

I had even talked to some of my counterparts in the propulsion engineering design group, and they said, "Oh, no, we would never have an explosion like that. No, no, no. That's not a credible scenario."

Based purely upon good design practice and prior experience, there was no specific reason to protect against this happening. But we went ahead and we designed the thing anyway. We had the capability, and to us, it was just the right thing to do.

Then, we had to decide whether or not to include this contingency flight control capability on the lunar module into the backup analog flight control systems. We brought it up with Grumman, and they said, "In order for us to have the backup analog system, it's going to cause hardware to be changed and we cannot afford the impact on our schedule."

So we said, "Okay we won't require it to be a function of the backup analog system, but the digital part can be done without changing hardware, changing software, or even changing code in the computer."

We took this idea to the Apollo program office, but they wanted us to prove that something might happen: "What is the problem, and what is the probability?" We didn't have the foggiest idea what the probability was that something might explode on the way over. So the initial response was, "Well, but you haven't proved yet that it is really needed."

But I went ahead and requested the Lab to go ahead and do a design, and to code it for simulation and testing. When we had done the software coding and knew that it wasn't that big a deal, that it would work, I brought this issue up before the Apollo Software Control Board, which was run by Chris Craft (before he became head of the center).

I made an impassioned plea to put it in, and I really believed that it was important enough, and it was logical enough, and even though we didn't have the explicit criteria for what we were protecting against, I made the argument this it was the right thing to do.

Chris listened to all this at the formal software control board meeting, and much to my surprise and chagrin, he said, "Ken, I think that you've done good work here, but you haven't proven that you need it, and therefore your request to put this in the basic capability of the Apollo program is disapproved."

I couldn't believe it. I said to myself, "I don't give a damn whether I can prove it or not! It's the right thing to do!" I was just crushed. But as I was walking out the door to leave, Chris motioned me over to the other side of the room, and he got me in a corner where there was just me and him. He looked me right in the eye, and there was a twinkle in his eye, and he said, "Put that mother in as soon as you can."

Immediately I realized that because of project politics, Chris did not want to open the gates for a lot of other changes that people had proposed that were not nearly as important as this.

So I called the MIT Instrumentation Lab and I said, "Put it in, put it in!" At this point it was a joint thing; it wasn't just me directing them. This was an interesting relationship between a civil service person and a contractor out to do something.

> We were totally, absolutely committed in a partnership sense to doing the right thing.

We agreed that we would put the design in and test it in the main program. Now this was totally against the rules, totally against the bureaucratic trend, but we did it. And when I came back three or four months later to the Software Control Board, I said, "We have done this action, we have put it in the main line configuration control and if you turn this proposal down at this point, it will impact the program because you will have to take it out." And Chris had a twinkle in his eye, and he just said, "Well, if that's the case, I think we just ought to keep it in and accept the design." So that's how it was done.

Well, so, when the explosion occurred on Apollo 13 in April of 1970, it did render the main propulsion system of the command service module inoperable. Had we tried to use that engine, it probably would have exploded. It was definitely not something we could have risked. So once they transferred to the lunar module, it became abundantly clear that we had done the right thing.

We're second-guessing history here, but I believe that it is probably the case, just in a probabilistic sense, that if we had not gone ahead and developed the digital control systems, Apollo 13 probably would not have made it back to Earth.

I was very happy, because I knew that I'd made a major contribution to the program itself. That's part of the intrinsic spirit and working together as a collective community that just flowed in the Apollo program. I think we were able to accomplish things like this because we had a very fluid organization in Apollo. We all had clearly defined goals, and we knew that this was an important international and national endeavor.

I suppose that part of our problem today is that the bureaucratic process began to take over as we got into the Shuttle, because it's a 30-year program. Any time you've got a 30- or 40-year program, bureaucracy just feeds on itself, people gradually develop turfs and stovepipe organizations and the whole bit.

Today, 30 years later, NASA is also burdened by the traditional don't-ever-throw-anything-away mentality. "We flight tested it, it works, keep it." So NASA applied the HAL to the early Space Shuttle, and today the Shuttle has something in it that's about 30 years behind the times. Even today, today!, we fly with some of that compiler language that was developed for Apollo. This is not a good story. It's probably the wrong thing to do.

• • •

So much depth and nuance is embedded in this story that even after all these years it is still moving and inspiring.

To help you understand the full context, we should add that during the Apollo program in the 1960s and early 1970s, Cox's job title was Manager of the Primary Flight Control Systems, and later he was also involved in the development of the Space Shuttle.

When Langdon met him in 1996, Cox was assistant to the director in the Engineering Directorate at the Lyndon B. Johnson Space Center, where one of his primary roles was leader of the Aerospace Technology Working Group (ATWG). Cox had established ATWG in 1990 at the request of NASA Director Richard Truly. The purpose was to ensure that NASA's thinking on the rapidly developing field of space technology was integrating many perspectives and viewpoints, and Ken worked closely with government scientists and engineers, the private sector, and academia to bring to NASA great insights into the future of aerospace.

For the first 20 years of ATWG, the focus was on semiannual technology conferences that Cox led, and more recently ATWG has published a series of insightful books on various aspects of space development. In his roles at NASA and with ATWG, Ken has been deeply influential on many people and many NASA technologies, and in the story of Apollo 13, we see many themes and elements that are entirely aligned with the Agile Innovation approach.

Is Failure an Option?

We began the story about Apollo 13 with Kranz's unforgettable comment that "Failure is not an option," and now as we reflect on the Apollo 13 story, what we first need to ask is:

> Is failure an option for you?

Or are you fully committed to building a systematic Agile Innovation capability in your organization, establishing authentic leadership, and moving ahead of the market by developing and executing innovations across the entire range of market requirements?

If innovation is going to play a critical role in the future of your organization, and it should, then you'll have to express your profound passion for it in a deep and enduring way. Your pursuit must transform into total commitment, for only that can lead to the accomplishment of great work.

The character of that commitment, so beautifully exemplified by Ken Cox, Gene Kranz, the astronauts themselves, and the entire Apollo program, is our topic here.

Leadership and Uncertainty

Part of the reason that leadership is so important is that the challenges that today's organizations face are, by and large, new challenges. If they weren't new, if we'd already seen and done everything there is to see and do, then our task might properly be called "management." As Keith Grint so concisely notes, management deals with *déjà vu*—that which we've seen before—but leadership is about the *jamais vu,* that which we've *never* seen.[2]

Guy Mansfield, an insightful author and executive with Total Oil, points out that leadership is most essential when there is high uncertainty. He notes that such problems are "inevitably complex, contextual and with no clear link between cause and effect. To achieve a solution, authority is passed from the individual to the collective because only collective engagement can hope to address the problem. The form of the 'solution' is therefore 'leadership'—asking questions."[3]

In these situations, of course, creating an innovation often *becomes* the solution, and this generally occurs only through the integrated efforts of many people, who work together to create and then solve the problem. Strong leadership plays a critical role in expediting this process, and is most effective when it comes from deep within, from your own profound, personal commitment.

DON'T SETTLE

"Your work is going to fill a large part of your life, and the only way to be truly satisfied is to do what you believe is great work. And the only way to do great work is to love what you do. If you haven't found it yet, keep looking. Don't settle. As with all matters of the heart, you'll know when you find it."[4]

Steve Jobs said that in 2005 in a commencement address to the students graduating from Stanford University. Greatness and commitment were his themes, not only in that talk, but also throughout his life.

When you experience the same level of determination not to settle, it may have an impact on your lifestyle in the short term, because the depth of your commitment will require huge portions of your time. Will you watch that movie, or study? Hang out with your friends and shoot some pool, or do some competitive research? Watch the latest, coolest TV shows on Netflix, or knock out another section of your thesis or your business plan?

These are the types of choices you'll be confronted with every day, and what you choose will go a long way toward both clarifying your own commitment, and doing the necessary work to fulfill it.

Exceptional individuals choose to pursue their visions, even though most realize full well that the hunt for great innovation, like the pursuit of great art, often requires sacrifices. Such sacrifices often reflect a state of inner clarity that emerges in people who commit themselves to achieving their full potential, a concept that is also referred to as *self-actualization*. In Part 2 we talked about inner motivation and intrinsic rewards, and how they're much more powerful than external motivations and rewards. Now, because the source of your motivation is so critical to your success, we will examine the nature of the intrinsic in more detail.

THE SELF-ACTUALIZED INNOVATOR

One of the most influential innovators in the history of psychology was Abraham H. Maslow (1908–1970), and among his many insights is a concept we now refer to as a *transpersonal theory of human needs,* which encompasses an understanding of human behavior from both social and cultural perspectives.

Maslow suggested that people are not controlled by mechanical forces (the stimuli and reinforcement of behaviorism) nor by the unconscious, instinctual impulses that psychoanalysis emphasizes. Instead, he suggested that individuals possess a unifying intent to achieve *self-mastery*. Because this focus on human potential fit so well with his times, his work spawned an entire movement.

This framework is a compelling source of insights for the Agile Innovator, precisely because self-mastery is exactly what innovative individuals and the leaders of great organizations aspire to achieve, and they understand self-mastery to be the foundation of future success as innovators. Further, because innovation is inherently a social process, the pursuit of self-mastery in great organizations is manifested at both the individual and social levels.

Maslow also believed that self-mastery is the basis of human happiness, and he developed his innovative approach by studying exemplary individuals, such as Albert Einstein, Abraham Lincoln, Thomas Jefferson, Albert Schweitzer, Eleanor Roosevelt, and Frederick Douglass. In explaining why he studied history's great minds, he poignantly noted that "The study of crippled, stunted, immature, and unhealthy specimens can yield only a crippled psychology and a crippled philosophy."[5]

In the same way, our study of exemplary individuals and innovative organizations has helped us develop the Agile Innovation approach to organizational growth and innovation. Central to both are the act of creation and the quality of creativity.

Maslow recognized that people who attempt to reach the frontiers of creativity, and who strive to reach higher levels of consciousness and wisdom, are self-actualizing individuals, and his transformational model of psychology consists of insights and techniques to enable healthy people to make their lives even better, to achieve their potential more fully. For organizations to achieve their full potential, they can follow the same principles and transform themselves at the organizational level.

Maslow recognized that people who attempt to reach the frontiers of creativity, and who strive to reach higher levels of consciousness and wisdom, are "self-actualizing" individuals, and his transformational model of psychology consists of insights and techniques to enable healthy people to make their lives even better, to achieve their potential more fully. For *organizations* to achieve their full potential, they can follow the same principles and transform the way they function and the relationships they foster.

Many companies already apply Maslow's theories in their marketing efforts, as they seek to understand the behaviors and attitudes that motivate their customers and better align their efforts with their customers' aspirations and motivations. Although organizations that look inward and seek to guide their self-development by applying Maslow's concepts broadly are rare, in the next section we'll explore how to do that successfully.

MASLOW'S HIERARCHY OF NEEDS

You may be familiar with Maslow's concept of the hierarchy of needs, a brilliant advance in our understanding of the human experience that is generally portrayed in the shape of a pyramid. The most basic physiological levels of need, the body's needs for survival, are shown at the bottom, with safety above that and psychological needs positioned still higher.

At the very top of the pyramid is self-actualization, where our concerns involve the highest existential and spiritual factors, including creativity, fulfillment, and meaning.

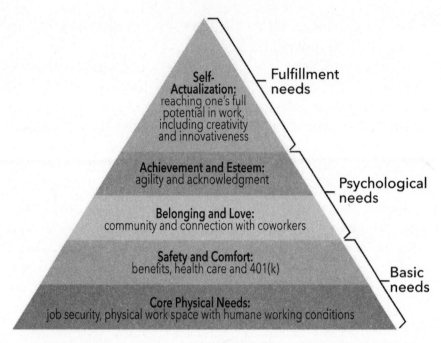

Figure 9.2 Basic needs are represented at the base of the pyramid, followed by psychological needs. When these are met, we then are able to consider and address fulfillment needs. This is one among many insights that Maslow developed during his long, innovative, and very productive career.

In defining the pyramid, Maslow pointed out that the most basic needs must be met before individuals can focus on fulfilling those at higher levels. For example, creativity and love would not be likely concerns of a person who was chronically deprived of basic survival requirements such as food, water, or safety.

As Figure 9.2 shows, the corporate analogy of Maslow's theory suggests that lower-level needs are issues of survival in basic operations, such as finance (profitability), project management, and human resources. These functions need to be fulfilled before an organization can focus on higher levels, which include innovativeness, business creativity, a healthy culture of aliveness, and ultimately fulfillment and meaning through great accomplishments.

Seen this way, excellence in operations is not the adversary of an innovation culture, but rather its foundation as well as its aspiration.

SELF-ACTUALIZING ORGANIZATIONS

It's important to note that there is a limit to how far we can take this analogy, and in thinking along these lines we have to be careful not to confuse qualities that can only be found in individuals with those of organizations. For example, we often hear it said that "Apple is a very creative company," but what this really means is that the people who work there are creative. The company isn't a person and it cannot actually be creative. Attributing to organizations qualities that they cannot possess is a mistake common in the English language; "organizations" are not caring, thoughtful, or even irresponsible, and if they manifest these behaviors, it's only because people in those organizations exhibit these qualities.

Nevertheless, we can carefully extend the concept of self-actualization beyond the individual to the organization if a significant proportion of the employees demonstrate the characteristics of self-actualization. Self-actualizing organizations therefore would likely have these qualities:

The Qualities of Self-Actualizing Organizations

- They're filled with creative people.
- They have lots of people who are passionate about solving important problems.
- They employ people who feel a closeness to the human condition, express respect for others, and are generally life affirming.
- They consist of individuals whose morals are fully internalized and independent of external authority.
- Many (or most) of the people who compose the organization aspire to do the right thing.
- Many (or most) of the people who compose the organization aspire to accomplish great things.

In the story about Apollo 13 that began this chapter, we see these very values clearly evident in the actions of Ken Cox and indeed throughout the entire NASA organization and the Apollo program team. In addition, people all around the world resonated profoundly with NASA's goals, and deeply respected the men and women who were working to achieve them. Hence, we see that the accomplishments you aspire to attain have a fundamental influence on the culture of your organization, on its manifestations in the market, and on how others perceive you.

Are you trying to grow sales by 3 percent, or do you intend to create a transcendent customer experience unlike any that your customers have ever had? Do you want to change the world, as Jobs said to John Scully, or spend your life selling sugared water?

The subtleties that emerge when you attempt to address fundamental issues and concerns related to human aspiration and human existence speak to many aspects of ourselves that are sometimes ignored in business, where "good enough" is too often the standard. Good enough is neither great nor is it inspirational, and a passion for greatness is what drives the innovator, the revolutionary, and the genius.

Hence, the goals you set for yourself and for your organization do indeed matter. Aim high.

> For you, the transformational and revolutionary leader, your ability to achieve greatness is determined by the goals you set. Aim high.

METAVALUES

Maslow also discovered that as self-actualized people progressed in their own development, they gradually spent less time concentrating on the lower survival values and became even more focused on higher values. Maslow called these *metavalues*.

Figure 9.3 shows a list of metavalues pertinent to organizations.

If we compare the concepts on these lists with the tedious issues that often preoccupy our days at work, the contrast is rarely inspiring and it can be downright discouraging. Do we worry over deadlines that are mostly artificial? Do we evade responsibility to avoid blame? Are we obliged to waste copious amounts of time on administrative trivia? Does the logic of compliance force us to do the wrong thing? Do we disregard

ORGANIZATIONAL METAVALUES
Organizational integration, Operational efficiency and Simplicity
Integrity
Completion
Aliveness
Richness (differentiation, complexity, intricacy)
Goodness
Uniqueness and Individuality
Effortlessness and Operational grace
The ability to see the future in terms of risk management

Figure 9.3 These nine metavalues describe aspects of fulfillment needs and opportunities for organizations.

the needs or concerns of our coworkers, or our customers, because we're on a deadline? Do we make choices to achieve trivial short-term goals at the expense of long-term value? Do we default to the letter of the rules while willfully violating the spirit?

Having observed and worked in numerous organizations where we saw all these behaviors and occasionally even found ourselves doing them, we know how easy it is to do only what's necessary to get along. But this condition is not inevitable.

Companies that self-actualize are those that enable peak experiences in which collaboration, joy, fulfillment, meaning, and peak performance are possible—and become the norm rather than the exception.

These organizations develop processes and systems that make life and work simpler and better. They eliminate drudgery.

"If you really loved me," an employee of a huge corporation once commented, "then you wouldn't make me use all this crappy technology." How often have you said that to yourself?

Organizations that demonstrate self-actualization also express resilience in the face of obstacles. They avoid setbacks, or quickly recover from them, because people readily and enthusiastically engage in finding brilliant solutions even in the midst of crisis. "Failure," said Gene Kranz, "is not an option." So it wasn't. In living and demonstrating this determination, NASA gained our deep and lasting admiration as a self-actualizing organization. It became a model, for a time, of what a great organization could be and what it could accomplish, as Ken Cox's description makes vividly clear.

Leaders whose organizations demonstrate self-actualization both enable *and* expect their employees to listen to one another, and they implement systems for effective feedback that enable new skills to be learned with speed and reliability. (And they get rid of crappy software.)

Do these qualities sound familiar? They should. These are natural principles and goals of companies that practice Agile Innovation. How, then, will you evoke and develop these behaviors in your organization?

ACTION STEPS: IT'S ALL ABOUT LEADERSHIP

Leadership, in all its manifestations, is of course the real topic here. Leaders set high and difficult goals, they articulate our aspirations, and they exemplify self-actualized attitudes and behaviors. Leaders create, design, innovate, and execute ideas, plans, strategies, concepts, and decisions as broad and aspirational generalists, and certainly not from narrow, limited, or bureaucratic perspectives.

We often relate this approach to the Renaissance, to the profound flowering of curiosity and discovery that marked Italy and then all of Europe in the sixteenth century. Hence, the notion of the Renaissance man or woman is deeply relevant to innovation, because many of history's best innovators have been generalists with numerous interests across a wide range of topics; they were certainly not narrow domain specialists. And a large part of their genius has been the ability to discover connections between ideas that no one else perceived.

Leonardo da Vinci was a great generalist, and history points to him as the very pinnacle of the Renaissance man, someone whose works we still admire today for their deep insights and profound beauty. His notebooks are considered priceless inspirations for good reason.

Other examples are the French leader Napoleon, the Chinese mathematician Zhu Chongzhi, the Greek philosopher Aristotle, the Indian politician Gandhi . . .

These are among the great figures from history to whom we look for inspiration in the midst of a revolution that has already begun. Out there, outside of your organization, people are busy inventing the next generation of products, services, and business models that will define the market landscape of tomorrow. Through inquiry, insight, and inspiration, they are busy innovating.

> To compete well and thrive over the long term, you must evoke a Renaissance in your own organization.

What Is Your Passion?

When Steve Jobs was in college he studied calligraphy because he was enthralled with its beauty, although certainly not because that would improve his chances of getting a job after graduation. He said, "I learned about serif and sans serif typefaces, about varying the amount of space between different letter combinations, about what makes great typography great. It was beautiful, historical, artistically subtle in a way that science can't capture, and I found it fascinating. None of this had even a hope of any practical application in my life. But 10 years later, when we were designing the first Macintosh computer, it all came back to me."[6]

Your passions may also find reflection in your work, although like Jobs, this may not be entirely evident when or how it will occur. But we know that to achieve greatness, which is what every aspiring innovator wishes to do, your passions and commitments must guide you.

Find them, explore them, develop them, and whether through analogy, metaphor, or the actual application of the knowledge you gain, those passions will inform your quest as an innovator and an Agile Innovation leader.

Questions to Reflect Upon

- In terms of Maslow's hierarchy of needs model, how would we characterize our organization?

(continued)

(*continued*)

- What is our highest aspiration?
- How does management in our organization set goals that align with our values and needs?
- How are our innovation priorities reflected in our leadership as a business?
- Toward what goals is the passion in our leadership directed?

10

CULTIVATING
CORE CREATIVITY

Innovation is different from many other business management con-
cerns in one important way: It requires processes, structures, and
resources to manage significant levels of creativity (developing new
concepts and ways of doing things) while executing (transforming
creative concepts into commercial realities.

—Tony Davila, Marc J. Epstein, and Robert Shelton[1]

As we discussed in the previous chapter, your passions are integral to who you are, and they must find expression in your work. To achieve the highest levels of success at innovation, a specific set of skills is also very helpful, including the abilities we've discussed in previous chapters, such as the ability to see and listen deeply, to unlock your own creativity and that of others, and to create and tell great stories.

Developing these skills throughout your organization will nurture the vital ability to envision and create the future and enhance your capacity to fulfill the vision that drives your organization forward.

SEEING MORE DEEPLY

The drive to innovate comes from the hope for, search for, and discovery of a better way, which stems from an implicit (or explicit) dissatisfaction with the way things are now. Sometimes that awareness comes spontaneously because of dissatisfaction with an unpleasant experience. At other times it can happen when we specifically hunt for new opportunities.

In both cases, the opportunity to innovate confronts us with two different and highly contrasting worldviews: One is the current way, possibly the accepted way. In many situations it can be labeled the *dominant paradigm,* the accepted way it's expected it to be, which may be so deeply embedded in thought, life, and lifestyle that it remains unquestioned.

However, when you so thoroughly and unquestioningly accept what is, then you may fail entirely to see the possibility of a new and improved world. Like a fish in a bowl of water, you may have difficulty seeing the context within which you're entirely immersed. Hence, it may be necessary to break the spoken or unspoken rules that block awareness, that prevent you from breaking through to fundamental insights and possible solutions.

Ignorance of an all-encompassing, immersive context is what often makes coming up with creative, disruptive, or revolutionary ideas so challenging. Hence, to spot their deficiencies, we must enter and master the contexts and paradigms in which our customers and we ourselves live.

Consider this definition of the ability to innovate, which we mentioned in Chapter 3:

When someone tells you that's not broken, or not to fix something that obviously is broken even if they can't see it, it's really an invitation to look deeper and discover latent innovation opportunities. This may require an expansion of your awareness, which will certainly serve you well thereafter.

Here are some examples of new business paradigms.

- Cell phones were just fine, but smartphones turned out to offer so much more.

- Horse-drawn carriages were fine, too, elegant and comfortable, but cars and trucks do things they never could.
- Ice delivery was a common service and a very big business throughout the world until refrigerators made them obsolete. (Did you know that 7-Eleven stores started out in the ice business?)
- A regular cup of coffee was fine, until there was Starbucks.
- A lumberyard had what you needed until Home Depot provided much more.
- Carbon paper was sufficient until Xerox (photocopying) came along.

> Every successful new technology or business model breaks an existing paradigm.

Indeed, in the context of Agile Innovation, that's the whole point. The question, then, is, How can we acquire the skill to see the unseen?

In art school, students are taught to see not just the objects in their field of view but also those in the negative space, the spaces between objects. They also learn to recognize a broader range of colors, and to appreciate types of art they may not naturally have found appealing.

For those interested in developing new ventures, a comparable skill is detecting tacit and unarticulated needs, which we discussed in detail in Chapter 3. As we noted, leading product development companies, including Apple, BMW, Procter & Gamble, and Intel, use the practice of ethnography to enhance their capacity to see and hear how their customers live, and this is a key technique they use to detect disruptive opportunities.

"Is Your Child *Still* in Diapers?"

This story highlights the role of ethnographic research in identifying a huge new market, leading to a product that addressed a fundamental, and entirely overlooked, market need. The story
(continued)

(*continued*)

summarizes a project led by Point Forward, one of the world's leading ethnographic research firms, which we also mentioned in Chapter 3.

By 1989, the disposable diaper market had become mired in a feature war. Messages touting "new and improved" absorbency and leak prevention were the primary advertising that all the manufacturers were using, but they weren't connecting with consumers.

By talking to parents not just about diapers but also about their broader emotional connections to their children, ethnographic research revealed the embarrassment and disappointment that parents felt if their toddler children were still wearing diapers.

As it turns out, diapers are not just waste disposal solutions; they also symbolize something critically important to parents, for they embody parents' expectations for their child's future success. Successful potty training was therefore not just a matter of convenience, but also a powerful and important symbol for parents.

The opportunity this discovery suggested was to make diaper products for toddlers that included elements of grown-up clothing and thus represented achievement and self-reliance. Huggies Pull-Ups were the first disposable training pants, and they created a new category.

Incremental revenues have exceeded $700 million per year, all based on the discovery that diapers are a lot more than just diapers.[2]

As you learn to see differently, you also learn how to expand the way you think. Since your brain was designed to automatically explore and create, this is your birthright, and indeed every human's birthright. However, our growth is shaped by both nature and nurture, and because many of our institutions are less than friendly toward these notions of curiosity and discovery, we may not have been raised in an environment that encouraged us to unleash our creativity. Many of us have thoughts, doubts, concerns, and fears that block our path.

Do you ever say to yourself:

"I'm not very creative."

"What if they don't like my idea?"

"I'd better not share my thoughts."

"They probably won't be interested."

Thoughts like these, so common for many of us, utterly block the flow of ideas and deeply or even totally inhibit our creativity.

Here's a simple example. Please take a quick look at Figure 10.1. What do you see?

Most people see the word *flop,* but if you look a little longer, you might notice another word. Do you see it?

To support our self-preservation, evolution has wired our brains to sense danger and to identify the worst possible cases so that we can (hopefully) avoid them. Hence, although nature gave us amazing capacity to explore and create, it also built into us a fear of change.

From a neurological perspective, potential threats are first sorted out in the brain's limbic system, and only after the nearly instantaneous reaction that the limbic system provokes does the neocortex then get the opportunity to analyze the situation. In other words, we react first and think later.

To avoid falling into the fear-first trap, the most creative among us flip the process around by allowing the neocortex to inhibit the limbic system so that they can operate more freely. As we discussed in the

Figure 10.1   What do you see?

previous chapter, this more thoughtful approach is, in fact, an expression of our higher values and our commitment to self-actualization.

> While evolution gave us an amazing capacity to explore and create, it also built into us a fear of change. Thus, we must reprogram our instinctive and subconscious mind to favor creative and innovative thought.

There are many ways to reprogram our subconscious to tap into more creative and innovative thoughts and thus to unlock the deeper resources of creativity. Breaking out of constrained thinking so that you gain new perspectives and insights on important problems overcomes inner constraints that hold you back from peak performance.

At many innovation workshops you'll experience creativity-building exercises for both individuals and groups that increase the flow of ideas and decrease subtle and unconscious inhibitors. Taking an art class and learning how to sketch or sculpt figures can also unlock your creative capabilities.

One approach we've begun to experiment with is the emotional freedom technique, or EFT, a therapy process developed to treat posttraumatic stress disorder. Using techniques borrowed from acupuncture and acupressure, EFT can lessen social anxiety that inhibits the ability to brainstorm in public.

A separate but related issue is unlocking the subconscious not just in yourself but also in an entire team—your team. That's a much bigger challenge. Brainstorming facilitators know that it's often the most shy and quiet participants who contribute break-out ideas . . . if they can only find the courage to share them. Once they do, it often lifts the energy level of the entire room because the shiest person in a group is often the one who expresses social anxiety that everyone else feels too.

For reinforcement to occur throughout the organization, it's necessary to exemplify the word and the spirit of openness, and this is precisely why your choices and the tone you set as a leader are so deeply influential. In essence, what you *do* is about 10 times more powerful than what you *say*.

Suppose you're the CEO and you announce an open innovation policy, but then you reflexively sneer when someone produces a less-than-perfect idea. Which message is more powerfully conveyed? The sneer will have much more lasting impact than the policy. Hence, the most subtle of mannerisms and reactions the CEO expresses will probably have an enormous effect on the culture.

Interestingly, Steve Jobs's reputation for abrasiveness tarnishes his legacy. Apparently he was not above humiliating others when he felt their ideas or actions were not up the level of his expectations, and surely this had a derogatory effect on the morale and even the performance of Apple.

This is not, however, a behavior pattern that was unique to Jobs. An engrossing study of genius by Howard Gardner examined the lives and works of Sigmund Freud, Pablo Picasso, Martha Graham, and others and found a consistency of abusive behavior across many of them. Whether this was because of self-absorption, arrogance, or simply opportunism is not apparent, but it is certainly a downside of many geniuses that has no place in the behavior of a truly great leader.[3]

Deep Simplicity

Seeing clearly also means being able to perceive the simplicity that may be hidden in layers of complexity.

The great British cybernetician Ross Ashby, who taught at the University of Illinois, engaged deeply in the study of complex systems. Toward the end of Ashby's career, a fellow faculty member commented to him that some students found his course to be a bit simple. "It took me a lifetime to make it simple," Ashby replied, for year after year he had stripped away the unnecessary details and layers, leaving only the essential core.[4]

Simplicity is a great virtue in innovation, and practicing the art of simple design can have the added advantage of helping you discover bottlenecks and shortcomings in your designs for

(*continued*)

(continued)

products and services. Extra steps or components tell you when something can be simplified, but you have to look, and to see.

Note that *simple* design is very different from *simplistic* design. Coming up with understandable, adaptable, simple designs often takes more time, but by eschewing nonessentials and focusing on customer value, doing less can free up the time required to do better at simple design.

Sir Jonathan Ive, chief designer at Apple and leader of the team that designed that paragon of simple elegance, the iPod, said when explaining the design philosophy behind iOS 7, "I think there is a profound and enduring beauty in simplicity, in clarity, in efficiency. True simplicity is derived from so much more than just the absence of clutter and ornamentation. It's about bringing order to complexity."[5]

Multivisioning

The term *brainstorming* was first popularized by ad executive Alex Osborn in his 1953 book, *Applied Imagination*.[6] After more than 10 years of refining the methods of creative problem solving, the inability of his firm's design teams to develop creative ideas for ad campaigns still frustrated him. To address this situation, he began leading creativity sessions, and discovered how to achieve significant improvements in the quality and quantity of the ideas generated.

Based on these experiences, Osborn devised some rules for effective brainstorming that can reduce social inhibitions among group members, stimulate idea generation, and increase the overall creativity of a group. These basic principles remain entirely valid today, and you probably already know them because they're deeply embedded in the way many of us work.

The noted design firm IDEO much later published its own list of principles to support brainstorming, simplifying and building on Osborn's work, which included these:

Simple Rules for Effective Brainstorming

- Start with a well-honed statement of the problem at hand.
- Defer judgment.
- Have one conversation at a time.
- Go for quantity.
- Be visual.
- Encourage wild ideas.
- Number your ideas.
- Write ideas down.
- Begin with warm-up exercises.
- Show examples of competing products.
- Build crude models of concepts.[7]

These elements are indeed important to success, and to build on them and help people and teams improve their creative abilities Moses developed an approach called *multivisioning,* a technique for continuously generating ideas by shifting the perspective on ideas as you brainstorm. This blends the best of Osborn's classic insights with recent discoveries in peak performance techniques and the best of today's advanced innovation methodologies.

The multivisioning technique came about as a result of research in the psychology of creativity. The *aha!* moment came while reading the journals of Leonardo da Vinci, who believed that to solve a problem you should begin by learning how to see it, or structure it, in many ways. He noted that the first way he looked at a problem was usually biased, but with each shift in his mind, his understanding deepened and he better understood the essence of the problem.

The next discovery came from the inventive processes used by physicists Albert Einstein and Richard Feynman. Einstein said that he found it necessary to formulate his problem in as many ways as possible, using diagrams and visuals to grasp it fully. Feynman felt the secret to his genius was his ability to disregard how past thinkers thought about problems, and instead "invent new ways to think." He called this "generating different ways to look at the problem, until you find a way that moves the imagination."[8] What these geniuses did, in fact, was invent new ways to invent, fully embodying the aspiration to innovate more deeply!

Like a sculpture that needs to be rotated so that the viewer can capture all angles, ideas need to be rotated conceptually so that they can be fully understood and developed, and Einstein, da Vinci, and Feynman all did it brilliantly.

Computer scientist Marvin Minsky, well known for his pioneering work in artificial intelligence and computing, also offers a very useful insight about connecting one thought with others. He notes:

> The secret of what anything means to us depends on how well we've connected it to all the other things we know. This is why, when someone learns "by rote"—that is, with no sensible connections—we say that they "don't really understand." Rich meaning-networks, however, give you many different ways to go: if you can't solve a problem one way, you can try another. True, too many indiscriminate connections will turn a mind to mush. But well-connected meaning-structures let you turn ideas around in your mind, to consider alternatives and envision things from many perspectives until you find one that works. And that's what we mean by thinking.[9]

Innovating at a higher level like this requires that you come up with fresh perspectives, new frameworks that evoke out-of-the-box thinking. As we noted in Chapter 6, we call this emptying the teacup, after the famous parable that reminds us that we must empty the cup of its existing contents before we can fill it with new insights.

Useful perspectives to consider are those that reflect the needs of your organization. "How does the customer see it?" emphasizes customer insight. "How does this affect compliance?" may be relevant if your industry is closely regulated. "What's the ecosystem around this product?" may inspire bigger thinking.

It also sometimes helps to try perspectives that might sound crazy or feel like Zen koans. "How would this be done on Mars?" "In zero gravity?" "How do children think about it?" "How would you get this done if you have no money?"

Multivisioning can be done individually or in groups. In a group setting, a given perspective is discussed and ideas developed in the normal back-and-forth course of the dialog until the group's energy winds down, and then the facilitator suggests yet another viewpoint to consider.

Another shift that works well is to flip the idea around, to invert it, and to reverse it, which you can do simply by asking a question that leads the group ideation down a different path. Perhaps we ask:

- "How would we do this if computing was free?"
- "How would our top competitors do this?"
- If it's a product idea, ask "What's the service version?"
- If it's a service idea, ask, "What products can we replace?"

A long list of useful and provocative questions and perspectives, which can also be referred to as *ideation lenses,* should be stored in a facilitator's database so that a scrum leader can easily browse a bunch and select a few to use in a productive session.

Multivisioning can also be done much more informally and is not limited to focused brainstorming sessions. Steve Jobs once noted that, "When a good idea comes, part of my job is to move it around, just see what different people think, get people talking about it, argue with people about it, get ideas moving among that group of 100 people, get different people together to explore different aspects of it quietly, and, you know—just explore things."[10] In this way multivisioning becomes an organizational habit and a way of socializing ideas.

GREAT STORIES

Stories have been the primary containers and expressions of human culture for hundreds of thousands of years, and they're still central today. Tender tales of romance or the thrill of danger, or a combination of both, can move humans in a profound way in books, in movies, in TV shows, and now on Facebook. Sitting together on the beach and at Starbucks, it's the stories we hear that engross and engage us.

Even our dreams come to us as stories, as sequences of impactful events and relationships that feel entirely real, and the experiences and images in dreams may stay with us for years. Stories remind us of the past, motivate us toward the future, and engage us to act in the present.

In the next chapter, we will discuss the importance of building your brand to gather support for your innovation revolution, which is, of course, all about building a compelling story, or narrative, around your business; our purpose here is simply to remind you that composing the story may be a critical factor in engaging the enthusiasm and support of those inside your organization as well as partners, customers, and all other stakeholders. This, too, is a fundamentally important creative act.

PRACTICE

How are you going to develop the skills you need to become an effective creator, innovator, and innovation leader? One very important thing for you to do is simply to practice.

You may have thought that these skills came naturally to the great innovators, but their writings consistently show that they did not take their skills lightly. Instead, they worked hard and persistently to develop and improve their abilities. Peter Drucker once remarked that, "Innovators do, of course, improve with practice." He then went on to clarify what he meant in more detail: "But only if they practice the right method, that is, if they base their work on a systemic analysis of the sources of innovative opportunity."[11]

The sources he refers to are outlined in detail in the same book, his pioneering work, *Innovation and Entrepreneurship*. They are:

- The unexpected
- Incongruities
- Process need

- Industry and market structures
- Demographics
- Changes in perception
- New knowledge

History tells us that da Vinci, Edison, and Jobs, among many others, were innovation virtuosos because they combined their natural curiosity and skill with literally thousands of hours of practice and training. Although they might not have given you this same list of sources, it's quite evident from their work that they tapped into their own sources perhaps as effectively as anyone in history has. Hence, it matters not only that you practice but also that your practice is guided in the most promising directions.

Recent studies of those with high-level skills in many disciplines have discovered a general rule, which reinforces the notion that effective practice is the differentiating factor. In the words of Geoff Colvin, "Contemporary athletes are not superior because they're somehow different but because they train themselves more effectively." He later goes on to mention that "A seventy-four-year-old man in 2004 ran a marathon in 2:54:44, which is four minutes faster than the gold medal performer in the 1896 Olympics."[12] How we practice and train is indeed decisive.

Researchers have now generalized this insight into what they refer to as the 10,000-hour rule, which Malcolm Gladwell described in his book *Outliers* and which notably draws upon work by K. Anders Ericsson, Ralf Th. Krampe, and Clemens Tesch-Römer at the Berlin Academy of Music. They found that the most proficient musicians were those who accumulated 10,000 hours of practice: "Ten thousand hours is the magic number of greatness."[13]

Hence, if you want to be great you, too, should probably ask yourself how many hours you've dedicated to perfecting your skills at ideation, innovation, and creativity, and how to find more time for it. Next, ask how your organization encourages, by its cultural norms as well as by its policies, the hard work of this practice, and facilitates the time required for doing it.

Effort and Practice

It's true in all sports that practice is obviously essential to success. Great athletes put in hour after hour in the gym, more hours of conditioning through roadwork, and still more hours lifting weights and studying films.

As a result, what appears to the casual observer as a natural talent may actually be the result of intense and prolonged practice and preparation. Hence, the great golfer Arnold Palmer said, "The more I practice, the luckier I get."

Although innate talent is a prerequisite for mastery in many sports, most of us already have the innate ability to create and share great ideas; we're just out of practice.

Consider the martial arts. Have you ever watched a kung fu master break a stack of bricks with his head? You might think, "Wow, that's amazing! I'd never be able to do that!"

But if you ask the master how he does it, he's likely to say, "There are no secrets. Just practice."

Indeed, the term *kung fu* consists of two characters: 功夫—the first, *kung*, means hard training or endeavor; the second, *fu*, means *man*, in the sense of *married man* whose commitment is for *a* lifetime. Together, even in colloquial use, these two characters express one single and compelling idea: *effort*. Mastering kung fu requires that one spend a lot of time training, and training hard—a dedicated and lifelong effort.

Basketball is no different. Ed Macauley, a great basketball player who was named MVP of the first NBA all-star game in 1951, once remarked, "When you are not practicing, remember, someone somewhere is practicing, and when you meet him he will win." Today's great players will tell you the same thing, and they have achieved greatness through hours in the gym, late nights, early mornings, and countless jump shots and free throws.

The point, of course, is that this is as applicable in business as it is in sports. To achieve success at innovation, you must also practice every day and train diligently.

FROM FEAR TO FLOW

In the end, you'll find that the greatest inhibitor to personal creativity is simply believing you don't have what it takes. As Henry Ford famously remarked, "Whether you think you can, or you think you can't—you're right." Many of us have beliefs that limit our creativity and our success, beliefs about our own capabilities, beliefs about what it takes to succeed, or myths that modern-day science has long since refuted.

Where does this negativity come from? For most of us, early childhood programming and the design of modern educational methodology have been major influences.

We carry these limits into adulthood, and then workplace mistakes and creativity-killing doubts reinforce them. In our heads we hear a voice that says, "My dad said I wasn't creative." "Why be innovative when someone else always patents it first?" "What if they don't like my idea?" Thoughts like these lock us up and inhibit our thoughts.

Conversely, believing that you really are creative is the first step to becoming so. The reality is that the human brain that was built to innovate, invent, and create. It is every human's birthright.

But to succeed, you must also take risks. Hence, perhaps the deepest truth about creativity is that the critical ingredient isn't necessarily brains; it's guts.

> As Henri Matisse said, "Creativity takes courage."

This is the essential modality in which would-be innovators work: There is no other way to learn how to walk but by falling; creativity is profoundly linked with experimentation, and experimentation includes the reality of failure.

Whenever you feel that fear, it may help to remember this handy acronym: *FEAR is false evidence appearing real.*

Overcoming the immediate fear reaction is a challenge, but it's absolutely achievable. Many techniques can help (see Appendix B), but the key to all of them is your commitment to personal transformation.

Creative Flow

The opposite of fear is *flow*. Creative flow is a peak experience, when breathtaking ideas begin to flow like water, similar to what athletes call being *in the zone*.[14] When this happens, your brain is flush with creativity-enhancing neurohormones and begins to work in special patterns that the emerging neuroscience of creativity is now exploring. In a study by Dr. Rex Jung, clinical neuropsychologist and assistant professor of neurosurgery at the University of New Mexico, a "first approximation" suggests that creative cognition might map onto the human brain by leveraging areas and networks of the brain used for daydreaming, imagining the future, remembering deeply personal memories, constructive internal reflection, making meaning, and social cognition. According to Jung, the brain's attentional control network helps us with laser focus on a particular task, but the imagination network is used for coming up with future scenarios and remembering things that happened in the past. Jung's theory suggests that reducing activation of the "executive attention network's" control modality and increasing activation of the "imagination and salience networks" of your brain is another way to enhance creative thought.

What this means is that you must allow your mind to roam free, imagine new possibilities, and silence the inner critic. Recent research with jazz musicians and rappers engaging in creative improvisation suggests that this is precisely what's happening in the brain while in a flow state.[15]

Daily creative practice has also proven effective. As we noted earlier, you may need 10,000 hours of practice to achieve genuine mastery, so don't hold back. The twenty-first century needs creative innovators like the Industrial Revolution needed factory workers, and in a world where information flows abundantly, your ability to come up with creative ideas and solutions may be the key to your personal and professional success.

Questions to Reflect Upon

- How do I come up with valuable ideas for innovation?
- Who in our organization exemplifies the search for new ideas?
- In our innovation efforts, what signs are we responding to, and where are they coming from?
- Are we practicing enough to attain mastery?
- What policies do we have in place to encourage, or discourage, innovation practice?
- In our innovation efforts, are we sufficiently dedicated, or do we give up too easily?

11

ACHIEVING AN ICONIC BRAND

Big, enduring brands become icons—not just of corporations, but of whole cultures. Coca-Cola not only has the most recognized brand logo in the world, but the logo also has become a symbol of Western way of life.

—Margaret Mark and Carol S. Pearson[1]

The creation of an iconic brand is one of the ultimate achievements in a career spent in pursuit of innovation, agility, and excellence. Brand building is also a critical task for the revolutionary leader, since creating a magnetic brand may be as essential to your success in communicating with colleagues as it is in communicating your vision, commitment, and even the performance of your innovations to customers. Without a properly tuned brand, great innovations often languish unrecognized in the marketplace, and thus branding is as essential to innovation as ideating and even research.

Brands are not just promises to the customer; they're also promises to ourselves. They are mirrors that we hold up before ourselves, mirrors in which we examine ourselves to see who we really are. As we learned in previous chapters, knowing who we are is critical in determining whom we would like to become.

Because "becoming" is all about what we create and innovate, we embrace the proposition that innovation and branding are two sides of a single coin.

We've already discussed the importance of ethnography as a method of uncovering hidden information about customers, and in the previous chapter we retold the story of Huggies, relating how a team of ethnographers exposed an entire world of insights about parents, children, and their diapers.

An important variation on ethnography is the study of character, the indwelling beliefs and ideals that characterize individuals and communities. The word for this discipline comes from the study of ethos—the Greek word for "character." Hence, *ethography* (without the *n*) explores the guiding beliefs and ideals that characterize a community, an ideology—or a Fortune 500 enterprise.

The Greeks also used the word *ethos* to refer to the power of music to influence emotions and behaviors, and we extend this to mean that you must use the power of music, particularly today in the form of media, to influence your customers. While eth*no*graphy is essential for navigating the space of human needs and need finding, brand eth*o*graphy is needed to identify and create meaning and identity at the brand level, helping you create the music that tells your story best.

BRANDING AND TOTEMS

A brand is essentially a totem, an object that carries significance far beyond its physical attributes. People identify with and select particular brands because of their totemic qualities, which is why a T-shirt or cap with the logo of your favorite football team may mean a lot more to you than one with no logo at all.

Given that modern clothing is covered with logos, and modern society is filled with totems, we see that leading brands develop and exploit the totemic nature of branding with great intention. Thus, your customers will purchase, use, or wear your brand only if the totem it embodies matches their self-identity, or even better, their aspiration. "Just do it" and the Nike swoosh beside it thus embody meanings on a great many levels.

In this regard, a brand also provides a magical form of protection. To be successful in creating a brand, you must therefore understand the meaning you intend for your brand to carry, and convey that authentically so that customers feel the brand means to them what you intend. You then must embed that meaning in your innovation, so when you bring all these dimensions into full alignment (which is by no means an easy task), and the brand itself embodies the spirit of innovation or creativity, then you can tap into a deeper source of meaning and aspiration that transforms *brand* into *icon*.

> In brand management the goal is to move toward the top of Maslow's pyramid, the place where only the most successful of brands can reside.

Overcoming Brand Blind Spots: A Case Study

This case study, an excerpt from his essential work *Soulful Branding*, was written by our friend, branding genius Jerome Conlon, who was working for the company in question at the time this story occurred. The firm, which we'll identify later in this chapter, had just experienced the first sales contraction in its 14-year history, which was itself a highly traumatic experience. Sales had declined 10 percent from the previous year, which necessitated a workforce reduction of 20 percent. Morale was totally shot, as was confidence. The company had missed a critical new market and had been outmaneuvered by an archrival that was simply doing a better job at marketing to a new target audience.[2]

The situation was further complicated by the company's culture. The company was historically distrustful of formal research or consultants and was managed by highly competitive people who felt they already knew what worked in the real world. Key decisions about products and marketing were intuitive, which had led to bold and gutsy decisions in the past. But management didn't realize that it was working in a closed information system and had serious blind spots and knowledge gaps.

The situation was precisely what Andy Grove, the former Intel chief executive officer, had labeled a *strategic inflection point.*

Conventional wisdom in marketing circles said that it would take about two years to reposition this national brand in the marketplace, which promised to be an excruciating and difficult process for everyone involved. The sense of dread was palpable.

The company described above was Nike; the year was 1986.

The new market that Nike was failing in was the women's market, which the company had thoroughly failed to understand. As a result, the field had been left wide open to Reebok, which quickly seized the opportunity.

By 1986 aerobics had become a national craze for women, and aerobic shoes were the primary style of sports footwear that women purchased. The market exploded during a five-year period, driving Reebok from an under-the-radar brand to number one in sports shoe market share in North America by 1987. Rob Strasser, Nike's VP of marketing at the time commented, "We never thought that a bunch of sweaty women jumping around in a dance room would ever amount to anything." This is a classic statement of a limiting belief that led to a major blind spot, and because of this type of thinking, Nike experienced a 60 percent decline in footwear sales to women between 1976 and 1986. It was critical to the future of the company that this be overcome.

However, Nike's brand positioning was not so friendly to most women. Nike's image highlighted elite athletes delivering powerful performances in various hyper-competitive sports arenas (think *Air Jordan*), and the advertising tone was loud, aggressive, and intentionally macho, often including male locker room humor and trash talking. This worked fine for most males, but generated brand perceptions that kept Nike from realizing its sales potential to women and a broader audience.

Recognizing the significance of the problem, top management called for a thorough assessment of the situation and asked Nike's marketing and advertising groups to examine the deeper root causes of the decline. The Market Insights team which Jerome led explored the mind-set of consumers regarding Nike's brands, products, and advertising, and also delved into the mind-set of its own leadership, meeting frequently with Nike executives in lively and animated conversations.

At that time, the hard-core competitive sports ethos within the company was so pervasive that it wasn't even discussed. It was the culture, period, so by going beyond the public face to get at the private voices of executives and of consumers, the team discovered hidden truths behind the market's choices and behind management's attitudes and feelings. On the basis of these insights, management was able to make significant progress in designing a new positioning.

Another limiting belief concerned the design of the shoes themselves. Nike designers believed that sports shoes needed to be sturdy, with lots of cushioning and lateral stability support. The upper materials needed to be thick and tough. Women, however, felt that Nike shoes were clunky, made their feet look big, and were not particularly comfortable. It was no wonder sales had declined by 60 percent, but because at the time no one was actually asking the women about these issues, the obvious information remained entirely hidden.

But not to Reebok. Its Princess and Freestyle models broke with the sturdy, overengineered paradigm. Made of thin and pliable garment leather, they had low-profile midsoles with minimal cushioning, resulting in a shoe that was immediately comfortable and required no break-in period.

At the time inside Nike there was a raging debate. One side held that Nike could never do shoes like Reebok because Reebok shoes weren't high performance, but of course, "high performance" was measured from the macho male perspective, not the perspective of the intended customer.

The motives that many women had for participating in fitness activities were also quite different from those of young males who participated in competitive sports. Women's exercise was more commonly an inner-directed form of therapy that improved their day. It was about personal empowerment, not high-performance status, and it was done for a sense of balance in their lives, often in playful ways. Such emotional benefits for engagement were completely different than for competitive males, and the desired product performance characteristics were entirely different, focusing on comfort and styling.

Ignorance of these hidden and largely unspoken beliefs was killing Nike in this critical market, but the research exposed these factors, so for the first time, Nike leaders had insight into who these consumers were, not as statistics on a sales spreadsheet, but as a different type of athlete with genuine feelings about how sport, fitness, brands, products, and advertising fit into their lives. Nike's leaders quickly understood that the company was out of alignment with market reality in its brand image, its advertising approach, its product design, and its perceived product value.

Nike leaders thus established a clear set of guidelines focused on expanding its market share, and quickly the company aligned and balanced the elements in the marketing mix to meet these needs. Within two quarters Nike had stopped the erosion, and sales started moving rapidly upward. Nike sales to women grew more than 75 percent each year for five consecutive years, and the company's stock value rose from $5 per share to $35.

Although this Nike case study is fascinating, it's definitely not an isolated situation, or one that is unique to Nike. In fact, it's a story as old as the parable of the fish that could not see the water it lived in and did not recognize *water* as the key constituent of its environment. Organizations often fall into this trap, and it's the role of researchers and brand leaders to expose the hidden dimensions of customer experience and company assumptions that result in these branding blind spots.

BRANDS AND ARCHETYPES

A useful way to think about the meaning of brands is to sort them into categories, which we call archetypes. The study of archetypes was the work of the brilliant psychologist Carl Jung, a friend, colleague, and sometimes rival of Sigmund Freud.

Jung was interested in how images, icons, myths, and objects carry meaning, and his studies revealed the same meanings across many human cultures. In cultures that had had no contact with one another he nevertheless found the same sets of personalities—warriors, rebels, nurturers, magicians, and tricksters exist in nearly all cultures—so Jung saw these as inherent in the human character, and labeled them *archetypes*. Brands are like myths, of course, and they carry archetypal meanings.

Jung once commented that the most important question anyone can ask is, "What myth am I living?" To the degree that we remember and retell our stories and create new ones, we become the authors, the authorities, of our own lives.[3] The brands we choose reflect the myths we choose to live, and this is as important for an organization as it is for an individual.

Hence, to create a brand requires that we understand archetypes and their meanings and then craft the brand's identity to suit the qualities and characteristics that we wish our innovations to embody. Here are some examples that will probably be familiar.

THE WARRIOR

There are warriors in every culture, and history is filled with their stories. Alexander the Great, David, and Napoleon were renowned for their skill in battle. The basketball great, Michael Jordan, also embodied the warrior archetype, his battlefield the hyper-competitive arena of the NBA. His unprecedented skills included an incredible 4-foot vertical leap, among the highest in the NBA, 20 inches more than average, because of which he could run and take off from the free throw line and dunk, appearing to fly. That led to the brilliant Nike Air Jordan brand, which became a phenomenal marketing success, generating billions of dollars of revenue. The phenomenon was based on Jordan's skills, and also drew upon his intelligence, personal charisma, and magnetism. Air Jordan shoes retain totemic value even today, more than a decade after his retirement.

THE MAGICIAN

Throughout history, those who possessed esoteric knowledge, special knowledge, became teachers, magicians, or shamans. Even Leonardo da Vinci leveraged his deep insights to portray himself as a magician, as for example in his job application to the Duke of Milan, in which he advertised his magical skills quite overtly, as we see below in the sidebar. Here he touts his knowledge of many secrets, and he concludes the letter with the offer of a demonstration:

> And if any of the aforesaid things should seem to anyone impossible or impracticable, I offer myself as ready to make trial of them in your park or in whatever place shall please your Excellency.

He got the job, where he remained for 17 productive years.

Da Vinci's Résumé

Letter from Leonardo da Vinci to the Duke of Milan, Applying for a Position

Having, most illustrious lord, seen and considered the experiments of all those who pose as masters in the art of inventing instruments of war, and finding that their inventions differ in no way from those in common use, I am emboldened, without prejudice to anyone, to solicit an appointment of acquainting your Excellency with certain of my secrets.

1. I can construct bridges which are very light and strong and very portable, with which to pursue and defeat the enemy; and others more solid, which resist fire or assault, yet are easily removed and placed in position; and I can also burn and destroy those of the enemy.

2. In case of a siege, I can cut off water from the trenches and make pontoons and scaling ladders and other similar contrivances.

3. If by reason of the elevation or the strength of its position, a place cannot be bombarded, I can demolish every fortress if its foundations have not been set on stone.

4. I can also make a kind of cannon which is light and easy of transport, with which to hurl small stones like hail, and of which the smoke causes great terror to the enemy, so that they suffer heavy loss and confusion.

5. I can noiselessly construct to any prescribed point subterranean passages either straight or winding, passing if necessary, underneath trenches or a river.

6. I can make armored wagons carrying artillery, which shall break through the most serried ranks of the enemy, and so open a safe passage for infantry.

(*continued*)

(*continued*)

7. If occasion should arise, I can construct cannon and mortars and light ordnance in shape both ornamental and useful and different from those in common use.

8. When it is impossible to use cannon, I can supply in their stead catapults, mangonels, trabocchi, and other instruments of admirable efficiency not in general use—in short, as the occasion requires, I can supply infinite means of attack and defense.

9. And if the fight should take place upon the sea, I can construct many engines most suitable either for attack or defense, and ships which can resist the fire of the heaviest cannon, and powders or weapons.

10. In time of peace, I believe that I can give you as complete satisfaction as anyone else in the construction of buildings both public and private, and in conducting water from one place to another.

I can further execute sculpture in marble, bronze, or clay, also in painting I can do as much as anyone else, whoever he may be.

Moreover, I would undertake the commission of the bronze horse, which shall endue with immortal glory and eternal honor the auspicious memory of your father and of the illustrious house of Sforza.

And if any of the aforesaid things should seem to anyone impossible or impracticable, I offer myself as ready to make trial of them in your park or in whatever place shall please your Excellency, to whom I commend myself with all possible humility.

Leonardo da Vinci

This isn't exactly the most humble of proclamations, but history also shows that it was not exaggeration, either. Then again, how much humility can we expect that a true magician actually should possess?

Centuries later, when Steve Jobs returned to Apple in 1997, the company's marketers were quite clever in how they positioned him as the magician, the master of intuition, confidence, action, and creation, who, like the Wizard of Oz, worked from behind the curtain to bring about transformation. And like da Vinci, he also delivered on his promises, perhaps more than anyone could have possibly expected. Apple remains to this day, now years after Jobs's sad and quite premature death, among the four or five most valuable corporations in the world.

THE TRICKSTER

Another Jungian archetype is the coyote, also known as Kokopelli, the monkey king, Kitsune (fox spirit), and Hanuman, the trickster demigod who prefers to disobey normal rules and convention. This is the usurper, the revolutionary and patron saint of rebellious behavior. In Norse mythology, it is Loki, recently returned to our awareness courtesy of the hit movies about his more conventional brother, Thor, who embodies the establishment as Loki fully reflects the anti-establishment.

This was also the elemental Jobs, for rebellion lies at the very heart of innovation. With his abrasive personality and rude demeanor, Jobs showed a bit of that dark side as well. Dismissive, hostile, spiteful, petulant, sometimes lacking respect for human dignity, Jobs took the trickster too far and belittled people, swore at them, and pressured some until they reached their breaking point.

Still, it is an important role, for when every thought you have tells you that there's a better way, and that you know what that better way is, and further that you have what it takes to bring it to the world, then you're experiencing the trickster archetype, who possesses self-confidence in abundance. The trickster openly questions and mocks authority while seeking out new ideas and experiences. In the process, the trickster also promotes impulse and enthusiasm, which leads inevitably to a little chaos and unrest—because it's all about rocking the boat.

But at the same time, the trickster brings deep knowledge and wisdom to his people, and even when punished horribly for his effrontery, his indomitable spirit keeps him coming back for more.

The trickster rebels against authority, pokes fun at the overly serious, creates convoluted schemes that may or may not work, plays recklessly with the laws of the universe. His role is to question and to cause us to question—and certainly not to accept things blindly.

In so doing he brings great value to societies that may otherwise become overburdened with ancestor worship and stagnation. Hence, the trickster often appears when a way of thinking becomes outmoded, needs to be torn down, and cries out to be built anew. He is the destroyer of worlds yet the savior of us all because he shows the way to the new world. Thus, the trickster is also a metaphor for the evolution of consciousness and therefore a central character in the archetypal myths of creation, and of innovation. Hence, if you're going to get very good at innovation, perhaps you should study the trickster closely, even if that's not the brand identity you want your new product, service, or business model to convey, because all innovations, even the most nurturing (like the Huggies Pull-Ups), carry at least a hint of the trickster's willingness to do things differently.

Perhaps the most rebellious act recorded in human mythology occurred in the Garden of Eden, when Eve bit into the first apple and thereby defied God's commandment never to taste of the tree of knowledge of good and evil. The consequences of this rebellion are hence forever connected to the archetypal apple—nakedness, sex for pleasure and not procreation, sin, kinkiness, and consorting with demons. The choice of the name Apple, embodying rebellion and sexual cathexis, churns at a subconscious level in the minds of Apple consumers, and whenever we see the Apple logo many of us subconsciously connect with the primordial rebellion, the delicious mischief, and the enthralling naughtiness.

If the Garden of Eden apple was the first mythical apple, then the apple that dropped on Isaac Newton's head was the second. When Newton proved that the Earth was not the center of the universe he launched another great rebellion in history, the scientific revolution that led to the modern industrial age.

With these many examples in mind—Michael Jordan, Nike, Leonardo da Vinci, Adam and Eve, Loki, Apple, Huggies, Steve Jobs, we can now ask the central question once again: How do we achieve iconic branding?

> Making a brand into an icon is a systematic process, not a lucky accident.

Through diligent research you can discover the inner workings of your brand's character, and the motives, values, experiences, and paradoxes embedded within it. What is the iconic image that expresses that character? What words and phrases express that character? What are the right colors and sounds? What are the right scenes and settings? Here are some examples.

- Ford pickup trucks—the right one to have on a construction site
- Coors beer—a bar filled with young and very attractive women
- Coca-Cola—the brand of sharing and love
- Progressive Insurance—a rather strange but somewhat attractive young woman
- Apple—the creative rebel

In addition to Jung's work concerning archetypes, a fine book that develops these themes specifically in a marketing and branding context is *The Hero and the Outlaw* by Margaret Mark and Carol S. Pearson, which provided the quote that we began this chapter with. Among the 12 archetypes they identify and explore in very interesting detail are those we have already mentioned, along with the lover, the caregiver, and the innocent.

STORYTELLING

More than anything else, a story—the sharing of insight and meaning—can unlock clarity, creativity, courage, and commitment. Since the beginning of time, human beings have transmitted the best of what they knew to the generations that followed through an oral tradition. The structure of story is built into our neurophysiology and into our evolutionary drive.

> The American poet Muriel Rukeyser said it well: "The world is not made of atoms. It is made of stories."

A story is the single most effective way to inspire a person—a team member, an investor, a customer—to shift from one state of consciousness into another. Therefore, the very best way to both ignite innovation and clarify your brand is to find your story and tell it well. Further, the DNA of your corporate culture is entirely based on this, because story is the genetic code of human culture and meaning.

Paul Zak, director of the Center for Neuroeconomics Studies at Claremont University, says that our brains produce the stress hormone cortisol during the tense moments in a story, which allows us to focus, but a story's happy ending releases oxytocin, the feel-good chemical that promotes connection and empathy and triggers the limbic system, our brain's reward center, to release dopamine, which makes us feel more hopeful and optimistic.

In one of Zak's experiments, study participants watched an emotionally charged movie about a father and son, and then were asked to donate money to a stranger. Those with higher levels of oxytocin were much more likely to give money to someone they'd never met.[4]

Learn from this, you aspiring entrepreneurs: To be successful, tap into the trust-inducing power of storytelling. What you need is thus the next generation of a business plan, which is less about the data and instead is a living document that holds the story and acts as an interactive operating guide for the venture.

Think in terms of a three-act structure:

Act I: Describe the opportunity and all the assumptions necessary to make your concept work.

Act II: Describe the central hypotheses and techniques you will use to test and validate these hypotheses.

Act III: Express the end state, the happily ever after, in clear and realistic terms.

The story-based approach puts important emphasis on learning, on constantly adjusting assumptions as you accumulate evidence, based on the fundamental premise that you are starting with incomplete knowledge and that things are likely to change as you progress. In this way, planning and operating are integrated, real-time activities, and instead of trying to achieve the static milestones of the old economy, you are focused on dynamic elements that constantly point you in the right direction.

Of course, there is still a need and a place for traditional metrics and milestones, such as financial budgets and human resource allocations, which form the framework for interfacing the real work of innovation with the real world of business and investing.

Hence, Agile Innovation storytelling is a way to integrate the scientific, systematic, and rational processes that are necessary, with the essentially human and metarational characteristics of observation, insight, intuition, communication, esthetics, and empathy.

THE BUSINESS PANORAMA[TM 5]

Lean start-up guru Steve Blank has said that "A business plan is a document that an investor makes you write that nobody ever reads." This is a perfect example of valuing comprehensive documentation over working innovations, and to solve this problem, he combined Alexander Osterwalder's Business Model Canvas with a focused Customer Development approach to create the Lean Canvas approach as a tool for developing new business models.

Whereas a comprehensive business plan can take weeks or months to write, your initial canvas could be sketched in under a day and then iterated over time. After you've figured out your unique value proposition and unfair advantage, and have fleshed out your shiny new model, it's time to turn the sketch into a masterpiece by using a tool called the *business panorama*[TM] to make the concept immediately attractive to your team, partners, stakeholders, and potential investors.

The business panorama is a way to make sure you include the one missing essential you desperately need to turn a business canvas into something you can sell: the story.

By merging the lean canvas with the Ackerman Scenogram, developed by UCLA screenwriting professor Hal Ackerman, you can adapt the lean canvas sketch into a *story spine,* the essential information that links story elements in a logical sequence that delivers an emotionally compelling ending.

Ackerman's model shows you how to create a visual representation of the story spine. Successful storytellers begin by focusing listeners' minds on a single important idea, and it usually takes no longer than 30 seconds to forge an emotional connection, which is the film script's opening dilemma. It is followed by the exposition, unifying devices, the act structure, and major turning points. This unites every element in the story, focuses it, gives meaning to events, and creates the forward momentum that advances the story to its conclusion.

Most important, the spine tells us *why* things are important, and why viewers, listeners, or readers should invest their emotions into staying with the story to its conclusion.

Conversely, if any part is missing then the spine is broken, and a true story does not exist.

Figure 11.1 shows the general layout of a business panorama. (If you'd like to download a template for a business panorama and some samples, you can do so via links available in Appendix B: Resources for Your Revolution.)

On the left is the inciting incident that is the raison d'être of your project or venture, and establishes the protagonist—who in most cases will be your customer. In a romantic comedy, this is what is called *meet cute*—and can be adopted as the strong opening for your pitch.

The primary shortcomings that you uncovered during your ethnographic research should comprise the pain points illustrated, with the last one summating all the others. These pain points become the vertebra elements of the full spine, and the solution points are the limbs that express the solution. These points integrate into the Big Vision, which explains your unique value proposition. Below, you explain how you validate the revenue model and become successful.

The climax and resolution of the story is in the final panel to the right, which is your vision for how the world has been transformed

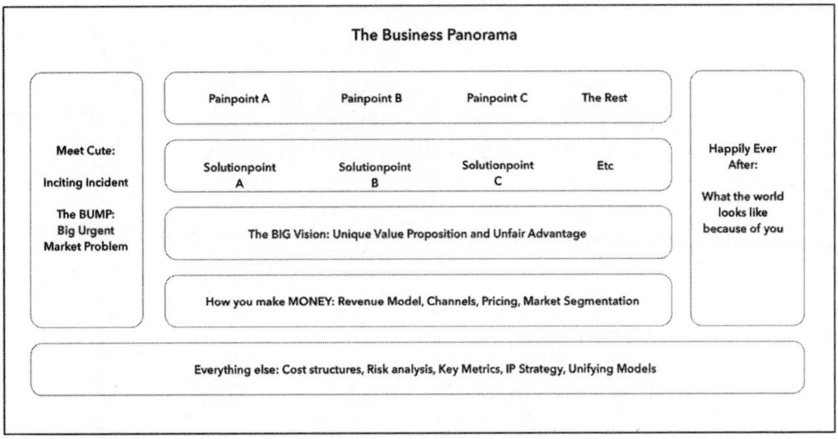

The Business Panorama

| Painpoint A | Painpoint B | Painpoint C | The Rest |

Meet Cute:
Inciting Incident
The BUMP: Big Urgent Market Problem

Solutionpoint A — Solutionpoint B — Solutionpoint C — Etc

The BIG Vision: Unique Value Proposition and Unfair Advantage

How you make MONEY: Revenue Model, Channels, Pricing, Market Segmentation

Happily Ever After:
What the world looks like because of you

Everything else: Cost structures, Risk analysis, Key Metrics, IP Strategy, Unifying Models

Figure 11.1 This way of visualizing the growth and development of a business captures the essence of the business in a story structure. Because storytelling is so essential to human thoughts and perceptions, using this format enables you to describe how the business creates value for customers, and how you can tell that story in the most compelling way to investors and other stakeholders.

because of your innovation. At the very bottom, include all other details that are pertinent to your stakeholders but would overburden the story.

The key to success is articulating the flow of the story from present experience, into the transformational aspects of your solution, and to a description of the future made better because of your efforts.

The business panorama gives you an approach besides the typical (boring) stack of slides that every entrepreneur shows to investors, or project leaders present to senior management. Printed out wall size, you can make your pitch without PowerPoint, and thus the business panorama is essentially a one-chart pitch. (This is similar to one-chart journalism and infographics, heralded by experts including Nate Silver and Ezra Klein, who seek to augment or perhaps replace the 700-word newspaper article with the single compelling image that tells a story so well that it's shared virally on Facebook and Twitter.) But what we're talking about is more than data visualization—it's the visualization of vision itself.

Remember, venture capitalists rarely think, "Wow, I really wish this guy would more accurately relay the data set underlying the business model." More likely they're thinking, "Oh my god . . . I must look

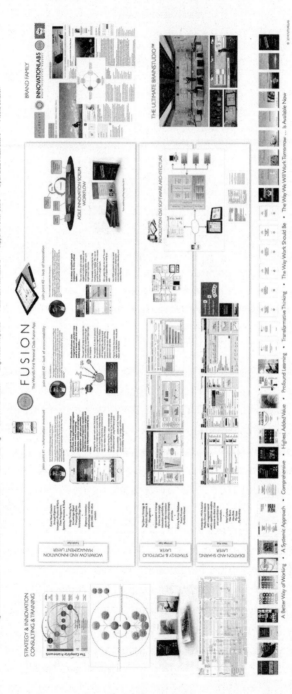

Figure 11.2 The business panorama of FutureLab. There's a lot of information here, but the flow and organization make it highly accessible to the reader. In addition, the fact that it's all in one image promotes integration and coherence, whereas the same information in a stack of PowerPoint slides might provide a fragmented view.

interested . . . must maintain a smile . . ." It isn't until they're engaged at an emotional level that it's possible to earn their trust.

Think Different[6]

Upon his return in 1997 to the wounded and nearly bankrupt Apple, Jobs realized that if he wanted to restore the company to its former glory, he would have to create a more inspirational brand narrative. The company needed, that is, a new story. He said,

> Marketing is about values! This is a very complicated world. It's a very noisy world. And we're not going to get a chance for people to remember much about us. No company is! And so, we have to be really clear on what we want them to know about us . . . Apple at the core . . . its core value—is that, we believe that people with passion can change the world for the better. That's what we believe! And we have had the opportunity to work with people like you, with software developers . . . who have done it. In some big, and some small ways. And we believe that, in this world, people can change it for the better. And that those people who are crazy enough to think they can change the world, are the ones that actually do! . . . And so we wanted to find a way to communicate this. And what we have is something that I am very moved by. And the theme of the campaign is "Think different." It's honoring the people who think different and move this world forward.[7]

Was the Think Different campaign an example of iconic, empathic, and soulful branding? Absolutely. Think Different projected Apple's heart and soul into a marketplace from which

(*continued*)

those energies had been almost completely removed, and then succeeded in attaching that magnificent positive energy to the Apple brand itself.

Of course, we would hardly remember the Think Different campaign if Apple had not also come up with three brilliant and iconic products in the years that followed: the iPod, iPhone, and iPad. We can suppose that the Think Different message resonated internally as well as externally, helping inspire the great work that transformed the Apple of 1997 as a company running on fumes from its past glories, to the Apple of 2014, the acknowledged world leader in creativity and innovation, and perhaps the world's most admired company.

The Think Different campaign brilliantly presents a microcosm of the art of iconic branding.

CREATING YOUR ICON

So how do you achieve status the status of an icon?

One of the reasons that successful innovations become so is because they convey meaning. A great product is more than a physical object; it's also valued for what it says about the owner, user, or wearer. By understanding the role of archetypes and totems in business and media, we learn to recognize how objects carry meaning, how to interpret that meaning, and ultimately how to embed meaning into products and brands.

An innovative product or service that we aspire to elevate to greatness, or a company we wish to make into a great one, must have a transformational approach to branding designed in from the very outset. That's how, and why, iconic brands are created.

What story does your brand tell?

And what will turn that story into an icon, a landmark that all future travelers along your path will have to acknowledge and honor? Certainly it requires great products and services, great relationships with customers, and a value set that embodies archetypes in provocative and authentic ways. None of these are easy to achieve, but all of them are entirely worthwhile goals toward which your innovation efforts at the level of specific products, services, business models, and ventures, and your brand as a whole, should strive.

Questions to Reflect Upon

- What is our corporate understanding of our brand, and how well does it match our aspirations?
- To what extent does our brand inspire our customers?
- What would characterize an iconic brand for us?
- Which of our competitors have achieved icon status, and how did they do that?

12

OPTIMIZING YOUR INFRASTRUCTURE

If you maximize the potential that people in an organization can and will communicate, you will vastly increase the likelihood of knowledge transfer, and hence innovation.

—Thomas Allen and Gunter Henn[1]

Your attitude, knowledge, and leadership skills are vitally important to success at innovation, and to nurturing and developing the innovation culture within your organization. So, too, are the business processes you implement to enable and support innovation, including Agile scrums for speed, portfolio management for risk mitigation, and the three innovation roles to nurture engagement.

For the innovation effort to reach its full potential, the right infrastructure, systems, and tools are also required, for they are essential enablers and catalysts. Because the performance advantage can be significant, it is an Agile Innovation leader's responsibility to design and implement the needed infrastructure. This chapter focuses on the key elements.

Four Elements of Infrastructure

The necessary infrastructure consists of four major elements:

- *The virtual infrastructure:* software tools for ideation, port-folio management, and workflow management.
- *Facilitation and collaboration:* the best ways of working together.
- *The physical infrastructure:* the work environment for innovation.
- *Open innovation:* the methods of engaging people from outside the organization in the innovation process.

The first three of these topics are discussed in this chapter, and the fourth is the subject of the next chapter.

EXPLORATION AND PRODUCTION

Innovation efforts benefit significantly from the right tools, but it's also important to note that the pursuit of innovation creates needs that are different from the operations part of the organization. We'll start by clarifying the distinction between operations and innovation by looking at the adjacent concepts of exploration and production.

You may already be familiar with these terms, especially if you're involved in the energy industry. In oil companies, the term *exploration and production* is a standard phrase that refers to finding oil, extracting it, and refining it into usable petroleum products, such a gasoline for cars, jet fuel for aircraft, and plastics for countless other essentials of the modern world, including clothing, building products, and toys. Because the notion of exploration and production is a standard organizational approach in the oil industry, most large oil companies have an E&P division, which is also referred to as *upstream,* and a separate distribution and marketing division, which is called *downstream.*

In the broader world of organizations struggling to adapt to a changing world, however, *exploration* means "innovating," whereas *production* means the "ongoing work of normal business operations." This distinction is important because, as we have noted, the processes and infrastructure required to support exploration and innovation are different from those for production and operations. Sometimes they are entirely different.

For example, creating and delivering new ideas, new products, new services, or new internal business initiatives requires approaches and tools that are quite unlike the set of methods and tools that the rest of the operation uses for monitoring and measuring the day-to-day work. The different core organizational culture and the management controls in these environments can be at odds with each other, often causing organizational distress.

Because the operations part is overwhelmingly larger, it usually wins out when there is a conflict of styles, which can result in crippling constraints suffered by the exploration and innovation parts of the business.

Infrastructure is one of the places where this difference of need and lack of alignment is most evident.

Dealing with Uncertainty

The core of the misalignment concerns how the two functions deal with the issue of uncertainty.

In the world of operations, a primary intent is to minimize or eliminate uncertainty. In fact, the operations mentality rightly values continuity, predictability, and repeatability, as these are the qualities from which growth and profits come.

However, the process of exploration inherent in the quest for innovation is entirely discontinuous, unpredictable, and fundamentally uncertain. Uncertainty in new product and service development is unavoidable, and even worse, numerous unknowns and risks are inherent in the process.

As the exploration factor ramps up, as design teams push technology to the edge (and preferably beyond), as market forces change rapidly, no process, not even the most brilliant team, can ensure success. However, the right people working in an agile, exploratory process can offer the best chance at success. Such projects succeed because of a team's ability to adapt to the environment, rather than follow a path prescribed by the past.

Effective, efficient operations are achieved by minimizing uncertainty. On the other hand, uncertainty is inherent in innovation. This difference has consequences that extend deeply into differing cultures, mind-sets, working styles, and even the types of required information and what we do with that information.

Our focus here is on understanding what this means for the infrastructure, and more specifically the tools we use.

THE VIRTUAL INFRASTRUCTURE

The virtual infrastructure that supports operations is often called enterprise resource planning (ERP). It's a massive software system, often from SAP or Oracle, that costs millions to buy and millions more to install. It manages accounting, finance, and perhaps human resources, making it the virtual backbone of the modern organization.

The quest for innovation, meanwhile, is supported by a more modest set of software tools that support the three critical functions of Agile Innovation: attaining top speed in the innovation effort, mitigating risk, and engaging the entire organization in creating and developing the best ideas. These were, of course, the main topics of Chapters 5, 6, and 7, and many of the sidebars you encountered in those chapters explained how the innovation management tools to support these functions work best, tools we've developed over many years of trial and (quite a bit of) error.

COLLABORATION AND IDEATION

- A powerful collaboration and ideation tool set enables sharing, discussing, refining, and disseminating ideas via the obvious and less obvious means. Obvious: e-mail, discussion groups, teleconferences, instant messages, and the phone. Less obvious: chat rooms, social workflow technologies, virtual whiteboards, and wikis.

- Online collaboration tools, such as Skype, enable people to connect anywhere in the world via simple video chats, often a significant improvement over voice-only or e-mail communications.

- Knowledge repositories enable you to store knowledge that you've gained throughout the organization so that you don't waste time and money recreating work and recreating knowledge that your organization has already found or accomplished. A knowledge repository that is easily searched and well organized can save tons of time and accelerate efforts when you're exploring new ideas.

- Similarly, new idea repositories are a great way to gather new ideas. Many organizations use idea-gathering systems that give people throughout the firm a convenient and efficient way to share their thoughts and ideas.

- Organizational archives and directories are very helpful for enabling people to access others inside as well as outside the organization.

- Open data interoperability, allowing integration with back-office systems and preventing lock-in with any single vendor.

WORKFLOW

- Creativity tools, such as mind-mapping software and visualization systems, can help people explore complex ideas, issues, and problems. These tools also help people find better ways to understand the relationship between the contributing factors, and can help them explain their ideas to others more efficiently.

- Social workflow assignment tools allocate tasks and then track them to completion, preventing missed deadlines and unpleasant last minute surprises.

PORTFOLIO MANAGEMENT

- As we discussed extensively, innovation managers need comprehensive project management and portfolio management tools that help them manage complex investment decisions.

- An analysis tool set that enables managers to assess portfolio management factors including concentration and concentration risk, strategic alignment, and overall progress.

- Managers can also analyze and manage collaborations, and move the more promising projects along the development pipeline as innovation milestones are met.

- An intelligent rating engine uses dynamically weighted voting and reputation engines to improve predictive skills around innovation, and helps to target the people best suited to contributing to projects in specific market and technical areas.

- Idea-voting systems are useful when new ideas are shared online so that others can study them and suggest which they think are best, and contribute to improving them. This enables innovation leaders to get quick insight into what people throughout the organization consider the best ideas, feedback that may help in the process of choosing which ideas should receive additional investment.

ENGAGEMENT

- A customizable incentive management system can help engage staff members and is thus also a way to influence the development of the innovation culture.

- An integrated social network can help deepen collaboration and form stronger teams. Such teams can also be extended into the extranet to enable powerful new partnerships, which is the subject of the next chapter on open innovation.

- Wikis and blogs are great tools to help individuals aggregate and organize their new ideas and personal knowledge, and if they choose, to make that information accessible to others.

- As mentioned earlier, one of the key characteristics of the innovation culture is a shift from hierarchical thinking to network thinking. Hence, networking tools, easily accessible archives, and directories help people find others who have similar interests or who are engaged in exploring similar questions.

- Innovation tutorials and online training systems help people understand the specific skills and methods involved in a company's innovation process.

Connectability

- The Internet was created by cobbling together disparate networks through a process similar to the evolution of multicellular organisms from unicellular eukaryotes in the pre-Cambrian era, roughly a billion and a half years ago. Similarly, whatever you build as a virtual infrastructure for innovation will eventually need to connect to the infrastructures built by your partners and customers. Someday, we expect this aggregated and unified infrastructure to become the *innovation grid*, a global innovation platform that will facilitate a new era of cooperative and collaborative innovation. Most likely, it'll be open, mobile, intelligent, adaptive, evolving, and Agile, and it could even hold the potential to help solve our world's greatest challenges. When you build your infrastructure, think about how you're building toward that vision.

Dashboards

- All facets of the virtual infrastructure should be accessible through visually-oriented dashboard displays that are accessible on all types of devices, including computers, tablets, and phones. (We'll have more to say on the dashboard shortly.)

Add all these elements together and you'll have an ideal virtual work space for innovation and high-energy collaboration.

Engagement in a Shared Mental Space

Innovation often happens as a result of interactions between individuals, whose creative ideas combine and recombine very quickly in the course of their conversations. The resulting discoveries and possibilities lead to new, different, and often quite unexpected conclusions. It's an open-ended, emergent process and thus highly unpredictable.

These discussions tend to differ significantly from those that occur in operations—they are multidimensional, ambiguous, and uncertain, and the root qualities of discovery and learning that characterize this form of dialog are not at all like the discrete and transactional nature of operations issues.

In the innovation realm it's essential that these conversations take place, and indeed, it is an accepted fact among innovation experts that encouraging such interactions is critical to success. They must be encouraged and supported.

Demos, prototypes, simulations, and models can be powerful catalysts for these interactions, as these artifacts define a shared engagement space, a mental construct in which an emerging problem and its solutions can be explored and then understood. This shared space is "where" researchers, designers, developers, marketers, customers, managers, and others can engage in meaningful and productive innovation efforts, and the *where* is in quotation marks because this can be a physical place as well as a virtual one.

When it's a physical space, it can be a hallway, a meeting room, or a space specifically designed to support innovation, such as an innovation lab, which we describe in detail later in this chapter. If it's virtual, then of course it's some sort of shared dialog on e-mail, through a website, or via an innovation management software tool.

In both physical and virtual instances, creating the shared mental space is critical to enabling and sustaining the innovation effort, and we define the requirements for a shared space in some detail. It has these fundamental components:

- *Commonality:* This means that objectives are clear for everyone to be able to participate productively in the innovation effort. The objectives be defined from the outset, and innovation champions or leaders are thus responsible for making sure that such clarity exists and that it's shared.

- *Inclusivity:* Innovators tend to be inclusive. That is, they discover and implement new ideas regardless of where in the organization the ideas originated. Their attitude is not focused on ownership of ideas or on pride in originating them, but in achieving objectives through the best means possible. They happily take and apply great ideas wherever they find them.

Steal Like an Artist

Here's what the very clever Austin Kleon says about art, originality, and stealing ideas:

> **How to look at the world (like an artist).**
>
> Every artist gets asked the question, "Where do you get your ideas?"
>
> The honest artist answers, "I steal them."
>
> How does an artist look at the world? First, you figure out what's worth stealing, then you move on to the next thing. That's about all there is to it.
>
> What a good artist understands is that nothing comes from nowhere. All creative work builds on what came before.[2]

- *Visualization:* This is the capacity to see what's different and transform what begins only in the mind's eye into a physical artifact—a drawing, model, diagram, rendering, video, or proto-type—so that others can also see it clearly and participate in understanding, developing, and improving it.

- *Simplicity:* The aim and ambition of creators and thinkers throughout history has been simplicity. Leonardo da Vinci, for example, wrote, "Simplicity is the ultimate form of sophistica-tion." You might have heard a similar comment from Steve Jobs or Jonathan Ive regarding the essence of the iPod or the iPhone, where tremendous complexity of function is accessed via systems and metaphors of great simplicity.

   Ive commented, "Simplicity isn't just a visual style. It's not just minimalism or the absence of clutter. It involves digging through the depth of complexity. To be truly simple, you have to go really deep. You have to deeply understand the essence of a product in order to be able to get rid of the parts that are not essential."[3]

In fact, leaders in many fields recognize creativity as a *subtractive* process—removing everything but the essential. This notion is typified by a comment attributed to Michelangelo, who was asked how he created his transcendent *David* sculpture: "I simply removed everything that was *not* David." Whether he ever really said that doesn't matter, as it conveys so simply and elegantly what we mean by subtraction.

Attaining simplicity is thus getting at the core, understanding its essence, and then making every element consistent with that essence. Although we may recognize simplicity when we see, touch, and use it, we also quickly learn that simplicity is difficult to achieve. Getting there takes time, thought, and effort: many design iterations, multiple prototypes, and thinking and rethinking the problem is necessary.

- *Networking:* Innovators are very likely to leverage alliances and partnerships as a means of accomplishing creative work. Most innovators are strong networkers, and they build their networks with people who, like themselves, get things done.

  A well-developed network can be a powerful asset when the external world starts to change because connections become invaluable sources of information that help innovators recognize that something's going on, find out where the leading edge is, and sort out the implications. As a result, innovators are often much more proactive in recognizing and responding to change than noninnovators.

- *Rigor:* Although innovative companies certainly value flexibility, they also have formal and structured processes to encourage and test innovations. The annual study published in *Strategy+Business* keeps coming back to the same key points, namely, the finding that it's not how much money your firm spends on R&D and innovation that will give you a competitive edge; it's the quality of your *process* that matters most. The study authors write:

> We continue to emphasize the key finding that our Global Innovation 1000 study of the world's biggest spenders on research and development has reaffirmed in each of the
>
> *(continued)*

(*continued*)

past seven years: There is no statistically significant relationship between financial performance and innovation
spending, in terms of either total R&D dollars or R&D
as a percentage of revenues. Many companies—notably,
Apple—consistently underspend their peers on R&D
investments while outperforming them on a broad range
of measures of corporate success, such as revenue growth,
profit growth, margins, and total shareholder return. Meanwhile, entire industries, such as pharmaceuticals, continue
to devote relatively large shares of their resources to innovation, yet end up with much less to show for it than they—
and their shareholders—might hope for.[4]

Of course what we've been describing here (and in our previous books)
is indeed a rigorous process that is fully intended to bring your organization great results precisely because it is a rigorous and proven process that's
in balance with the open-ended nature of exploration and discovery.

Creating and managing the shared mental space will advance significantly as the next wave of technology arrives over the next few years. We
can expect to see innovation apps for digital whiteboards, genuinely useful
artificial intelligence (beyond Siri) to assist in the process of refining ideas,
social workflow tools that leverage business and social activity frameworks
to map and codify workflow optimizations on the fly, and comprehensive
systems for dynamically measuring and tracking intellectual property
value, which will be particularly useful for real-time innovation audits.

In summary, the Agile Innovation approach unleashes creativity by
offering powerful infrastructure tools that enable new behaviors, new
collaborations, and the expansion of your core creativity skills and methods.

The Downside of Technology: A Company Swamped by Meetings

At a company we worked with recently, just about everyone
complained bitterly of meeting sprawl that seemed to be taking

over. The amount of time spent in meetings had ballooned, and many thought that meetings had fully taken over the entire work week. We heard complaints such as, "I don't know why, but over the past couple of years, life's become so much busier. I can't find time to think anymore. I'm trapped in eight meetings a day."

Research conducted by the Annenberg School of Communications at UCLA and the University of Minnesota's Training and Development Research Center shows that executives spend on average 40 to 50 percent of their working hours in meetings, and although some estimate that the national average is three meetings per day for a typical business executive, a quick survey in our client firm found that the average midlevel executive was locked into six.[5]

Consequently, many of our client's staff members were coming into work at 7 AM to respond to e-mails before the deluge of meetings began at 9. The whole group was headed for a disastrous burnout.

When we analyzed how this came about, we found an interesting and entirely hidden root cause. The company had recently implemented a popular networked meeting scheduler, and the software required full transparency to everyone's calendars. But because the software didn't understand how humans use their time productively and made no provision for think time, the result was that meeting requests filled every open moment without restraint or control. Employees were in meetings literally around the clock.

Once this was recognized, though, the problem was not so difficult to address. People were encouraged to book meetings with themselves a few hours a day to ensure they had private time for important work that otherwise was not getting done.

FACILITATING INNOVATION

The second major element of the innovation infrastructure is also a key role played by innovation champions, the job of facilitating productive interactions that help structure and speed along the problem-solving, learning, and design processes that characterize innovation efforts. To enable these efforts to be most efficient and effective, facilitators constantly apply the best ways to accelerate the work of creating innovation, whether that is in the research phase, in meetings, in workshops, or in the idea evaluation and decision process.

Why is this necessary at all, you might ask? Simply because we cannot assume that any team is capable of organizing its own work in the most effective manner. Many teams, unfortunately, tend toward being dysfunctional if left to their own devices, easily distracted from the focus on attaining the required results because of personality issues, time conflicts, or lack of clarity about roles or objectives. Hence, facilitators can indeed add tremendous value to the day-to-day work of innovation teams by helping to deal with these types of issues proactively.

The authors have been designing and facilitating innovation projects and teams dealing with complex business problems for more than 20 years, engaging large groups in structured work activities in the quest to achieve progressively better solutions in less time. Through the course of this work we've developed many design principles and guidelines to help facilitators bring about significant productivity enhancements.

> The goal of facilitation is simply to make it easier to accomplish meaningful work.

In fact, that's literally what *facilitation* means—making something *facile* (Latin for "easy"), or easier. This definition enables us to contrast the old way of working—in meetings, typically—with new ways that aim to dramatically compress time while significantly increasing the quality of the results. Is it possible to get weeks or months of innovation work done in a few days? Consider the following:

- In the old, traditional way, people gather in a meeting room, typically a boring space with a big rectangular table sitting squarely in the middle of it, and probably too many chairs squeezed around it. In the new way, the facilitated work way, people gather in a space designed to support effective innovation and collaboration, definitely not a traditional meeting room, but a fluid work environment that isn't dominated by the monster table.

- In the old way there's a lengthy agenda listing topic after topic, a linear death march. In the better way, a carefully structured flow enables people to learn quickly and assess new information in the shared mental space, and then develop specific ideas in response, moving progressively and building through cycles of design work to valid and comprehensive conclusions.

- In meetings, conversation typically jumps around and may converge on conclusions apparently at random, or not. In facilitated work, activities are prepared in advance and follow a logical structure of exploration that may include both divergent or lateral thinking exercises and convergent or analytical steps in a proper sequence that leads progressively toward specific design goals.

- In meetings, people usually lobby hard for the ideas that they already liked best before the meeting even started, whereas in facilitated work the goal is for new ideas to emerge through dialog and then to be developed through iterative cycles. In this way the best ones emerge and they're improved through dedicated and focused attention. And since all the participants made contributions to the emerging solutions, they likely feel a deeper level of enthusiasm and support for the ideas that are, frequently, better than any they had when we came into the room.

- At the end of a meeting the next steps may or may not be clear, but facilitated work aspires to a high degree of alignment along with explicit agreements about specific next steps that need to be accomplished.

Having applied these methods successfully in many cultures throughout Asia, the Americas, and Europe, our experience shows this to be a universal, human-centric approach to achieving high performance work, and not a style of working that is specific to any one culture.

Great things often happen by applying these principles of facilitation and doing so in a work environment specifically designed to help people reach a dynamic of high performance and dynamic creativity. Let's look at that work environment now.

THE PHYSICAL WORKPLACE FOR INNOVATION

The next element of the infrastructure is the design of the physical work spaces that support innovative efforts: the offices and meeting places, small and large, where formal and informal meetings, planned and spontaneous interactions, facilitated workshops and work sessions all occur.

These spaces are important and can contribute significantly to productivity improvements. And due to the evolving nature of work, most organizations now require much more meeting space than they needed in the past. Twenty years ago the right ratio might have been one meeting room for every 40 or 50 people, but the constant increase in the speed and complexity of the business environment creates new problems and opportunities at a rapid rate, which in turn evokes a need for much more meeting and collaboration space. The increasing complexity and accelerating rate of change in global markets also results in the need for larger meeting spaces for the greater numbers of people who participate in collaborative efforts.

Today the right ratio is likely to be one meeting space for every 10 people, and in organizations where large numbers spend significant amounts of their time working collaboratively, it could even be one meeting space for every five people.

However, most existing office facilities were not designed to support this extent of collaboration, and when new facilities are being developed, the architects should be directed to provide more meeting spaces in recognition of these changes.

But it's not just that *more* space is required. Equally important is the recognition that traditional meeting spaces simply aren't good enough. An entirely different approach to meeting space design can yield tremendous benefits, because spaces specifically designed to enhance and augment collaboration provide a significant benefit by elegantly supporting innovation project teams, brainstorming, and creative development projects.

Sometimes these spaces are referred to as innovation labs, innovation zones, skunkworks, or perhaps even sandboxes. They're rich with information, and they're equipped with the right tools, like large whiteboards that stretch from floor to ceiling that people can use to develop their ideas much more easily than by using small flip charts. Furniture is on wheels, easily reconfigured to meet the needs of any work group, and much better than heavy, immovable arrangements that impose a rigid work process for meetings simply from the lack of flexibility that's been designed in. New, flexible space designs also enable a much greater variety of meeting spaces to be created from hour to hour, so different types of gatherings can be well supported in a single meeting space throughout the day.

For organizations that frequently have large gatherings, a specific type of meeting space, sometimes called a collaboration or innovation center, supports a high performance work style that far surpasses what conventional meeting spaces can achieve. Attributes of these vastly improved meeting spaces are abundant natural light, open spaces, and high ceilings that feel expansive and are easy to move around in, books and other learning objects to stimulate exploration and creativity, support for multimedia and remote collaboration, and a great deal of flexibility.

Why is all this important? The need for new types of workplaces addresses one of the key issues facing creative individuals who are dealing with significant business and innovation challenges, which is that the kinds of problems that they're working on tend to be quite complex and require the integration of lots of information and knowledge. In traditional conference rooms there just isn't room for all the information that a team needs to have on hand when designing a new product, creating an innovative business model, or conceiving of a new service, brand, or entity. Crammed into spaces that are too small, they don't have all the charts, diagrams, and raw data they need to display and refer to, so critical information is buried in piles, hard to find, and harder to include in the design process.

Project teams benefit enormously when they can use a dedicated work space for the weeks or months of their IdeaScrums, where they can keep important information on display, meet any time they need to, store their reference materials, and keep their prototypes and prototyping tools. In this way, the room itself becomes part of the project's physical memory, and helps with the difficult work of concept integration. This enables people to effectively manage much more complex sets of information than they can view on their computer screens, and posting information on the walls also promotes better sharing of ideas, which is also essential to innovation projects.

If yours is a large organization then your innovation center may be a dedicated environment that could include 10, 20, or even 30 project rooms that are constantly in use by various project teams. Even if they're working in the room for only 5 or 10 hours a week the space investment is worthwhile because the space itself does so much to facilitate and add value to the process of addressing complexity, and thus the team will likely achieve better results in less time.

●   ●   ●

Your innovation labs can also help people overcome the obstacles that are built into the typical corporate environment by encouraging would-be innovators to conduct their work and play in free innovation zones, where experimentation is expected, and where reliability or stability is not expected. The modality is trying, testing, failing, reflecting, and experimenting further, making these ideal settings for people who are exploring new concepts, exploring boundaries, and taking risks where they can learn and thrive. In this organizational context and the right physical environment, they receive explicit and exceptional management support that encourages the right sort of thinking that leads to exceptional innovation results.

Figure 12.1 Exterior view of an innovation center. The center was built in the midst of the company's courtyard, making it the symbolic and actual center of the office building, fully accessible to the entire organization. The curved wall defined a large meeting space; the inside of the curve was covered with whiteboard material (see Figure 12.3), enabling everyone working in the space to see the full scope of ideas as they emerged during workshops and design activities.

Figure 12.2 The new workplace: digital whiteboards, analog whiteboards, smart (digitally enabled) seating, videoconferencing, etc. This is the right environment for the globalized and digitized innovation effort.

Figure 12.3 Inside the curved wall, a continuous white board.
Source: Pascal Baudry

During our many years of innovation work we've successfully designed quite a few of these environments, and we've seen them flourish as centers of learning and discovery, and hence as essential elements in the overall innovation efforts of their organizations.

SUMMARY

Organizational leaders are now recognizing that they need to take control of the physical and virtual work environments to support and stimulate innovation. This can mean different things in different organizations, but the point is to pay attention to this issue and not to assume that conventional approaches are right for you.

The right technology, a facilitated work process, and well-designed workplaces can all make significant contributions to the quality of the innovation effort. Together with the practices of open innovation, which we explore in the next chapter, they compose the essential infrastructure for effective innovation.

Like great artists who put significant effort into designing studios that enhance their creativity, organizations can do the same. For example, consider the great sculptor Manuel Neri. His financial success enabled him to design the ideal studio for his own needs, so he purchased a grocery store refrigerated walk-in container—completely soundproof, climate controlled, and painted white—creating a perfect distraction-free environment so that nothing would interrupt him while he was creating his masterpieces. He became one of the most prolific sculptors of the twentieth century.

Questions to Reflect Upon

- Which of our tools are the easiest to use? Which are most difficult?
- Is the quality of our innovation work improving over time? Can quality improvements be linked with increased quality of our tools?
- Are more and more people clamoring to have access to our innovation infrastructure?
- Is the depth of engagement in the innovation process also reflected in more widespread usage of the tools?
- How effective is our virtual infrastructure? Where is it strong or weak, and how should it be improved?
- Does our organization have the right facilities to support good collaboration for groups of all sizes, from a pair of people to hundreds?
- Do we have people who are skilled at facilitation? Are they called upon enough to use those skills?
- How well are our work spaces set up for innovation?
- In our organization, how does collaboration work?

13

ADVANCING OPEN INNOVATION

The pace of innovation will increase when innovators learn to harvest interactively from the incredible amount of information out there.
—Jorgen Randers[1]

ENGAGING SMART PEOPLE IN YOUR INNOVATION EFFORT

The concept of open innovation, the fourth essential element of the innovation infrastructure, is well documented in a number of fine books, and is widely practiced by organizations all over the world. The underlying principle is that by opening up the innovation process to broader participation by outsiders (that is, anyone who's *not* part of your organization), you'll be able to engage a larger number of smart people in thinking about and solving your problems and creating new opportunities.

Open innovation is a compelling term that evokes the promise of profound and confident success, whereas its opposite—*closed innovation*—brings the impression of silos, fear-based decision making, and failure to leverage the power of networks. So how could anyone question the wisdom of opening up innovation?

For some organizations, open innovation means partnering with universities and other research organizations to address specific technical or organizational challenges. They use open innovation services such as InnoCentive and NineSigma to access large pools of technical experts who help them solve scientific, technology, and business questions.

Open innovation also means company-branded Internet portals that gather ideas from partners, customers, and anyone who shares their thoughts, needs, and solutions, which can then be applied in the innovation process. Some well-known companies that do this include Dell, BMW, P&G, and even Shell Oil, all of which developed snazzy Web presences to promote their open innovation efforts.

A quick Web search finds a Unilever site named, not surprisingly, "Open Innovation." Here is an excerpt:

> We all want to create a better future—for consumers, for the environment, and for our business. To achieve that vision, we need to innovate—to improve existing products and create new ones.
>
> We have world-class research and development facilities, making breakthroughs that keep Unilever at the forefront of product development. But we know that the world is full of brilliant people, with brilliant ideas—and we are constantly looking for new ways to work with potential partners. We call this way of working Open Innovation.[2]

The statement is not particularly original but it's effective nonetheless. But why, you might ask, would Unilever be so interested in open innovation? One reason is that its archcompetitor P&G is a premier exemplar of open innovation. P&G's innovation platform, called Connect+Develop, or C+D, allows customers and partners to share ideas and co-create products with P&G.

A recent P&G press release announced C+D's second decade:

> P&G launched its Connect+Develop program more than 10 years ago and has developed more than 2,000 global partnerships, delivered dozens of global game-changer

products to consumers, accelerated innovation development and increased productivity, both for P&G and its partners. The website has served as P&G's "open front door to the world," allowing any innovator anywhere to share their innovations with the Company. The site, which includes translations in Chinese, Japanese, Spanish and Portuguese, receives about 20 submissions every weekday—or more than 4,000 a year—from all over the world.[3]

By leveraging outside talent, P&G taps into more brainpower and brings new concepts and perspectives that it might not otherwise become aware of at all.

P&G may have been one of the first to embrace open innovation, but it will not be long before this is the common and accepted practice. As open innovation expert Stefan Lindegaard reminds us, "Here's something very important that I want to emphasize. In five to seven years, we will no longer talk about open innovation. The term 'open innovation' will disappear and we will just view this as 'innovation.' The key difference is that innovation will have a much higher external input than what we see today."[4]

The Netflix Prize

A clever approach that brilliantly exemplifies these notions about open innovation and ecosystem innovation was used by Netflix when the video-streaming firm invited outsiders to help improve the important algorithm that is central to its movie recommendations system. Because recommendations are one of the key aspects of the company's value proposition, improving the quality of recommendations offered the potential to significantly enhance the value of its service.

In 2006 Netflix compiled a sample data set from its own database and announced the $1 million Netflix Prize, an award to be given to the programmer that developed an algorithm that could improve recommendations within the data set by more

(continued)

(continued)

than 10 percent, using the company's own algorithm as the benchmark. In the event that no team won the prize within a year, Netflix also promised a $50,000 annual progress prize to the best-performing solution, until the ultimate prize was won. By June 2007 more than 20,000 teams from more than 150 countries had registered for the competition, and 13,000 submissions had been received.

The contest continued for three years, and two progress prizes were awarded. In July 2009, a team consisting of researchers from AT&T, Yahoo!, and two other firms won the prize by submitting the winning algorithm a mere 20 minutes ahead of the second-place team, whose members came from IBM and other firms.

The contest received massive media attention worldwide, so the publicity that Netflix received was worth far more than the $1.1 million the firm paid out in prize money.

Interestingly, a planned second contest had to be cancelled when Netflix was sued for misuse of customer data, as it turned out that customer privacy laws were apparently violated in the original contest. The data that had supposedly been scrubbed of customer information turned out to be not so clean.

But that's beside the point, which is that by tapping into a huge ecosystem of brilliant programmers and analysts, Netflix improved its service, built its brand, and created an unparalleled learning environment in which its specific business objectives were met in a stunning and elegant way.

The Netflix story featured here also highlights a potential downside of open innovation, which is the challenge of protecting confidential and proprietary information. Although Netflix's issue was with customer data, a more common problem is related to intellectual property. How do we open up the innovation process while protecting our company's valuable IP? For this we offer a new next-generation model of open innovation, agile openness across the entire ecosystem.

AGILE + OPEN = ECOSYSTEM INNOVATION

Beyond the obvious benefits that firms like Unilever, P&G, and Netflix are seeking from openness, there is an additional layer of advantages, deeper and more subtle, which will also become critically important in the future. This is where Agile + open becomes meaningful.

> From a broader perspective, open innovation at its fullest marks a significant shift, an evolution from the notion of a company tasked to generate all the knowledge it needs from within, toward an organization that functions as a knowledge broker among and across companies, individuals, and indeed across an entire global business ecosystem. Open innovation represents the evolution of a company into a powerful network that accesses and leverages knowledge across an entire global ecosystem.

This broader concept is a significant reframing of the very notion of what constitutes an "organization," and what constitutes *our* knowledge. Done well, it can also be transformative in that it unleashes a much larger pool of creative talent, analytical capacity, and valuable foresight. In essence, open innovation is most useful when it alters the boundary between a given firm and its environment, enabling it to capture more resources while providing new channels through which it can learn, innovate, and communicate.

When we think of the business world surrounding a given firm as an ecosystem, which is a useful and popular idea, then we can also consider how the ecosystem as a whole can and should evolve toward higher performance. In this case, evolution is not a random process but one that can be directed. It can also be accelerated.

From an evolutionary perspective, organizations that engage in open innovation are actually becoming new types of business entities. P&G's 2,000 global partnerships make the firm a fundamentally different one from what it had been before. Talented people, creative thinkers, and all the physical resources at their disposal have become part of P&G, and they are assets that P&G benefits from *without* owning them.

This is a profound and potentially transformative force.

Likewise, the Netflix organization grew to include hundreds or thousands of super-smart programmers and mathematicians who worked on the challenge of the Netflix Prize, including people who were at the time working for AT&T, IBM, Yahoo!, and hundreds of other top firms, as well as students from hundreds of universities. Without the open innovation and the Netflix Prize context, there was essentially no way in the world that Netflix would or could have ever engaged these people in improving its business.

Hence, open innovation clearly transforms the very shape of an organization and alters its boundaries. In summary, then, the continuing development and success of open innovation efforts shows how to gather ideas from the broadest range of possible sources. This approach also means that a firm's innovation efforts will gather and utilize the very best information available, potentially much better quality information than it would otherwise have access to. No firm henceforth needs to be limited by the ideas and information sourced only internally when new insights and opportunities emerge in this compelling space of external dialog.

In addition, firms that practice open innovation are actively participating in yet another way in the broad external dialog that is occurring constantly throughout society. We as a global community are struggling with massive, complicated challenges that affect everyone: energy, water, environmental damage, health care, etc., all in various stages of crisis. Intensive, multistakeholder efforts are directed toward the development of innovative solutions to these seemingly intractable problems, and this innovation-focused dialog is a critical one for every organization to participate in. In particular, by putting forth its brand message and organizational values in a very positive, solution-oriented context, the best thinking and aspirations of a given firm are thus present in the broader social conversation for the benefit and thus the learning of all.

> In this way, open innovation promotes better and faster evolution of ideas in society.

Government also has a role in supporting and protecting openness, as these thoughts from Elliot Maxwell highlight clearly:

> Even in the midst of the enormous dislocations resulting from the collapse of the dot-com bubble, the strong positive effect of new information and communications technologies on U.S. productivity and innovation is clear. The openness inherent in the Internet has played a key role in this. It is important to define, in various domains, the right degree of openness that will encourage innovation and stimulate growth. If the benefits of openness are not understood and protected, where appropriate, the U.S. may have a future where some individual interests may benefit, but at the expense of a vibrant, competitive, and growing economy.[5]

OPENNESS IN BUSINESS ECOSYSTEMS

In the previous chapter, we discussed the importance of creating a shared mental space wherein problems and innovative ideas reside during their early formative stages. Here, the same concept is now present in the context of the entire business ecosystem. Firms that are active and effective in the broader dialog are able to influence how people think and feel, and thus they can contribute to social progress while achieving specific business or commercial objectives.

Hence, opening the innovative boundaries of firms also leads to new innovation dynamics. This can be of enormous help to organizations that happen to be located in territories that are less endowed with innovation resources (both physical and human ones). Just because you're not in California's Silicon Valley, the Silicon Plateau of India, or any other global innovation hub, you're no longer doomed to underperform your counterparts located in other more favored places. Indeed, undertaking collaborations with innovation actors outside of a given territory allows firms to access needed diversity of resources, thus enhancing efforts everywhere. The innovation potentials of different regions can align, enabling each region's strengths to be more thoroughly utilized.

The underlying motivation for any firm to engage in open innovation is the significant advantages that can result. The practices that need to be facilitated, then, are those that achieve even more openness while taking on less risk. But how can this paradoxical outcome be achieved?

TECHNOLOGY-ENABLED OPENNESS

Despite all the benefits of openness, openness does have some obvious drawbacks. The potential to inadvertently reveal important secrets to competitors is a legitimate concern. Consequently, open innovation practitioners put considerable effort into protecting their own IP, even as they work to leverage their external networks.

The other major concern with open innovation approaches has to do with the sharing of knowledge that does not lead directly or immediately to a solution but proves to be valuable only later on. Suppose, for example, that someone submits a proposed solution to a problem that has been posted by a given firm on a crowdsourcing solution platform. If the firm looking for solutions does not use this proposed approach immediately to solve the original problem that has been crowdsourced, but later relies on the knowledge in addressing a different problem that arises subsequently, how do these actors account for and share their rights?

From the opposite perspective, by revealing a problem it is confronting, the firm posting a call for proposals on a crowdsourcing platform diffuses private information on its strategy or its internal organization, which might be quite useful to competitors working on similar technologies. In this case, the firm relying on crowdsourcing to develop its innovation may be the victim of a technological holdup whereby someone leverages this valuable information to offer a solution at an exorbitant price. (On that point, it is worth noting that the crowdsourcing of innovation challenges is generally restricted to a limited number of industries, such as chemistry and pharmaceuticals, both of which are characterized by efficient intellectual property rights (IPR) protocols.)

By leveraging technology with cleverness, Agile offers approaches to help address these issues.

As noted throughout this book, the practices of Agile Innovation are about increasing the speed of innovation, reducing its risk, and creating the broadest possible engagement in the innovation effort. These goals also describe the intent of open innovation, so the marriage should be a fruitful one.

In particular, the Agile approach to open innovation offers a way to make corporate boundaries more porous and thus easier to move ideas in and out, while at the same time making them more secure in an intelligent manner. These boundaries can be thought of as *smart data membranes,* achieved by developing a different approach to trust based on an electronic IP policy server using a new standard for information sharing, which we call *IdeaXML.*

(Please note: This discussion of IdeaXML and the topics that follow will require us to engage in a deeper level of technical terminology than we have used in the previous chapters.)

IdeaXML

IdeaXML is a proposed open standard that will allow enterprise software applications to interoperate over an intelligent and secure framework for collaborative innovation. What this means is that a computer from your company and computers from your partners will be able to exchange information more freely, in a secure way, and then analyze the shared set of data to identify and suggest ways in which both firms could benefit. This will enable a new generation of interenterprise ethnography services that may unlock the next layer of productivity gains possible during the coming phases of the Information Revolution.

In current practice, ideas are either shared or not shared, and sharing typically means total transparency, whereas not sharing means total opacity. What's needed instead is the ability to share partially, in a much more nuanced way, to support progressive discovery of collaboration opportunities, and doing so without prematurely disclosing confidential information, but also without unnecessarily withholding the information that could enable a productive collaboration to occur. Hence, the objective is to create a set of standards that enable the exchange of useful information without compromising protection for IP, enabling new and more powerful forms of both intracompany and intercompany collaboration.

This requires a specific set of XML tags to be devised and applied to all the records in the system, creating a set of metadata that enables sharing of information to be much more nuanced than is currently possible. The information contained within IdeaXML repositories would then enable many innovation methodologies and approaches to flourish by creating a unified approach to the underlying taxonomy of innovation and ideation. This would allow ideas and team formation data to cross between disparate applications and systems.

IdeaXML will also embed contextually meaningful geolocation and time information, as well as idea ownership information in all data records. New types of applications could thus be developed and deployed over this framework, and even sold through an innovation app store.

An IdeaXML service requires the establishment of an authenticated identity with location and time stamp notarization authority, which would permit a registry that records the who, what, where, and when of each idea.

There are additional capabilities that could be unlocked by the adoption of the IdeaXML standard, such as nonbinary trust models, electronic IP policy servers, and social workflow, as we explore below.

NONBINARY TRUST MODELS

Nonbinary trust means technology-enabled trust using machine learning to assess the actual content of documents to identify affinities, similarities, and complements. By conducting information assessment using neutral, trusted, third-party computers, companies can exchange valuable information through such intermediaries without disclosing the actual proprietary content to one another.

Nonbinary trust models will simplify the management of intellectual property and enable a win-win-win platform for all stakeholders, one that provides benefits to everyone in equal measure, including management, employees, partners, customers, and shareholders in multiple organizations.

The key to digitizing innovation is an electronic IP policy server (described next), and the key to enabling openness is to deploy an enterprise social extranet. This is the most compelling part of the open innovation promise, where the nature of enterprise social networks can fundamentally change to allow everyone to locate better talent and ensure success more reliably.

ELECTRONIC IP POLICY SERVERS

The cost and overhead for IP policy is quite significant in open innovation practices, notably when crowdsourcing and open-source communities are involved. Networks of IP policy servers containing automated confidentiality and IP ownership logic determine how confidential ideas will be secured, shared, and collaborated on.

Additionally, policy servers should do the following:

- Provide an automated processing system for managing IPR exclusions and tracking so that they do not unreasonably prohibit any person or firm in an anticompetitive manner.
- Provide an audit trail for IPR policy changes.
- Provide an audit trail for compliance data.
- Provide an audit trail for spot checks, which ensure that confidential information is not misused.
- Provide an automated processing system for handling exportation prohibitions.

SOCIAL WORKFLOW

Social workflow can be effectively automated by applying an "action requirement tag" to messages, which thereby transforms them into work requests, work commitments, and work-tracking data. Hence, messaging generated in a social network is transformed into workflow, which makes complex collaborations trackable as projects and measurable by counting activities, such as tasks per user and work required to complete tasks. It can also be used to assess performance, leading to assignments of work to individuals within a group according to skills and previous results. This extends and provides much more nuance to the Agile Development approach, which uses "on schedule" or "behind schedule" notifications to monitor progress. By extending this approach to social workflow throughout the organization, a higher level of performance can be facilitated, but the true power and potential for such systems lie between organizations.

Innovation Collaboratories

In high-technology research it is sometimes costly and burdensome for large firms to develop relationships with university researchers because confidentiality and IP constraints make it impossible to freely disclose internal discussions without significant managerial overhead. In this situation, an interlinking social network, with nuanced transparency of IP, can simplify and empower the management of external researchers. We call this a collaboratory, where researchers outside of an organization can more easily collaborate with researchers inside.

The collaboratory concept enables automated entitlement and tracking of idea origination to ensure that confidential information is not divulged. Paired with partial transparency searches, the system also allows research teams to search for and identify likely participants. Confidential information is then released only under explicit circumstances after initial dialog has proved fruitful, but because those dialogs are more fully informed, finding the right match of skills and interests becomes much more efficient.

Transactionalized Idea Search

By pairing an IP Policy Server with partial transparency searches, people can easily search for collaborations and potential project team participants while retaining the capability to release confidential information only under specific, assured circumstances.

> In this way search becomes a transaction, which will unlock new capabilities that can benefit companies by enabling them to seek resources and ideas without requiring them to expose their IP.

Blind searches are easy, enabling trusted development companies to query inventor offerings to locate promising ideas for license or purchase. Thus, idea creators who want to license or sell their work could set the privacy level as a function of the position and trustworthiness of searchers, also turning search into a transaction for their benefit. Thus, creators of protected ideas could enable an automated process to unveil the confidential data incrementally to prospects, based on their identity and trustworthiness.

THE ENTERPRISE SOCIAL EXTRANET

An enterprise social extranet is perhaps the most compelling part of the open innovation promise. The goal is to fundamentally change the nature of social networks, allowing everyone to more reliably locate partners they can trust.

An IdeaXML standard for open innovation would also enable all idea-catching applications to interoperate. This has the potential to become a significant enabler of more effective creation and selection, particularly for very large companies with disparate divisions that host different idea collection systems and processes. Through the deployment of IdeaXML, enterprise innovation resource management tools could become extranet collaboration solutions, in which people from outside the organization could safely (in terms of intellectual property rights) participate in confidential product development discussions. IdeaXML could enable an intelligent, fine resolution entitlement capability to ensure that confidential information is not divulged inappropriately.

Hence, scientists in academia and in corporations would be able to work together more easily through the automated orchestration of complex collaborations that are normally daunting and laborious to initiate and manage. IdeaXML could also enable a greater diversity of participants in the innovation process, using IP Policy Servers to allow innovation to flow more easily through corporate data membranes and social networking technologies to help form more optimal teams.

Finally, the system would enable automatable data collection for the study of cross-organizational collaboration, industrial psychology, entrepreneurship, communication sciences, and group decision sciences. Fully implemented, it could spur development of a next-generation, global innovation smart grid that could enable powerful new business models and functionality to emerge, which will enable the effortless formation of vibrant innovation partnerships between academia, government, and industry. That will dramatically increase global innovation capacity and competitiveness.

The Global Innovation Smart Grid

Digitally enabled open innovation will be built on the foundation of a multienterprise collaboration framework.

Advanced technology tools could further enhance the open innovation process by providing tools supporting many important innovation functions, including:

- Innovation project tracking and measurement
- Social workflow
- Enhanced idea search
- IP policy servers
- Digitally enabled external idea incubation (aka *excubation*)
- Self-optimizing innovation team formation
- Powerful visualization systems for managing the flow of innovation
- External networks of innovation portals and hubs across multiple companies and industries

Ultimately, the connection of multiple digital innovation hubs would enable the emergence of an innovation smart grid, which could enable much higher performance for the innovation efforts within a company or industry ecosystem.

There are many benefits possible through the development of such a system:

- The system would allow internally focused corporate innovation platforms to evolve toward secure and open innovation platforms.

- It would enable disparate corporate innovation applications to communicate and interoperate.

- It would facilitate intelligent, fine resolution entitlement capability to ensure that confidential information is not divulged inappropriately, essentially enabling innovation search to become a transaction.

- It would foster the formation of more effective innovation teams and partnerships within and across organizations, and increase licensing of technologies from academia to industry along with improved feedback about user needs.

- It would allow participants to gather and analyze meaningful metrics for innovation and best practices.

- It would enable an "open app" store approach to easily creating compatible innovation applications.

- Enterprises would be able to provide ideas to partners and customers and have their implementation and value realization tracked dynamically, facilitating the development of innovation ecosystems.

- The framework would serve as a blueprint for building a national innovation grid.

THE NEXT GENERATION TOOL SET

As we transition into the fast-moving world of twenty-first-century ecosystem-based business alliances and ventures, three additional factors will enhance the traditional approach to innovation diffusion: viral adoption, critical mass, and IP meta-coordination.

Viral adoption means that growth is propelled via positive feedback, and open innovation is an essential tool for engaging viral networks in generating and gathering that feedback, which is the critical factor in brand building and growing scale and scope for ideas, products, and services.

Critical mass occurs when feedback from users, possibly rare at first, grows geometrically or even exponentially so that the majority of supporters have arrived to what seems like an overnight success. In predicting the impact of the Web, Everett Rogers, the inventor of the innovation diffusion model, mentioned that "A critical mass occurs when the diffusion process becomes self-sustaining. After the critical mass point, individuals in a system perceive that 'everybody else' has adopted the interactive innovation. With each successive adopter of an interactive innovation, the new idea becomes more valuable not only for each future adopter, but also for each previous adopter."[6]

The next generation innovation tools will enable individuals and organizations to share information such that the growth to critical mass adoption can occur stunningly fast; the downside, of course, is that the energy can dissipate equally fast.

IP meta-coordination involves using a higher order of strategic intelligence to bring greater coordination to complex business processes, such as IP management. We believe that meta-coordination is the key to a next generation approach to Agile management.

Consider, for example, the problems faced by the current patent system, which has fallen far behind the pace of innovation. Originally designed to protect the brilliant independent inventor of a better mousetrap, the patent system is being severely stressed. Some business analysts estimate that almost a third of the United States' IP portfolio is under attack, and the number of patent infringement actions filed annually in the United States has increased by about 300 percent over the past two decades.[7]

By adopting a meta-coordination approach to optimizing IP collectively, new strategies can evolve to support a more complex model of managing a multienterprise consortium. When a trustable third party sits at the hub to drive and adaptively target the innovation capacity of all members, an adaptive patent pool for the consortium can be generated.

This could go a long way toward addressing the plague of patent trolls—nonpracticing litigation entities—that are a growing burden on the IP system. For a country, the trusted hub partner could be a governmental agency, such as Japan's Ministry of International Trade and Industry (MITI). Armed with a predictive forward IP landscape model, the trusted entity could make valuable recommendations to individual participants that would help optimize the aggregate performance of the entire country's innovation ecosystem.

Such techniques have already been used. Patent defense companies and consortia have been formed to counteract the problems patent trolls caused in the high-technology industry. In 2008, a group of 11 high-tech companies, including Cisco Systems, Ericsson, Google, Hewlett-Packard, and Verizon, formed Allied Security Trust with the goal of identifying and obtaining key patents and preventing them from falling into the hands of the trolls. Also in 2008, RPX Corporation introduced the RPX Defensive Patent Aggregation service to purchase patents on the open market and reduce the risk of nonpracticing entities' assertion and litigation against e-commerce, financial services, hardware-manufacturing, networking, software, and wireless companies.

Looking forward, technology-enabled meta-coordination of collaboration, the next generation of Agile management, can help us achieve a quantum leap in productivity and fulfill the promise of intelligent openness.

THE PROMISE OF INTELLIGENT OPENNESS

Although the concept of open innovation holds great promise for invigorating and reinvigorating the enterprise, a clear vision of multi-organization collaboration and integration is necessary to guide the design, deployment, and management to realize the full potential. Current techniques concerning open innovation are grounded in the thinking and procedures used in previous generations of technology.

Metaphorically, then, most open innovation systems use traditional warfare techniques to address market competitors. But today's market is more like guerilla or terrorist warfare, where nimble competitors try to outsmart the frontal strategies of traditional armies. The leading companies will be those that adapt their strategies to address this new kind of business threat.

More intelligent openness is possible with multienterprise collaboration frameworks that will allow organizations to connect with customers and partners to collaborate in new ways, for example, with IdeaXML and social workflow. These frameworks will enable digital innovation hubs that could transform current corporate innovation processes by enabling the advances we described earlier.

The many benefits are clear. First, the proposed frameworks would allow internally focused corporate innovation platforms to evolve toward IP-secured open innovation platforms that can exploit entire ecosystems of super-smart players. Second, these frameworks would allow disparate corporate innovation and collaboration applications to begin to interoperate in an Agile way, leading to safe interoperation outside the enterprise firewall.

> The true promise of social workflow is between organizations, not just within them.

Next, the use of IP policy servers would facilitate intelligent entitlement capability to securing confidential information, enabling functions such as idea search to be transactionalized. This is, in effect, "Google searching for IP management," and it would in turn foster the formation of more effective innovation teams within and across organizations, and increase the effective licensing of technologies from academia to the market.

Finally, these frameworks would allow participants to gather and analyze key metrics for innovation, improving the monitoring of progress and thus all aspects of innovation management. The evolution of such frameworks could serve as a blueprint for any country to build its own national innovation grid.

Our vision is that some day in the future scientists in academia and in corporations will be able to work together more easily through the automated orchestration of complex collaborations that are currently laborious to initiate and manage. The system would also enable a greater diversity of participants in the innovation process, and allow innovation to flow more easily through corporate data membranes.

Fully implemented, the innovation smart grid could enable powerful new business models and functionality to emerge, facilitating vibrant innovation partnerships between academia, government, and industry, thereby increasing global innovation capacity and accelerating global GDP growth.

Furthermore, these frameworks would enable automated data collection for the study of cross-organizational collaboration, entrepreneurship, communication sciences, and group decision sciences. In addition, by defining a standardized set of innovation metrics, we could theoretically create a fourth standard financial statement addressing innovation portfolio valuation, which could be as powerful a predictor of future investment value as the balance sheet. This could significantly benefit astute investors by enabling them to channel capital toward companies with stronger innovation practices, which would also, of course, be a powerful form of feedback to corporate managers.

Like single-celled organisms that slowly combined to create life on our planet, individual computer networks slowly connected to form the Internet. In the same way, Agile open innovation could lead to an inter-network for innovation. This could lead to a fundamental increase in the rate of innovation so radical that it enters a phase beyond linear predictability. This is the definition of mechanical singularity: a position or configuration of a mechanism where the subsequent behavior cannot be predicted, or the forces or other physical quantities involved become infinite or nondeterministic. (We prefer this simple definition to the idea that someday we'll want to upload our brains into computers.)

In other words, we recognize that humanity is only at the beginning of a new arc in the evolution of the art and science of innovation, and that something like an Internet—one that is specifically built to support invention and collaboration—is not only possible, but may be the next evolutionary step for business management in the twenty-first century.

This is the true potential of open innovation.

Questions to Reflect Upon

- How open are our innovation processes?
- How much benefit are we deriving from being open?
- How are we measuring how to benefit from being open?
- If our organization is not open, what are the reasons for this approach?
- What are our concerns about trusting partners in innovation?
- Are we getting cool new ideas from outsiders?
- Are we thinking about our entire ecosystem as a source of valuable ideas?

14

TRAVELING THE ROAD TO REVOLUTION

The philosophers have only interpreted the world, in various ways; the point is to change it.

—Karl Marx[1]

As we have noted throughout this book, the synthesis of Agile and Innovation can readily become the basis for a fundamental transformation of your organization. In other words, this synthesis offers the promise of a genuine revolution in how you operate. Fulfilling that promise, however, will require quite strong leadership and carefully crafted actions.

10 (EASY) STEPS

In the event that you have never imagined yourself as the leader of a revolution, we'd like to offer some guidelines that we hope will enable you to succeed in this new and somewhat unconventional role. Here, then, are the 10 easy steps of revolutionary leadership.

1. *Educate yourself:* Know why this transformation must happen and how to achieve it. Identify the goals and the most efficient means of achieving them without compromise. Appreciate and respect a diversity of tactics and supporters. The revolution must be directed toward *making things better.* This creates a positive vector and defines a winning position. After all, will anyone argue that we need to be *less* efficient, *less* productive, or *less* innovative?

2. *Know your goals:* You're about to dedicate a good portion of your life to the goal of making your organization considerably more successful by implementing the principles of Agile Innovation. So should your goals be big picture and strategic, or more focused and tactical?

   The strategic perspective defines what you intend to accomplish as an organization, so it's important to assess the rate of change today, to forecast what it will be tomorrow, and to design your overall innovation goals to intersect with future realities in the market and in society.

   Strategic goals also express specific aspirations for your organization. Are you ready to lead the world in your field? Are you ready to accomplish great things that no one has ever attempted? You can then set about to organize the effort and engage the people.

   At the tactical level, Agile Innovation is a set of methods and tools intended to advance the effectiveness of your unique way of creating and managing innovation, so two good questions to ask yourself are, "What's *ineffective* about the current ways of working in my organization?" and "What kinds of *systems* do I need to create and implement so that my coworkers and I can do what must be done in the most effective way possible?"

   You may conclude that social workflow and the technology infrastructure are the keys. "Perhaps," you might tell yourself, "we could automate bureaucracy out of existence!"

   You could also work to bring automated, intelligent filtering and machine learning into your innovation process and apply Agile-inspired social workflow to make the completion of tasks more efficient.

Remember that the goals you choose become the heart of your revolution, so please choose them carefully.

3. *Build support and consensus:* Nothing much is going to happen if the only rebels (change agents) are you and your mates (unless you happen to be the CEO). Build support for change, progress, and agility by getting the word out that there are better ways of working. Start a blog. Hold meetings. Evangelize. Share. Promote. Network.

    The supporters of the Agile revolution don't have to meet together, agree on any actions, or even know each other, but they must be united under a common vision and shared fundamental principles: We can make the work better.

    Experiment with methods and tools, find out what works best in your organization, and share your findings.

4. *Leverage discontent:* One of the most important elements of any revolution is the instigating cause: People aren't happy with the current state of affairs. The root cause of discontent may come from a commitment to a higher level of performance, and thus the expectation and conviction that we can and ought to do better.

    In discontent there must also be discipline and commitment not just to complain, but also to drive toward improvement. Hence, this revolution is an idealistic one, carried forward by lofty aspiration and high expectations, not by blood lust or base anger, and it is a practical one based on sensible actions, measurement, feedback, and results.

    Beware, however, that any revolution can be co-opted. If you notice signs that this may be happening, it could be that your idea was not popular enough to attract support, so prepare to overcome attempts at splintering. Return to the aspirational message repeatedly: more effective, more efficient, more success!

5. *Find like-minded people who are ready for action:* Set up a field of communication to attract those who, like you, are committed to doing and being their best. This will probably work best in a nonhierarchical group in which all voices are heard. Even in a small group dedicated to the same cause, it may be useful for one individual to serve as spokesperson, someone humble who will not be identified

as *the* leader or *the* innovator, but a person of unimpeachable integrity who speaks for a broader, aspirational objective and a broader consensus.

6. *Work for collective liberation:* Everyone's liberation is linked. If our organization is going to be innovative and agile, all of us have to aspire to be innovative and agile. If we are to have a voice, it must be a voice that speaks from many of us, or better, all of us.

7. *Demonstrate the popularity of the movement:* The greater the popularity among society, the less the likelihood of repression. Attract broad support (this is another dimension of the concept of critical mass that we discussed in the previous chapter).

8. *Revolution is really a search for freedom:* Revolutions are about making major changes in some aspect of society that result in greater freedom. This revolution is about the freedom to do great innovation work, the very best work imaginable, work that is transformative to the organization and to the marketplace.

   Are you ready to work more efficiently? Do you intend to become more innovative? To accelerate the workflow?

   These qualities will indeed free you and free everyone else in the organization to do his or her very best, to make the greatest difference, and perhaps even to ignite the market and light the customers on fire with enthusiasm.

   Achieving this is why a revolution is worth creating!

9. *Take action:* Any revolution dies without action. You must take action to avoid the fate of the umpteenth proposal (that gets ignored), of still more meetings (that are repeatedly rescheduled), or of promised pilots (that are planned but never funded).

   Why might this occur? Perhaps because the powers in place will defend themselves, simply because that is the nature of power.

10. *Persist:* This last step is clearly the most important. Your resolve will be tested, and only through persistence will you win out. Setbacks may discourage you, and morale may sink, but remember that many others have struggled through similar challenges to finally defeat overwhelming adversity. The march may be long, but it's the right and necessary march.

THE REVOLUTIONARY LEADER: WHAT KIND OF REVOLUTIONARY ARE *YOU*?

Famous revolutionaries and change makers tend to fall into six categories, six revolutionary archetypes, all of which are necessary contributors to successful revolutions. Which of these descriptions fit you best?[2]

THE VISIONARY

Visionaries see possibilities in the tiniest of inspirations. As you focus on your goals, you will devote yourself to what you see emerging, the possibility of a better future. Your goal is to achieve this better reality.

Throughout this book, we've offered many quotes from Steve Jobs and other great leaders who exemplify many of the great (and some less great) qualities shared by visionaries who have shown the rest of the us the way forward.

THE SCHOLAR

Perhaps you're the one who works out the important details and establishes the philosophical tenets of your movement. Are you an Agile Innovation scholar? Although you may tend to isolate yourself from others, the knowledge you have gathered will be invaluable to the movement as a whole, and as you get excited about the type of work that many others might find boring, your contribution becomes all the more essential.

Noteworthy scholars, such as Betty Friedan and Rachel Carson, both of whom published powerfully transformative books in the early 1960s, took on the battles of gender equality and environmental awareness respectively, and convinced millions through their research, storytelling, and experiences that something was seriously wrong. Great change resulted from their efforts.

THE REBEL

Are you unafraid to confront the forces of oppression head-on? If this is you, you might find yourself defending others and forging ahead in uncertain situations, leading those who lack your courage and fire. Be careful, though, that you don't find yourself accidentally fighting against those who are really trying to help you.

Carson is a terrific example of a rebel as well as a scholar. Unafraid to challenge authority, she was even accused of being a traitor to her country because of her views. She took on very powerful business interests, including the chemical industry, but was able to set in motion forces that laid the groundwork for modern-day environmentalism and environmental protection.

THE GENERAL

Does your strength lie in planning? A visionary might see the goal, but generals and their staffs determine the best and most effective routes to get there. You are good at making serious decisions and organizing others to play their parts, but you risk becoming bogged down if you stop to examine every detail before making decisions. Generals must keep things realistic and have a good sense of what can actually be accomplished with available resources and time.

In the recent history of China, the difference between the visionary and the general is evident in the relationship between Mao Zedong, the visionary who transformed Chinese politics, and Deng Xiaoping, the general who then transformed the Chinese economy after Mao's death. Deng's leadership merged the communist political system with Western capitalism, and the resulting explosive economic growth has transformed the lives of hundreds of millions of Chinese people, as well as millions more in other countries who have benefited from Chinese economic growth.

THE DIPLOMAT

Are you the person whose sense of perspective can smooth things over and ensure that effective communication happens? Your natural calm attracts others to reveal the truth, and you know how to get people to open up. Don't let your pride take over if someone turns against you, for inevitably not everyone will be on your side.

Martin Luther King, Jr. combined scholarly characteristics with the diplomat's abilities in his quest for civil rights and equality for all races in the United States. He struggled with criticism from all sides, but managed to strike the right balance that inspired a large majority of

Americans to join the cause of civil rights, and thereby transformed law, culture, and society.

THE SECRET AGENT

If you're excited by challenges, especially those that come from authorities that you do not recognize as such, then perhaps you're ready to work in secret, surreptitiously behind the front lines. You may be in senior management, yearning to be a revolutionary, and able to work from within the dominant paradigm to overturn it for the betterment of the organization and society. Being a spy is really about gathering information, so if you want to start a revolution this way, study your market and competitors until you become the definitive expert at your organization.

Applying this model, the pharmaceutical giant Merck believes in open innovation so strongly that its product managers are required to use half of their time tracking research being done outside of the company, that is, gathering information. Because progress in biochemistry, neurochemistry, and genetics is advancing so rapidly, product managers must be agile, ready to redirect their internal efforts when better approaches surface elsewhere.

● ● ●

Each of these revolutionary archetypes can make significant contributions to the successful social movement, and of course, they can be most effective when they work as a team.

THE POWER OF COMMITMENT

We end this chapter with the story of the epic Battle of Thermopylae, which took place in 480 BC, when the Spartan king Leonidas led a small but unified Greek army to fight off the Persian invasion led by the great Xerxes. The Persian army was enormous, and because they so vastly outnumbered the Greeks, they felt entirely confident that they would prevail. The Greek historian Herodotus, who left us a brilliantly detailed account of the battle and this entire era of intense warfare, estimated that Xerxes's force numbered more than 2 million soldiers, and noted that these troops could "drink a river dry."

Today's historians estimate that Xerxes's force numbered closer to 150,000, but in any case they far outnumbered the 7,000 Greeks, so their confidence was justified.

Knowing full well the magnitude of his advantage, Xerxes sent an envoy to propose to Leonidas that the Greek defenders of Thermopylae should surrender. He offered that they could become his allies and proposed to give them farms in exchange, promising that they would be resettled on land better than that they possessed. Leonidas, committed to defending his homeland, refused.

Xerxes's envoy then demanded Leonidas lay down his weapons, to which he famously replied that the Persians could instead "Come and take them."

The envoy then told him, "Our arrows will block out the sun," to which Leonidas answered, "Fine, then we shall have our battle in the shade."

So the battle was engaged, and the Greeks held on for seven days before the Persians succeeded in defeating them. Leonidas led the mythic 300 (plus about 1,000 others) and held the well-positioned Greek force together long enough to inflict at least 20,000 casualties on the Persians before the Greeks were finally overwhelmed, and the Persians went on to occupy most of Greece. Following the Greek defeat at Thermopylae, however, the Greek fleet lured the vast Persian navy into the Straits of Salamis, where it was destroyed.

With the destruction of his navy, Xerxes feared that his army might be trapped in Greece, and he retreated to Asia. However, nearly all his soldiers died of starvation and disease along the way, essentially ending the Persian threat to the Peloponnese and bringing to an end a long period of warfare.

What can we learn from this story, one of the most well-remembered events in all of military history?

The point we think is most important is the immense power that a small number of committed people can accumulate and express: For seven days, 1,500 Greek soldiers held off 150,000 invaders. So suppose that a few hundred of your most courageous employees formed a cadre of innovators. What if they bravely proclaimed, "We know there's a recession and a salary and hiring freeze, but we aren't afraid—we intend to help. We will work nights and weekends, we will create breakthrough innovations, we will find new ways to accelerate sales . . . We will transform our organization!" With the right support, even against impossible odds, they can succeed; with the right vision they can even change the world.

Wouldn't that choke you up, just a little bit?

That's the spirit needed to transform a company and to achieve innovations worthy of history. It's also the spirit that revolutionary leaders seek to engage among those whom they lead, throughout their organizations and in the broader networks of partners and other stakeholders who can contribute so much to the brand building, the innovation creating, the storytelling, the service delivering, and ultimately the creation and recreation of great and enduring enterprises.

Do you feel any one among the types of revolutionary leadership styles fits you? Excellent! Now go find others whose skills and commitment complement your own, and set forth together along the revolutionary's road!

Questions to Reflect Upon

- What will it take to effect transformational change in our organization?
- What role might I personally play in effecting change?
- Who might be my most helpful natural allies?
- Who might resist change the most?
- How might we overcome their resistance?

Using Agile Strategy to Shape Your Organization's Future

The future enters into us in order to transform itself in us long before it happens.

—Rainer Maria Rilke[1]

Computers started out as large, remote machines in air-conditioned rooms tended by white-coated technicians. They moved onto our desks, then under our arms, and now into our pockets. Soon we'll routinely put them inside our bodies and brains. By the 2030s we will become more non-biological than biological. By the 2040s nonbiological intelligence will be billions of times more capable than our biological intelligence.

—Ray Kurzweil[2]

ACCELERATION

Humans invented writing about 5,000 years ago, and around the same time, they gathered in cities, thus giving birth to the ideas of as well as the realities of both civilization and history. Through documented knowledge that grew progressively from generation to generation, waves of invention spread steadily around the globe from city to city. As various civilizations grew, they recorded their greatest ideas and events, and so began the journey toward the modern world.

In Egypt, on the other hand, the mythical figure Thoth was credited with the invention of writing. He also served as a mediating power between good and evil and served the gods as their scribe. Not long after the Egyptians began writing, across the globe another mythical figure, Fu Hsi, became the first sovereign of China, and was credited with the invention of writing, fishing, cooking, and the I Ching. Legend states that the trigram of the I Ching was revealed to him on the back of a large turtle that emerged from the river Luo, and this subsequently led to the invention of calligraphy.

Writing also developed spontaneously around the same time in Sumeria, the region we presently we call Iraq, where cuneiform script was created. As the brilliant Peter Watson has noted:

> In 1946, Samuel Noah Kramer identified no fewer than twenty-seven "historical firsts" discovered or achieved or recorded in the cities of the early Iraqis. Among them were the first schools, the first historian, the first pharmacopoeia, the first clocks, the first arch, the first legal code, the first library, the first farmer's almanac, and the first bicameral congress. The reason for this burst of creativity is not hard to find: cities were (and remain) far more competitive, experimental environments than anything that had gone before, and sometime in the late fourth millennium BC, people [first] came together to live in large cities. The transition transformed human experience.[3]

Cuneiform was also invented in pre-Columbian Mesoamerica, where Mayans, Olmecs, and Zapotecs drew glyphs and carved their symbols on stones.

Then, a little more than 500 years ago, Johannes Gutenberg's invention of movable-type printing changed the world. Although each of the components of his wooden engraving press was already in common usage, he combined these elements into a practical system. His design was similar to the screw-driven olive presses and winepresses of the period and used ordinary oil-based ink. His metal alloys and a practical mold for casting type created movable type and was immediately a major improvement on handwritten manuscripts and woodblock printing.

Although Gutenberg personally did not achieve financial success (the fast followers did better), his technology spread rapidly. Because it facilitated large-scale publishing and knowledge sharing across long distances, it became a major catalyst for both widespread literacy and for the scientific revolution that subsequently triggered the European Renaissance.

Fast-forward 400 years to the middle of the twentieth century and the invention of computers. In the early 1940s, John W. Mauchly and J. Presper Eckert, Jr., created the electrical numerical integrator and calculator (ENIAC) machine at the University of Pennsylvania. ENIAC used 18,000 vacuum tubes and punch card input, weighed 30 tons, and occupied 1,500 square feet (about 150 square meters) of floor space. It was programmable literally only by changing the wiring, but it was productive from 1946 to 1955, computing artillery firing tables for the army.

Decades later, the evolution of computing capability led to the creation and deployment of the Internet and the World Wide Web, also funded by the military, and eventually to the smartphone sitting in your pocket, a compact 3 × 6 inches and a feathery 4 ounces. In 60 years, that's a tidy reduction in size by a factor of nearly 13,000 and in weight by a factor of 240,000. Impressive improvements, eh?

Leveraging these miniaturized technological miracles, Facebook and Twitter achieved the milestones of 100 million users within five years of their founding, thus giving birth to the social web. This is especially notable because previous revolutionary technologies, such as the telephone, the automobile, and electricity each required about 50 years, or 10 times longer, to reach similar levels of usage and market penetration.

Things are getting smaller, faster, and more powerful, all at once.

The Information Revolution is taking over the world precisely because these multiple factors of speed (accelerating), size (shrinking), and penetration (exploding) are relentlessly improving while compounding one another, amplifying the impact enormously. Did we mention that the cost has also plummeted?

When we look at these trends and inventions from a more elevated perspective, even more compelling than their specific circumstances or impact is the realization that they reflect the acceleration of humanity's overall rate of progress and development. History itself, in other words, is speeding up.

In summary, it took 5,000 years to progress from the invention of writing to movable type, 500 more years to get to the computer and Internet, 50 years to get to the creation of the social web, and five years to reach penetration measured in hundreds of millions of users.

This leads us to ask, "What will life be like five years hence?"

Yes, this is the world, the market, the ecosystem of blinding change in which your organization must now learn to succeed. It is a world of relentless change, stunning acceleration, and intense competition.

In such a world, we are not exaggerating when we say that innovation is your only hope for success. We go further, and we say that *mastery of innovation is your only hope for survival.* In this challenging world, we would also assert that Agile Innovation could reasonably be seen as utterly mandatory.

Given these pressures, nothing less than a systematic and comprehensive approach to innovation management can provide the outcomes you seek.

AGILE STRATEGY: THE EVOLUTION OF INNOVATION

We hope that the previous chapters have given you a deep and useful understanding of Agile Innovation; that the concepts, tools, and techniques we've described can help you and your organization achieve stunning proficiency in innovation; and that this, in turn, supports you in assuring your organization's survival and achieving success.

Yes, this is all important stuff, and there is an additional dimension that must also be examined, which is the nature of the strategic effort that must guide the innovation effort. In this concluding chapter we will thus explore the theme of Agile Strategy.

Making sense of the Information Revolution and adapting to the accelerating rate of change is a personal journey, an organizational journey, and a societal journey. Success requires that enterprises learn how to reshape themselves with no fixed end point in an environment where the rules are often changing faster than you can figure them out. This is what we mean by *Agile Strategy*.

Developing and applying Agile Strategy requires that we explore two critical themes.

> First is the recognition, at long last, that the survival of your enterprise critically depends on investing, perhaps heavily, in the development, refinement, and promotion of the *tools and capabilities* required to facilitate the management of innovation. The first step is acknowledging that this is essential to assure your organization's survival.

Because innovation is so important, and because the performance of the innovation effort is so deeply dependent on methods and tools, these are themselves strategic assets that must receive proper attention.

> Perfecting the practice of innovation is itself a strategic priority.

The second dimension in which Agile Strategy must come to the fore pertains to the rate of change, the fact of acceleration, and the multitude of challenges that this presents. In fact, the rate of change itself constitutes an existential threat such that the organization must adopt a fundamentally different approach to the formulation of strategy itself.

What's necessary is not strategic planning and long-range foresight in a traditional sense, because the rate of change threatens to make such plans and forecasts obsolete long before the ink on the paper is dry. Instead, the very formulation and execution of strategy must itself reflect the principles of agility—it must be a *social process* that moves fast, engages very large numbers of people in detecting and responding to change, and is guided by an underlying foundation of risk management.

We will look first at the question of tools, and then at the dynamic process by which history is accelerating and its deep implications for strategy making.

THREE ERAS OF INNOVATION TOOLS

If we look at humanity's rise from prehistory we can identify three waves, or bursts, of evolutionary acceleration. The first was the transition from hunting and gathering to the agricultural age and the first permanent communities, propelled by religious awareness, and the ability to breed plants and animals, to fashion basic tools such as hammers, spears, and plows. This occurred 5,000 to 10,000 years ago.

The second was the Industrial Revolution, propelled by metallurgy, which led to the invention of machines, and then assembly lines, organized workflow, and standardization. This happened at scale beginning a few hundred years ago.

The third is the emergent Information Revolution, which is rapidly evolving humanity's relationship with the very tools that are being invented in a dynamic process of accelerating feedback. It started a few decades ago and is so new that we don't have clear enough perspective to really understand what it means, where it's headed, or even what to call it.

As history has advanced the methods and tools of innovation have naturally evolved, and the processes and technologies that comprise the art and science of innovation have progressed in three phases. In the BC (before computers) era, innovators were hunter-gatherers of ideas. Innovation systems or methods were haphazard, and the best that even the mighty IBM could do, in terms of innovation methodology, was to put up inspiring posters requesting its workers to think harder. The village shaman would cast an occasional fishbone diagram and invoke the Pareto Principle (the so-called 80–20 rule) to conjure up a little quality for the organization, and like totems hung around the office, such items have become artifacts for the social ethnographer. But their actual impact was questionable.

In the AD (After Digital) era, computers changed everything in much the same way that hand tools changed life for early humans. Today, though, we're building brain tools, not hand tools—brain amplifiers, or what Steve Jobs called bicycles for the mind, which are changing how we learn, how we create, and indeed, how we think. Now, to paraphrase Apple, we don't care to think harder; we prefer to "think different," and innovation is at the forefront of our thoughts.

Early innovation tools included mind mappers, idea catchers, and online bulletin board system (BBS) forums that allowed discussions to be distributed temporally. The next wave provided innovation pipelines and stage gate methodologies that allowed the production of ideas to be industrialized and automated. This was the era of the *idea factory*, and a leading innovation consultant of the time, John Kao, even used that term as his brand signature.[4]

Now, at long last a third wave of innovation tools is emerging, with a focus on agility, on simplifying and automating the production and processing of ideas to enable inventors to create fundamentally better and more impactful ideas, faster, with less risk, and with broader engagement within and across organizations. Because it's not just ideas that we aspire to produce; it's innovations that move the market.

Innovation managers in the future will use the kinds of tools that today's project managers and financial managers use, tools that will not only measure innovation but also actively assist in assessing what might be wrong early enough that fixes are cheap. They'll also help by refining ideas and designs to maximize customer delight, intimacy, and value. Running on big screens and smartphones, in real time, with dynamic dashboards and reliable value calculations, these powerful new tools will be innately social. They will be mobile, usable anywhere and everywhere, and especially they will be fast.

This, we believe, is where the road leads, and those who get there first will gain significant advantages over their competitors.

Teaching Revolution, Teaching Innovation

Teaching innovation is different from teaching anything else.

The core of innovation is a dynamic way of thinking, rather than working with a static body of knowledge. A brilliant example of someone who taught a profound way of thinking is the brilliant physicist Richard Feynman.

(continued)

(*continued*)

In Feynman's now-famous Physics X lectures for freshman physics majors at the California Institute of Technology, bright minds sat in absolute wonder, watching the Nobel Laureate magically derive Maxwell's equations from nothing more than the uniformity of time and space. I myself (Moses) sat transfixed during these lectures and thought to myself, "This must be what it felt like to watch Aristotle or Socrates!"

Feynman didn't teach from a textbook or a lesson plan, and he didn't teach formulas or techniques for solving equations. Instead, deep inside of his physics lectures he was actually teaching a profound philosophy of life. He exuded genuine excitement and a relentless curiosity not only about how the world works but also why it is so amazingly beautiful.

He once commented, "Poets say science takes away from the beauty of the stars—I too can see the stars on a desert night, and feel them. But do I see less or more? What is the pattern or the meaning or the why? For far more marvelous is the truth than any artists of the past imagined it... Science only adds to the excitement, and the mystery, and the awe of it."[5]

Innovation is best taught in the same spirit. Socrates insisted that the greatest teachers were not those who had the most information (i.e., the experts) but those who best created the "space of learning." Those who teach innovation must do the same thing—they can't focus on the nuts and bolts for coming up with ideas and shepherding them through the organization; they must instead teach a new way of seeing, listening, thinking—and interacting.

An excellent analogy for teaching innovation is teaching martial arts. Both disciplines require years of study and diligent effort to master. Both require that you continuously test what you're learning in the ring, and adapt your theories to fit reality. Finally, both rely on a sensei (master) to lead you in the right direction.

One of the most innovative martial artists was Bruce Lee, whose book *Tao of Jeet Kune Do* is exceptional in that it was not a how-to manual for learning a form (or *kata,* a specific, defined set of movements in karate) but rather a distillation of his remarkable philosophy.

The essence of Jeet Kune Do is to let go of form, to allow the student to become formless and dynamic in every way—while staying grounded in what really works. Lee said, "If you follow the classical patterns, you are understanding the routine, the tradition, the shadow. You are not understanding yourself."[6]

In the same way, teaching innovation must, at some point, let go of textbooks and techniques and allow the student to achieve formlessness.

But before you can allow yourself to imagine what it might be like to be a formless Zen-master samurai, you have to put in long and painful hours doing basic exercises. As we noted in Chapter 10, most significant human skills and forms of expertise, such as learning to play the piano or the violin, speaking a new language, or mastering a sport—require about 10,000 hours of practice to achieve complete proficiency. Martial arts and ideation—the skill of creating ideas—are no different.

Does this mean everyone can learn to become an Einstein or Edison? Of course not. Some of us will inevitably demonstrate a natural-born genius that others can never match. But all of us can learn to be a lot more than we've been led to expect of ourselves.

Another similarity between martial arts and innovation is the linkage between theory and execution. In both activities, you must think and plan strategically and creatively—but in the final analysis, if you're poor at execution or if you can't "bring it" in the ring, the system or invention will not succeed. Therefore, effective teaching of innovation must include a self-contained process for continuously improving execution as well as ideation. In other words, you have to continuously test what you're learning to find what really works. Then, adapt and improve your theories constantly to reflect what really does work, what really counts, and what really matters. This is why a quite accurate definition of innovation is *creativity + execution for business.*

(*continued*)

(*continued*)

Perhaps the most important similarity between the martial arts and innovation is the spirit of the sensei. If your innovation coach is actually lousy at innovation, or is basically a politician rather than an innovator (sometimes we refer to such people as the ones who put the *no* in in*no*vation), then you probably won't be able to go very far under his or her tutelage.

The ideal innovation guru has to be 50 percent innovation and 50 percent guru—someone who, as the great samurai Miyamoto Musashi wrote, "truly understands the smallest things and the biggest things, the shallowest things and the deepest things. From one thing, he can know ten thousand things. When you attain the Way of [Innovation] there will not be one thing you cannot see."[7]

AGILE STRATEGY AND THE ACCELERATION OF HISTORY

Our second major theme concerns the rate of change, or as Gerald Piel put it, *The Acceleration of History*.[8] Acceleration has brought us to what technology analyst Michael Murphy refers to as the Fourth Wave, the latest stop in the progressive computerization of society.[9]

The First Wave, he says, was driven by mainframe computers. Semiconductor sales for mainframes peaked at about $5 billion in 1974. In the down cycle following the peak, no one knew what, if anything, would drive the next up cycle.

Unpredicted, largely unrecognized at the time, but driven by mountains of brilliant research and stunning innovation, the PC then emerged, and semiconductor sales took off in a new up cycle, peaking at $26 billion. The PC cycle topped out 10 years later in 1984, though, and in the down cycle that followed no one knew, again, what would drive the next up cycle. Many believed that there would not be a next up cycle.

But research and innovation continued, unexpectedly yielding networking and the Internet, which kicked off a still more dramatic up cycle. It peaked in 2000 at $204 billion in chip sales, about 8× higher than the second peak and 40× higher than the first. The cycles were shortening but the peaks were much higher.

"Where do we go from here?" Murphy asks, and indeed that's what we all ask. A conservative estimate based on the first three waves is that the next up cycle should be at least 5× the Internet peak—$1 trillion in chip sales—but once again no one knows what will drive the next up cycle.

So the obvious question is, "How much further can the computer revolution take us?" Today's laptops have more memory, more flexibility, more functions, more versatility, and more speed than any top secret government computer that was in existence in 1970. Indeed, your smartphone is the supercomputer that fits in your pocket, with more computing power than you could buy for even $3 billion in the 1970s.

If we plot this increasing power of computers on a graph we get a steadily rising exponential curve, which we also know as Moore's Law, named for Intel cofounder Gordon Moore, who noticed this trend in 1963. The declining cost of computers also shows up on a graph as the reciprocal downward curve, and when we put the two curves together they intersect to form a tidy, little space in which the letter D fits perfectly, and hence we call this the D-curve.

In addition to describing the shape of the curve, the D also stands for "double," because it is, in fact, two curves, and it represents two

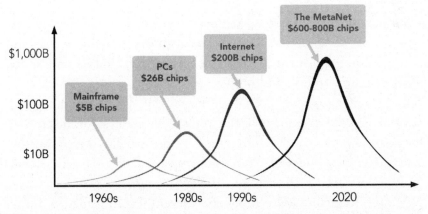

Figure 15.1 Each generation of chips has sold 5 to 10× more than the previous generation. How long will this trend continue (y-axis is exponential)?

enormously important themes. The first is *digitization*, which refers to the use of digital technology in all aspects of the economy, and the second is *disruption*, which is what follows from digitization.

What sort of disruption are we talking about? We mean fundamental economic disruption, characterized by the rise of an entire generation of digital powerhouse companies such as Apple, Samsung, Google, eBay, Alibaba, Baidu, Amazon.com, Yahoo!, Cisco, etc., and alongside them are companies that have *applied* digital technology to fundamentally alter the economic landscape, firms such as Wal-Mart, FedEx, Home Depot, Ikea, and Carrefour.

Building a Winning Team

Consider the task of team optimization. Yesterday, the typical approach to building a start-up team was to hire people you knew and trusted, and then hire more people whom those people knew and trusted. However, because trust isn't transitive, the reliability of subsequent generations of hires erodes quickly down the line.

The emerging model, a much better approach, is to leverage social networks and innovation reputation ratings to more effectively build teams of diverse yet compatible, motivated, trustworthy, and entrepreneurially minded people.

In industry after industry, the digitally savvy have transformed how business is done: advertising, airlines, autos, banking, education, energy, film, government, health care, investment, music, publishing, retail, telecom, and on and on it goes.

Even agriculture has been transformed by digital technology, as farmers use GPS to guide their tractors; satellite analysis of soils to help them seed, water, and fertilize their fields; satellite-driven weather forecasts to help them care for their crops; and live data feeds from multiple markets to contract for delivery on the best terms.

Venture capitalist Marc Andreessen recently commented about all this digital action very cogently, noting that "Software is eating the world,"[10] a very accurate description of what's happening.

As long as the twin trends of the D-curve continue, and there is every reason to expect them to persist for many years, the impact throughout society and the economy will grow stronger still, becoming utterly inescapable. No sector, industry, or company will be left untouched, and many will not be touched so lightly.

We also know that sustaining these trends will require new fundamental technologies, as current chip-making techniques are rapidly approaching the physical limitations of silicon. Although some observers believe that the progression will end, and others think it will continue ad infinitum, this is not our concern at this moment. Even with known technologies that are already in the engineering pipeline, such as 3-D circuit designs and new substrate materials, we can anticipate significant progress in microprocessor development and thus further disruption throughout the economy.

Perhaps in the future computing will be based on the switching of molecules, atoms, or even quanta, rather than 1940s vacuum tubes or 2010s crystals, bringing us to yet another plateau in computing and communications power. Some of the theoretical possibilities do indeed boggle the mind, such as real-time language translation that fits inside an earplug, or reliable weather prediction weeks in advance, or mastery of the genetic code and reliable diagnosis of your personal genome's susceptibility to disease. In all likelihood, these are coming.

Looking further ahead, the factoring of a 400-digit number, which would take 10 billion years using today's supercomputers, could be cracked by a quantum computer in less than 30 seconds, which would mean that sci-fi level possibilities become realities. What would *this* mean for your organization, your industry, and your marketplace?

At a minimum, mounting an intelligent response to all this requires a fundamental transformation in how you think about strategy, and in how you execute it, and hence Agile Strategy will become an imperative.

And before you dismiss this as what appear to be futuristic dreams, consider that only 30 years ago science fiction writers predicted that everyone would have mobile communication devices, that a 60-second medical operation could repair myopia, that cars could drive themselves, that we'd put video cameras into our watches and eyeglasses, that the human genome would be completely sequenced, that long-distance video-telephony would be ubiquitous and free, that . . . well, you get the idea. Yesterday's science fiction has become today's everyday reality, so what does today's science fiction tell us about tomorrow?

THE APPROACHING SINGULARITY

In some respects, it gets only more intense, for the data on increasing computer power make it absolutely clear that social change and its underlying technology is accelerating exponentially, and that we're heading for something . . . interesting. In mathematics, this sort of "something interesting" is sometimes called a *singularity*, a time at which a given mathematical object is not defined or fails to be well behaved in some particular way, such as differentiability, and takes on entirely unprecedented behavior. In other words, it undergoes a fundamental transformation.

In engineering, a mechanical singularity is the configuration of a mechanism or a machine whose subsequent behavior cannot be foreseen. Hence, we're dealing not only with the unprecedented, but also with the unpredictable.

Is this where we are headed?

Such a description, unprecedented behavior that points toward transformation, could hardly be a more accurate way to describe our era, so yes, perhaps it is precisely where we're going.

Accordingly, futurists, including Ray Kurzweil (whose book was titled *The Singularity Is Near,* thereby revealing in the very title what he believes), have announced the impending technological singularity, which he defines as the emergence of artificially intelligent machines with greater-than-human intelligence.[11]

The concept was originally popularized by computer scientist Vernor Vinge, who saw that "superintelligence" would take control of the world. He predicted that computers would demonstrate human-level thought and intelligence amplification via brain-to-computer interfaces that would enable people to "jack in" and dramatically increase the power of human thought.[12] He referred to this as an "intelligence explosion," and if this sounds like a story element in every third sci-fi movie, that's because it is. Except it may not be shelved in the fiction section for much longer.

Welcome to your future, which, by the way, has already arrived.

Because all this actually describes today, not tomorrow. Computers *already* beat humans at complex cognition tasks, such as tournament-level chess, and most of humanity is already "jacked into the matrix," where we access all (or nearly all) the human knowledge created and collected throughout thousands of years of human history, across thousands of miles of geography, and by millions of scientists, scholars, and students. We do so daily.

"Jacked into the matrix" is the scene at any coffeehouse, any class-room, any library, any bus or airplane, and many street corners in hundreds of nations, where humans are augmenting their natural intelligence by accessing static data and open-source web applications that communicate instantly and provide immediate answers to questions simple and questions sophisticated. What's the best route from here to there? Where's the nearest Starbucks? What's the recipe for sake-infused steamed Chilean sea bass? What's the difference between string theory and quantum mechanics? How do I tie a half-Windsor knot in my necktie? Detailed answers to all these questions, both the trivial and the utterly profound, and video instructions pertaining to many of them, are at your fingertips instantly.

Yes, the singularity is already happening, and cascading inventions are following at breakneck speed, bringing further disruption with them. In the process we are creating a new kind of economy.

THE AGILE ECONOMY

For at least two centuries the forces driving the world's economies have remained more or less unchanged. Every nation and each border is the site of countless marketplaces where products and services are exchanged, whether for seashells, rice, computer chips, or NASDAQ securities. The economic structures of these diverse markets have run the gamut from loosely organized trading outposts to highly structured marketplaces. Some of these structures have failed, and some have been very successful, but the rules underlying all of them have been stable and consistent—until now.

The world is changing in a fundamental way, and this transition from an industrial age to an Information Revolution is marked by steadily increasing utility, activity, and opportunity that will lead to a new form of economic structure.

The interlinking of humanity that began with the emergence of language has now progressed to the point where information can be transmitted to anyone, anywhere, at the speed of light. Billions of messages are continually shuttling back and forth in an ever-growing web of communication, linking the billions of minds of humanity together into a single system.

Amidst all these relentless macro forces, your enterprise is in for the ride of its life. Innovation will inevitably be one of its critical core skills, and the better and more capable its innovation skills become, the more likely it is to survive, and indeed to thrive, in the macroeconomic tumult and chaos and the explosion of competition and opportunity that is coming. Or perhaps it has already arrived.

Our hope is that by applying Agile Innovation, perhaps you will create your own future, and also have a positive influence on our shared future.

OUR CONCLUSION: AGILE CAPITALISM

We close this book where we began it, with a simple question.

> To innovate or not to innovate?

Is that the question you're asking yourself?
Is that the question you should be asking yourself?
Is that the question your company's board of directors is asking?

We think that the best answer is probably "to innovate," but of course you have to decide for yourself.

This book is about our experiences working with companies that were and are facing big challenges, and it's about how exceptionally talented groups of people have succeeded in addressing challenges through innovation. At a broader level, it's also about the fact that innovation is now central to our economy, central to the very structure of how we create and exchange ideas and products all around the world. Innovation is central, that is, to capitalism.

The capitalist model has been studied and critiqued by some of the world's most brilliant economists, philosophers, business leaders, and politicians, and passionate opinions about the value of labor and capital have spanned millennia, from Aristotle's time, to Marx's, to Joseph Schumpeter's, and right up to today. During the past few centuries, dramatic revolutions in France, Russia, and China have tried and tested alternative ways to structure industries and economies, and these three, along with all the rest of the world's national and regional economies, continue to evolve.

A century and a half ago, Marx postulated that capitalism's inbuilt conflicts would eventually cause its collapse. A century later, Schumpeter took a more positive view and pointed out that capitalism's inherent process of creative destruction drives development in every industry, and thus constitutes a built-in feedback loop that helps sustain the system itself. The twin forces of creation and destruction constitute a powerful adaptive force, an evolutionary force.

The historical context of both theories is important. The examples Marx and Schumpeter studied were based on the production of physical goods from physical raw materials. The production processes that most concerned Marx were the beginnings of modern industrial automation, and the social forces he saw as the system's downfall were exploitative and dehumanizing. But capitalism did not collapse, and Schumpeter's work in the middle of the following century reflected a later stage in capitalism's development, by which time manufacturing had in fact achieved the promise of automated mass production at high quality, while new social protections addressed some of Marx's concerns.

For both Marx and Schumpeter, the definitions of a *unit of production* and a *unit of labor* were clear, because both were based on physical materials and physical effort. Efficiency increased when mechanical devices did work that humans had previously done, and the progressive lowering of commodity prices formed the foundation of a supply-driven economy.

Today, however, we are in a much different economy, a new Relationship and Knowledge Economy. It's still capitalism, but now connectivity is the critical currency rather than raw materials. This is a profound and fundamental shift from physical asset-based business models to new ways of doing business based on leveraging intangible assets that we often don't own.

This new economy is built on intellectual capital that dramatically alters the zero-sum approach; now highly valued assets are widely shared in win-win scenarios. As an example, consider how Apple's App Store and iTunes business models serve as economic platforms, a new type of infrastructure that creates billions of dollars of transaction revenue for developers of new apps (including teenagers who are still in high school).

How did this happen?

> The answer is that capitalism has evolved and has driven itself to become a new form: Agile Capitalism.

Progressive development of knowledge, technology, and business models, driven from within the capitalist system itself, have transformed into new forms that could not have been foreseen in the time of Marx and Friedrich Engels. Emerging in Schumpeter's era, capitalism is something new, now global, electronically connected, and utterly knowledge and relationship based. This process of self-transformation is sure to accelerate, continuing to self-transform because of the innovative efforts of individuals and organizations all around the world who, in the grand tradition that capitalism uniquely empowers, seek economic advantage for themselves. Agile capitalism may define our era, and the accelerated method of innovation, Agile Innovation, is at its core.

> Hence, innovation is at the core of every manmade thing in the world, and it ubiquity affects every individual, every corporation, and every nation.

• • •

We have worked in the field of innovation for many decades, and when we had the good fortune to participate in developing and implementing innovative solutions, we learned as much if not more than our clients did. Hence, one of the most important lessons for us has been that we must keep exploring and learning—being agile and adapting—because given the rapid rate of change, what worked and what we believed to be true yesterday often needs to be reexamined for its relevance today and tomorrow.

Consequently, our offering in this book represents a beginning, not an ending. This is a journey that you have also started, if only by reading this book, and we hope that you will also recognize the need to discover new truths for yourself, and better ways to make innovation work for you and for your organization.

> Innovation is not imitation, but adaptation.

Innovation is also a natural path to growth, an essential process of self-renewal. Markets mature as industries grow, by progressively addressing human needs and society's needs. Markets evolve as people gain access to more knowledge, to new tools, and to more choices. That last word is the key.

When people have more choices, how does that affect markets and the competitive position of companies?

For on the other side of the system, not the production side but the consumer side, the result of large-scale automation is that increasing billions of consumers are offered vastly more choice. This is causing the second major shift, for in the new abundance, the market is demand driven rather than supply driven.

And commoditization, offering lower prices, is only one of the ways to enlarge market share, and sometimes an ineffective way. In the demand-driven market, companies increasingly must deliver many other, less tangible aspects of value, including aesthetics, convenience, user interface, reputation, brand, social responsibility, and even individualized personal preferences. All of these require innovation.

Intense competition in the knowledge-relationship marketplace is itself a powerful and valuable feedback loop, one that's built right into the system of capitalist innovation. The organizations that best interpret and act on this invaluable feedback are the ones that win. They are, in other words, the Agile Innovators.

> Agility is now a matter of survival of the fittest.
>
> Agility in the ability to innovate effectively is also a matter of survival of the fittest.

Like Schumpeter, we believe that the strength of the capitalist system lies in the fact that it evolves from within, driven by innovation and entrepreneurship and now also driven by consumption and by choice.

What impact does that have on us, the consumers? The inherent contradictions in human nature were and are viewed by some, like Marx, as weaknesses to be controlled. But that has never worked. To the contrary, we appreciate and value the delightful paradoxes that define our identities and differences as unique individuals, and we believe in the power of the human spirit to rise and meet new challenges, to adapt by finding or creating opportunities to make life better, and to help make us all more joyful, more creative, and more productive.

As an Agile Innovator in your organization, you bring together people with different talents and skills and facilitate their interactions in a systematic, purposeful manner, providing vision, leadership, and coordination. This is how innovation transforms a company, an industry, and the world, not by imitation, but when each finds their own way . . .

●   ●   ●

We close by noting that as relentless optimists we see tremendous innovation opportunities for all who are brave enough to try. Our global society faces a great many complex and difficult challenges—water, energy, environmental damage, health care, poverty, human rights, etc.—and although it's all too easy to complain and criticize others for whatever they do or don't do, we have a different response.

We focus our energies on *what we can do.*

We express our creativity and commitment through innovation to deliver value to society.

Our world may be at a tipping point. Which side will you be on?

Questions to Reflect Upon

- Does your organization have a strategy statement?
- How deep is your executive team's understanding of the critical forces that are driving change in your markets?
- Do you have a clear view of the six global forces of change (commoditization, digitization, social media and networking, globalization, turbulence, and acceleration), as well as the forces specific to your industry?
- Is your leadership team fixated on a single model of the future (very risky), or do you have alternative models of possible futures that you're monitoring attentively and thoughtfully? (The latter would come from a strongly recommended, robust scenario-planning process, one in which the leadership team participates energetically.)
- Does your strategy provide a clear sense of what ought to be in your innovation portfolios?
- Does your CEO talk about the strategy, and has he or she linked the organization's goals and expectations to the execution of the strategy?
- Which wave of innovation is your company surfing?
- Are you ready to implement Agile Innovation?

Appendix A

CRITICAL QUESTIONS

At the end of each chapter we included a short list of questions related to the content that we hoped would be useful and provocative. Questions open the doors of learning and discovery, and they can be tremendously powerful allies in the important work of strategy, design, and, of course, innovation. As Thomas Berger has told us, "The art and science of asking questions is the source of all knowledge."

In addition, we have prepared a more detailed list that relates broadly to the entire scope of the book. These are mostly deep questions that we hope will help you consider what innovation and Agile Innovation in particular may mean for you and your organization.

QUESTIONS ABOUT YOU

If your life were a novel, what would be the title? How would the story end?

Who has been the most important person in your life?

What was the happiest moment of your life? The saddest?

Who has been the biggest influence on your life?

Who has been the kindest to you in your life?

What are the most important lessons you've learned in life?

What are you most grateful for?

In your ideal job, what would be your greatest fear?

Are you more of a follower or a leader, and why?

What one thing have you not done that you really want to do? What's holding you back?

Have you ever seen insanity where you later recognized creativity?

Are you holding on to something you need to let go of?

Do you push the elevator button more than once? Why?

Has your greatest fear ever come true?

What is your happiest childhood memory? What made it so special?

At what time in your recent past have you felt the most passionate and alive?

If you just won a million dollars, would you quit your job?

What is the difference between being alive and truly living?

If you only learn from your mistakes, why are you always so afraid to make a mistake?

Have any of your recent actions openly expressed the love you feel?

Five years from now, what from the past month will you remember?

Do you make eye contact 100 percent of the time?

Do you keep 50 percent of your time unscheduled?

What do you see as the biggest challenges to innovation in your organization?

Who in your organization do you admire for his or her contribution to innovation, and why?

What is your leadership style in the context of innovation efforts?

How much urgency do you personally feel regarding the need for innovation in your industry?

If you could create for yourself the ideal job as a member of an innovation team, what would that be, and why?

Which is worse: failing or never trying?

If you could do it all over again, would you change anything?

If happiness were currency, what kind of work would make you rich?

Are you doing what you believe in, or are you settling for what you are doing?

If the average human life span were 40 years, how would you live your life differently? How about if the average human life span were 400 years?

How old are you on the inside? How old are you in terms of your creativity?

What is the one thing you'd most like to change about the world?

If you could offer 1 million newborn children one piece of advice that they would receive when they turned 18 years old, what would it be?

What makes you, you?

INNOVATION AS A PROCESS

How do you innovate in your company?

How do you spot opportunities for innovation?

How do you learn from failures?

How can you learn more about your ideas?

How do you invent a new way to come up with ideas?

What types of innovations have been created in your organization?

What would you like to change about the way your processes work?

What is your biggest dream of what you might achieve?

If you have participated in an innovation effort, what aspects of the process were the most frustrating for you?

If you have not participated in an innovation effort, and would like to, why has that not happened yet?

What have you learned from the advice (from consultants and others) you received regarding ways to improve your innovation capability?

How well integrated are your innovation efforts with your organization's long-term growth strategies?

How do you encourage innovation in your organization?

How can you create a safe space for innovation at your company?

How should you form and manage innovation teams?

How can you tell whether an innovation strategy is any good?

How can you invent a new kind of business model for your organization?

What's the best way to manage your firm's innovation portfolio?

What role should senior executives play in innovation?

How can you personally become a better innovator?

Are you harnessing technology effectively?

Are you thinking big enough?

What was the last experiment you ran? What was the last new thing you measured?

Why is true innovation so difficult?

How do you build innovation to scale like Google, Apple, Procter & Gamble, Amazon.com, etc.?

Corporate Culture and Management

Describe your corporate culture using three words.

Within your organization, what are the greatest roadblocks to change?

How does your corporate culture support innovation?

How do you share information and insights that might help your innovation efforts?

How open are your innovation efforts? How well does your organization collaborate with outside innovators or other organizations?

Is your company more worried about doing things right, or doing the right things?

How is resistance to change manifested in your organization?

What types of change are the most challenging, and which are the easiest to implement?

What sorts of changes energize people in your organization?

What sorts of changes demotivate people in your organization?

What does your top management, including the board of directors, expect in the way of innovation?

What is your theory of human motivation, and how does your compensation plan fit with that view?

What historical or fictional character would you want to hire, and why? What does this teach you about whom you want to hire next?

How do you stay inspired?

What level of tolerance for uncertainty and acceptance of risk taking does top management exhibit?

What did you miss in the interview for the worst hire you ever made?

Who, on the executive team or the board, has spoken to a customer recently?

What's your appetite for risk?

How can you make your organization more responsive to change?

How can you get other people behind your idea?

How long does it take a new business to scale and why? Can you do it faster?

Are you measuring the right things?

During the past five years what kinds of accomplishments have been most celebrated in your organization?

Are people in your organization rewarded for experiments that succeed and penalized for those that fail? How?

From where in your organization are innovation efforts typically initiated?

Is your organization changing as fast as the world around us?

It's 2020 and your company was just honored with a Best Company to Work for Worldwide award. In hindsight, what three things did you do to earn this award?

Are there effective innovation champions in your organization? If so, what are they like? What makes them effective? What might help them to be more effective?

How do you see an ideal innovation team functioning?

You've just written a tell-all book about your company: What secrets does it reveal?

Are you burning out?

COMPETITION

Which of your competitors do you think is the most innovative and why?

What would be necessary to overtake your most admired competitor?

Which of your competitors is the least innovative and why?

If you could recruit the most innovative person in your industry, who would that be? What makes him or her most innovative?

Who in your innovation team would be the biggest loss if a competitor recruited him or her?

How does your organization respond when competitors launch innovative products or services that challenge your market share?

What might be the most disruptive kind of innovation in your industry?

What are examples of disruptive innovation that have already occurred in your industry?

INTELLECTUAL PROPERTY (IP)

How might the sharing of your organization's IP affect your innovation efforts?

How leading-edge is your organization's IP?

How does your organization benchmark the value of its IP?

How actively does your organization manage its IP assets (buying, selling, licensing, and prosecuting patents)?

In your market niche, which competitor has the strongest IP portfolio? How does it manage that portfolio?

Where is the most IP activity taking place in your market niche or product area?

Are you outsourcing the right tasks?

CUSTOMERS

What are the characteristics of your ideal customers? How could you transform all your customers to become similarly ideal?

What is the shortest path to your customer?

How does your organization gather feedback from existing and potential customers?

How is in-depth market research done in your organization?

How do your marketing and innovation teams interact to share insights into customer habits, needs, and aspirations?

How much unsolicited feedback (positive and negative) do you receive from your customers?

How do your customers respond to innovation in your product or service areas?

What one word do you want to own in the minds of your customers, employees, and partners?

STRATEGY AND LEADERSHIP

Can you name a person who has had a tremendous impact on you as a leader? Maybe someone who has been a mentor to you? Why and how did this person impact your life?

What are the most important decisions you make as a leader of your organization?

As an organization gets larger there can be a tendency for the institution to dampen inspiration. How do you keep this from happening?

How do you encourage creative thinking within your organization?

What is your big hairy audacious goal?

In your organization, where do the great ideas come from?

How do you help new employees understand the culture of your organization?

When faced with two equally qualified candidates, how do you determine whom to hire?

What is one characteristic that you believe every leader should possess?

What is the biggest challenge facing leaders today?

Do you set aside specific times to share your vision with your employees and other leaders?

What resources would you recommend to someone looking to gain insight into becoming a better leader?

What firm are you going to put out of business next?

What should you stop doing?

What do you need to start doing?

What is one mistake you observe leaders making more frequently than others?

What is the one behavior or trait that you have seen derail leaders' careers more than any other?

Can you explain the impact, if any, that social networking and Web 2.0 has made on your organization or on you personally?

How do the decisions you make today help people and the planet tomorrow?

If you weren't already in the business you're in, would you enter it today?

Which is the most important to your organization—mission, core values, or vision?

How do you ensure your organization and its activities align with your core values?

How do you or other leaders in your organization communicate your core values?

How do you encourage others in your organization to communicate your core values?

What advice would you give to someone going into a leadership position for the first time?

What are you doing to ensure that you continue to grow and develop as a leader?

How can you become the competitor that would put your own firm out of business?

Will your organization be relevant five years from now?

What awards do you want your organization to win? What will it take to win them?

Appendix B

RESOURCES FOR YOUR REVOLUTION

We have established an online repository of useful tools and materials about Agile Innovation at the following website: http://futurelabconsulting.com/agileinnovation.

Please feel free to visit and peruse the offerings.

The following are resources that might be of interest to you.

THE 12 AGILE PRINCIPLES ADAPTED FOR INNOVATION

The following 12 principles were derived from the core values of the Agile Manifesto to guide the practice of Agile Development. These guiding principles can help teams determine what practices are appropriate, generate new practices when they are necessary, evaluate new practices that arise, and implement practices in an agile manner.

You can download a PDF poster of these principles at http://futurelabconsulting.com/agileinnovation.

The 12 Principles of Agile Management Adapted to Innovation:

1. Delight the customer through rapid delivery of a minimal key feature set.

2. Welcome changing requirements by building in a rapid pivot innovation model.

3. Deliver value continuously that fulfills progressively deeper tacit customer needs.

4. Implement Agile Innovation as a team sport, daily.

5. Build projects around incentivized and empowered innovators.

6. Convey information face to face using a co-facilitation process.

7. Measure progress by completion of working innovations.

8. Maintain a consistent cadence of progress by adopting proven methodologies.

9. Aim to simultaneously master customer insight and technical excellence.

10. Simplify, simplify, simplify.

11. Unleash ideation by unlocking your team's core creativity.

12. Hold innospectives to continuously learn and improve.

THE EIGHT CS OF TRANSFORMATIONAL CHANGE

You can also download a PDF poster of the eight Cs of change at: http://futurelabconsulting.com/agileinnovation.

1. Customer insight must be expanded to discover unarticulated customer needs.

2. Creativity must be amplified through continuous brainstorming.

3. Constructive leadership takes appropriate risks by adopting incremental business cases to enable faster product cycles.

4. Collaboration happens more effectively in smaller Agile teams and stand-up meetings than monolithic projects and traditional death march meetings.

5. Continuous learning must be implemented through retrospectives.

6. Compensation models need to be modified to incentivize business creativity and accountability.

7. Comprehensive software tools and systems must be deployed to provide measurement and management of both ideation and execution.

8. Cultural norms must encourage leaders to inspire new behaviors and new competencies.

THE ELEVATOR TEST STATEMENT

The elevator test statement—an explanation of a project to someone within 2 minutes—generally takes the following format:

- For (target customer)
- Who (statement of the need or opportunity)
- The (product name) is a (product category)
- That (key benefit, compelling reason to buy)
- Unlike (primary competitive alternative)
- Our product (statement of primary differentiation)[1]

Every product and project needs a core concept from which its details can flow. Without a core concept, team members often spend time investigating blind alleys and racking up costs without contributing much to a project's success. Particularly with new products for which the risks and uncertainties are high, having such a core concept, a unifying vision is essential to keeping the cost of exploration appropriate to the scope of the opportunity, and the elevator test statement should vividly depict the vision behind a product.

It also emphasizes that projects produce products. Some projects (e.g., internal IT projects) may not create products for the external market, but viewing them as products for an internal market keeps the team grounded in a customer-product mind-set. Whether the project produces enhancements to an internal accounting system or a new digital camera, product-oriented thinking reaps benefits.

IDEATION LENSES AND PERSPECTIVES FOR MULTIVISIONING

Multivisioning, a technique for continuously generating ideas by shifting the perspective on ideas as you brainstorm, blends the best of classical brainstorming with recent discoveries in peak performance techniques and advanced innovation methods.

The underlying principle is that just as a sculpture needs to be rotated so that the sculptor can capture all views, an idea needs to be rotated conceptually through various perspectives, or what we call *ideation lenses*.

The authors maintain a repository of ideation lenses and perspectives, which you can download and contribute to at http://futurelabconsulting .com/agileinnovation.

Here are a few to stimulate your imagination:

What would it take for us to become more passionate about this idea?

How can we enlarge this idea, maybe turn it into a global idea?

How can we open it up, maybe do open systems thinking here?

How would we have dealt with this 10 years ago? How about 10 years in the future?

How would they solve this problem on *Star Trek*? (Then put on a skit.)

How would Steve Jobs solve this problem? Warren Buffet? Albert Einstein? Thomas Edison?

Let's become the customers and think about it from their perspective.

What is the gap that exists between A and B? What are all the things we need to fill up this gap? (Make a list and find out how to attain them.)

Let's create a visual picture, a mind map of the situation.

How does the Medici Effect manifest here? (The Medici Effect concept, described in the book of that title, refers to how ideas in seemingly unrelated topics and fields intersect to add more value.)

Let's invite someone to play the challenger—and challenge all the assumptions in our situation.

Let's do a force analysis and map the forces that are impacting this project.

What if money, time, people, and supplies were not issues at all?

How do we billion-ify a half-baked idea? (Many ideas may seem like small ideas, but in reality, they could be seeds of billion-dollar ideas, if we only knew how to enlarge, deepen, and modify them.)

What are the root causes of the issues we are investigating?

What are other applications of this solution in other markets?

How has the world changed since we started this project? Are those changes important for us to consider?

What is known and unknown about our project?

To what category of ideas or objects would our work belong? What other categories could we shift to? What happens when we shift categories?

What is a high score in the game we're playing?

How do we flip around, invert, or reverse this idea? (Reversing an idea may sound crazy, but it can lead to brilliant thinking.)

Other techniques to support multivisioning include:

Let's do a SWOT (strengths, weaknesses, opportunities, and threats) analysis to open up our thinking.

Let's play Finish the Idea. Everyone takes a piece of paper, starts an idea, and then hands it off to the next person to finish.

Let's create a laser focus on some aspect of the idea.

Let's play Change our Hats—we brainstorm each idea from different perspectives: just the facts (white hat), the positive aspects (yellow hat), the problems or negative aspects (black hat), the emotional reactions (red hat), and the alternatives building upon the initial idea (green hat). The hats model is the work of Edward de Bono.[2]

Let's play Body Swap—everyone become someone you're not, and let's keep brainstorming in character.

THE BUSINESS PANORAMA™

After you've developed your business model using a business canvas or another conceptual sketching tool, you can turn that sketch into a masterpiece using the *business panorama.* This is a way of injecting the one thing you desperately need to turn a business canvas into something you can sell: *the story.* The right story will make the concept more attractive to your team, partners, stakeholders, and potential investors.

You can download a tool kit for making your own business panoramas, which contains detailed instructions, templates for PowerPoint and InDesign, and other tools at http://futurelabconsulting.com/agileinnovation.

Appendix C

DEFINITIONS

Comparing Agile Software, Agile Innovation, and Classical Innovation

Agile Software Process	Agile Innovation	Classical Innovation
Pushed up from research and development	360° innovation	Pushed down by chief executive officer
Measures work using points and Fibonacci series	Measures innovation using points and Fibonacci series	Is difficult to measure
Customer collaboration	Pervasive ethnography	Design ethnography
Reduces unproductive meeting time in exchange for behavior change and real-time work tracking	Provides a model for innovation behavior change throughout the organization	Does not request deep behavior change—for example, "Let's run a contest for the best idea."
Use of dashboards to drive management of engineers	Use of dashboards to drive innovation, because we can now measure innovation	Use of dashboards difficult to implement

Working software over comprehensive documentation	Progressive business cases with rapid prototyping for customer testing and insight	Business cases with fast failure

Tools and Techniques of Agile Innovation

Agile Software Process	Agile Innovation	Classical Innovation
Stand-up meetings	Stand-up staff meetings	
Burn down charts	Innovation burn down charts	
Scrum	IdeaScrum—innovation feed, plus collaborative and social workflow	Ideation
Retrospectives	Innospectives	Intermittent learning
Planning poker	Agile group voting using Fibonacci numbers to amplify differences	Weighted voting
Stories	Vignettes—structured stories that encapsulate features with benefits for integrated value case, leading to business panorama	Personas
Releases	Innovation systems	Initiatives
Iterations and sprints	Planned ideation sprints with staged focus on each sprint, using multivisioning of idea perspectives	Brainstorming

Glossary of Agile Innovation Terms[1]

Agile Manifesto	"The Manifesto for Agile Software Development" is a historical document authored in February 2001 by 17 people who came together at a ski resort in Utah to discuss

	different approaches to lightweight, responsive, adaptable software development.
Agile practices	Procedures defined as being highly efficient to productivity, including user stories, cross-functional teams, unit testing, refactoring, continuous integration, planning poker, and burn down charts.
Backlog	Also known as *product backlog,* a prioritized list of user stories and defects in order from most valuable to least valuable. Backlogs include both functional and nonfunctional user stories, as well as technical team-generated stories.
Best practices	Processes, skills, and systems that are considered to deliver optimal performance. These are often associated with market leaders.
Brainsprint	Iterative brainstorming effort within an IdeaScrum.
Brainstorming	A method of generating new ideas on a particular topic within a group situation. The key is to make an initial list quickly without discussion before evaluating the list as a whole.
Burn down chart	A chart showing the number of hours remaining for completion of a project, that shows a downward trend of work remaining to do.
Business model	Conceptualization of the value proposition that distinguishes a firm or product from its competitors.
Cadence	Representation of the flow or rhythm of events and the pattern in which something is experienced. Cadence is a state that Agile teams strive to achieve, because it indicates that they are operating efficiently.

Cannibalization	The scope of demand for a new product that causes reduction of demand for an existing product or service.
Champion	The person who ensures that a new idea is implemented effectively. This person is often a senior or middle manager with a high degree of passion and vested interest in the success of a new idea.
Chickens and pigs	From the popular story by Ken Schwaber. A chicken describes someone who, while involved in the process or project, is not committed and accountable for any specific deliverables. Chickens are often interested stakeholders, managers, and executives. Because these individuals are not directly involved or accountable, it is encouraged that chickens' participation in the process be limited to observation only. Pigs, however, are individuals who are committed, because they are directly accountable for specific project and product deliverables. Pigs are encouraged to participate wholly in the process, because they will be held accountable for their involvement and estimates. *The Chicken and Pig Story* A pig and a chicken are walking down a road. The chicken looks at the pig and says, "Hey, why don't we open a restaurant?" The pig looks back at the chicken and says, "Good idea. What do you want to call it?" The chicken thinks about it and says, "Why don't we call it 'Ham and Eggs'?" "I don't think so," says the pig. "I'd be committed, but you'd only be involved."
Convergent thinking	A method for reducing the number of ideas or concepts to a manageable number, possibly using structured criteria. Contrast with *Divergent thinking.*

Corporate culture	The values, operating principles, or shared beliefs within an organization that the people in the organization adhere to. This is often heavily influenced by the founders or the chief executive and should significantly affect the development of a culture of continuous innovation.
Corporate utility function	A measure of the value achieved by the fulfillment of goals. The function is quantified by combining profitability, cost, return horizon, competitive durability, impact to intellectual property (IP) strategy, and impact to internal learning and processes.
Cross-functional team	A team composed of members with all the functional skills and specialties necessary to complete a project from start to finish.
Crossing the chasm	Successfully making the transition from the innovation stage of introducing a new idea to adoption by the mass market. Geoffrey Moore pioneered this concept in his book, *Crossing the Chasm*. Moore expanded on the insights Everett Rogers developed in his book, *Diffusion of Innovations* (see *Adoption curve*).
Dashboard	An electronic (computer) or manual display of information relating to the performance of a team, process, product, or business.
Divergent thinking	A process to encourage more creative thinking in the early part of the overall innovation process by thinking broadly across many possibilities. Contrast with *Convergent thinking*.
Electronic IPR policy servers	Computerized system that automates processing and managing of intellectual property rights (IPR).
Enterprise Agile	The adoption of specific Agile practices in an organization that works in conjunction with other non-Agile practices. Enterprise Agile

	comprises highly efficient and customized practices for large organizations that have difficulty making a complete transition to Agile, as well as for organizations that already practice efficient development processes.
Epic	A user story that describes a large number of customer value statements and is then broken down into many smaller user stories around which actual features can be developed.
First to market	The first product or service in a new or emerging market. These products will often gain what is called first mover advantage, or prime mover advantage.
Gatekeepers	A group of managers and subject matter experts who will make the formal go or no-go decision on new ideas at regular formal review points, sometimes called gates.
IdeaScrum	Using the Agile scrum process to drive brainstorming.
Ideation	Activities that generate creative new ideas.
IdeaXML	A proposed open standard that will allow enterprise software applications to interoperate over an intelligent and secure framework for collaborative innovation.
Incremental innovation	Small improvements in performance resulting from the introduction of a new idea, similar to continuous improvement.
Innospective	Meeting held at the end of every IdeaScrum to review and reflect on what went well and not well during the effort and what can be improved upon during the next scrum.

Innovation	The implementation of a new or significantly improved product (good or service), process, marketing method, or organizational method in business practices, workplace organization, or external relations that adds value in some discernable way. The end user or customer provides the determination of value, and hence customers' experiences ultimately determine the existence of innovations.
Innovation management	The principles and practices that encompass integrated approaches to managing all dimensions of innovation, from innovation in products, services, and business processes to organizational and business models, through continuous monitoring, development, and improvement processes.
Innovation master plan	An overall plan for the innovation efforts of an organization, encompassing the themes of innovation strategy, innovation portfolio design, the innovation process, innovation culture, and the infrastructure and tools necessary for success. Based on the book *The Innovation Master Plan* by Langdon Morris.
Innovation smart grid	The result of a connection of multiple digital innovation hubs that could enable much higher performance for the innovation efforts within a company or industry ecosystem.
Innovation strategy	A plan for the future, expressing the extent and direction of innovation, which may include process improvement; extended or new product or service development; extended or new market or channel development; and diversification. These choices will reflect the firm's goals, required investment levels, and attitude toward risk.

Intellectual property (IP)	Private or proprietary information relating to an idea, including proprietary knowledge, designs, and brands, that can be formally protected by law.
IPR server	A computer server system that administrates intellectual property rights (IPR).
Iteration	A microcosm of a traditional systems development life cycle (SDLC), each of which produces working software. Iterations can be as long as three months but are more typically one to four weeks. See *Sprint*.
Kanban	Production methodology that comes from Toyota Production System and lean manufacturing, applied in software development with three main components: visual system for managing work, limiting work in progress, and pulling, versus pushing, work through the system.
Knowledge transfer	The processes for capturing, collecting, and sharing explicit and tacit knowledge, including skills and competence.
Meta-coordination	Using a higher order of strategic intelligence to bring greater coordination to complex business processes, such as IP management.
Metrics	Key performance indicators used to assess the value of a new idea, or the performance of an individual or an organization. Use of metrics is essential for management and should be balanced across financial, operational, and strategic indicators.
Nemawashi	A Japanese term meaning to "nurture the roots" of an idea. Many ideas stand a better chance of being supported by others if the seeds of the idea are planted in meetings and discussions before any formal decision point is reached.

Nonbinary trust models	Technology-enabled trust process wherein trust is not required to go in both directions between the parties. Because technology and machine learning in secure computer systems assess actual content of documents to identify affinities, similarities, and complements, useful information is shared, and new information is created without the parties actually revealing proprietary information to one another.
Open innovation	The emerging paradigm for innovation, involving methods that use partnering, licensing, and venturing to seek and combine internal and external sources of ideas and technologies.
Pareto profile	A graphical representation of a series of ideas, products, or markets ordered to show those with the highest value or contribution at one end and those with the lowest contribution on the opposite end. This technique is useful for getting a team to identify and focus on priorities. Developed by economist Vilfredo Pareto, who is also famous for Pareto's principle, the 80–20 rule.
Pipeline	A set of ideas that are in various stages of development and that may ultimately be evaluated and implemented.
Planning poker	A consensus-based technique for estimating the effort or relative size of future tasks in software development. Planning poker is useful for soliciting independent inputs from team members, building team cohesion, and fostering self-organizing teams.
Portfolio	A group of ideas, projects, products, or markets, managed as a set.

Product backlog	The backlog of elements or ideas in an Agile Software project. They are the responsibility of the product owner.
Product owner	One who manages the product backlog, addresses questions that arise during development, and signs off on work results. This role originated from scrum but has now been widely adopted independently of scrum (see *Scrum*).
Prototype	A model of a proposed final solution that can be tested to assess its completeness or performance across critical dimensions.
Refactoring	The practice of continuously improving the usability, maintainability, and adaptability of software code without changing its behavior.
Retrospective	In Agile Methodology, a communication forum in which Agile teams come together at the conclusion of a process or project to celebrate team successes and to reflect on what can be learned and improved.
Return on innovation investment (ROII)	A standard measure of the financial rewards associated with an idea as a ratio of the investment required to make it happen.
Scenario planning	A process of identifying and evaluating alternative, possible future states. Future scenarios are identified by assessing driving forces, future trends, and possible outcomes in the market or the broader environment.
Scrum	An Agile Development project management framework based on sprints. The framework of scrum leaves most development decisions up to the self-organizing scrum team, where decisions are reached as a whole team.

Scrum master	A person trained to facilitate daily scrum meetings, remove project impediments, oversee a team's progress throughout a project, and track scrum team updates.
Self-organizing	A method of team problem solving and development by deciding on the best solutions through the inputs of team members via various means of communication and reoccurring structured meetings. Self-organizing teams are distinct from those that are guided or managed from outside.
Sensitivity analysis	Assessment of the overall performance or result as a consequence of changing a single variable.
Social workflow	The conversion of social network activity into work requests, work commitments, and work-tracking data to enable and promote more effective management and thus better results.
Sprint	An iteration of work as done in a scrum by a scrum team.
Sprint backlog	The list of features that a development team plans to complete.
Sprint planning	A meeting for scrum teams, scrum masters, and product owners wherein the product owner describes priority features. The scrum team gains enough understanding about the tasks discussed that they are able to choose which ones to move from the product backlog to the sprint backlog.
Stage gate process	A structured process or methodology used in innovation project management to check progress and minimize risks throughout a project's life cycle. Each part of the project has clearly defined outputs (stages) or deliverables,

	and progress is checked and deliverables are assessed (gates) before further effort and investment are authorized.
Stand-up meetings	Daily meetings to quickly and efficiently resolve obstacles that any team members may be experiencing. By doing the meeting standing up (literally), people are not particularly comfortable, nor do they bring loads of materials. The meeting duration is thus held to a minimum.
Strategic partnering	Forming an alliance or partnership between organizations at a strategic level to improve operational processes, create new products, or exploit new markets. It is generally assumed that strategic partners will invest capital or people in their joint efforts and will mutually benefit in some significant ways.
SWAG	Scientific wild ass guess.
Task board	A physical or electronic board showing the state of tasks in a current sprint, often divided into *to do*, *in progress*, and *done*.
Technology road map	A top-level plan or graphic that shows how technology is expected to evolve over future periods and how it will affect the evolution of an organization's products and processes.
Technology transfer	The process of transferring expertise, knowledge, and IP from one organization to another.
Think tank	A group or environment set up specifically to generate and evaluate new ideas. Often very distinct from a typical operations environment to attain more creative and distinctive solutions.

Time to market	The time required to develop a new idea from concept to implementation or initial sales in the market.
Time boxing	The practice of constraining the amount of time for performing any activity to promote efficiency and eliminate waste.
Transactionalized idea search	By pairing an IP policy server with partial-transparency searches, people can easily search for suitable collaboration partners and potential project team participants while retaining the capability to release confidential information only under specific, ensured circumstances.
Unique selling proposition (USP)	A distinctive set of features and benefits that deliver a competitive advantage in the market. The USP can be identified only as a result of achieving a detailed understanding of customer wants and needs together with systematic assessment of competitor performance.
Value chain	As an idea or product moves through each stage of its development from idea to implementation, value is added. The value chain identifies each link (step) and assesses the relative value each link adds.
Velocity	A measurement of the number of story points that an Agile team completes over a given period, often one to four weeks.
Virtual team	A team working toward a common purpose but not located in the same facility or location.

NOTES

PART I THE INNOVATION REVOLUTION

1. Kuhn, Thomas S. *The Structure of Scientific Revolutions*. 4th ed. Chicago: University of Chicago Press, 2012.

CHAPTER 1 STARTING AT SPRINT ZERO

1. Schwaber, Ken, and Jeff Sutherland. *Software in 30 Days: How Agile Managers Beat the Odds, Delight Their Customers, and Leave Competitors in the Dust.* Hoboken, NJ: John Wiley & Sons, 2012.
2. Associated Press. "Oregon Drops Online Health Exchange for Federal Site." *San Francisco Chronicle*, April 25, 2014. http://www.sfgate.com/default/article/Oregon-drops-online-health-exchange-for-federal-5431148.php#photo-6217082.
3. Nelson, R. Ryan. "IT Project Management: Infamous Failures, Classic Mistakes, and Best Practices." *MIS Quarterly Executive* 6, no. 2 (June 2007): 67–78.
4. Institute of Medicine and National Research Council Committee on the Science of Adolescence. *The Science of Adolescent Risk-Taking: Workshop Report.* Washington, DC: National Academies Press, 2011.
5. Freiberg, Kevin, and Jackie Freiberg. *Nuts! Southwest Airlines' Crazy Recipe for Business and Personal Success.* New York: Broadway Books, 1997.
6. Srinivasan, Raji, Gary L. Lilien, and Shrihari Sridhar. "Should Firms Spend More on R&D and Advertising During Recessions?" *Journal of Marketing* 75, no. 3 (May 2011): 49–65.
7. Razeghi, Andrew. *Hope: How Triumphant Leaders Create the Future.* San Francisco: Jossey-Bass, 2006.
8. Jobs, Steve. Commencement address, Stanford University, Stanford, CA, June 12, 2005.
9. Tharp, Twyla. *The Creative Habit: Learn It and Use It for Life.* With Mark Reiter. New York: Simon & Schuster, 2006.
10. Harris, William Torrey. *The Philosophy of Education*, 1906.
11. Baldwin, Neil. *Edison: Inventing the Century.* Chicago: University of Chicago Press, 2001.

12. Biddle, Sam. "Peter Thiel Just Paid 20 Kids $100k to Not Go to College." *Valleywag* (blog). May 9, 2013. http://valleywag.gawker.com/peter-thiel-just-paid-20-kids-100k-to-not-go-to-colleg-498525048.

Chapter 2 Becoming Agile Rapidly and Painlessly

1. Saddington, Peter. *The Agile Pocket Guide: A Quick Start to Making Your Business Agile Using Scrum and Beyond.* Hoboken, NJ: John Wiley & Sons, 2012.
2. Beck, Kent, Mike Beedle, Arie van Bennekum, Alistair Cockburn, Ward Cunningham, Martin Fowler, James Grenning, et al. "The Manifesto for Agile Software Development." Agile Alliance. February 2001. http://www.agilealliance.org/the-alliance/the-agile-manifesto/.
3. Hammer, Michael, and James Champy. *Reengineering the Corporation: A Manifesto for Business Revolution.* New York: Harper Business, 1993.
4. Boehm, Barry. *Software Engineering Economics.* Upper Saddle River, NJ: Prentice Hall, 1981.
5. Miller, William L., and Langdon Morris. *Fourth Generation R&D: Managing Knowledge, Technology, and Innovation.* Hoboken, NJ: John Wiley & Sons, 1999.
6. Aulet, Bill. *Disciplined Entrepreneurship: 24 Steps to a Successful Startup.* Hoboken, NJ: John Wiley & Sons, 2013.
7. Kahane, Adam. *Transformative Scenario Planning: Working Together to Change the Future.* San Francisco: Berrett-Koehler, 2012.
8. Tichy, Noel M., and Stratford Sherman. *Control Your Destiny or Someone Else Will.* New York: Currency Doubleday, 1993.

Chapter 3 Transforming How We Work

1. Tzu, Sun. *The Art of War.*
2. Ibid.
3. Beck, Kent, Mike Beedle, Arie van Bennekum, Alistair Cockburn, Ward Cunningham, Martin Fowler, James Grenning, et al. "The Twelve Principles of Agile Software." Agile Alliance. February 2001. http://www.agilealliance.org/the-alliance/the-agile-manifesto/the-twelve-principles-of-agile-software/.
4. Intel Corporation. "Healthcare and Ethnography." Video, 3:27. 2007. http://www.intel.com/content/www/us/en/healthcare-it/healthcare-ethnography-video.html.
5. Point Forward. "About." Accessed May 24, 2014. http://pointforward.com/about.htm.
6. "They Really Ought to Have Known Better." Accessed May 24, 2014. http://zimmer.csufresno.edu/~fringwal/stoopid.lis.
7. Ibid.

Chapter 4 Thriving in Change

1. Schumpeter, Joseph A. *Capitalism, Socialism, and Democracy.* New York: Harper & Brothers, 1942.
2. Boaz, Nate, and Erica Ariel Fox. "Change Leader Change Thyself." *McKinsey Quarterly,* March 2014. http://www.mckinsey.com/insights/leading_in_the_21st_century/change_leader_change_thyself.
3. Schumpeter, 1942.
4. Gerstner, Louis V. *Who Says Elephants Can't Dance? Leading a Great Enterprise through Dramatic Change.* New York: Harper Business, 2003.
5. Foster, Richard, and Sarah Kaplan. *Creative Destruction: Why Companies That Are Built to Last Underperform the Market—and How to Successfully Transform Them.* New York: Broadway Business, 2001.
6. Barsh, Joanna, Marla M. Capozzi, and Jonathan Davidson. "Leadership and Innovation." *McKinsey Quarterly,* January 2008. http://www.mckinsey.com/insights/innovation/leadership_and_innovation.
7. Kuhn, Thomas S. *The Structure of Scientific Revolutions.* 4th ed. Chicago: University of Chicago Press, 2012.

Chapter 5 Accelerating Success

1. Blankenhorn, Dana. "Barnes & Noble's Rude Awakening: Tech Markets Are Winner-Take-All." TheStreet. April 4, 2014. http://www.thestreet.com/story/12625819/1/barnes-nobles-rude-awakening-tech-markets-are-winner-take-all.html.
2. Personal interview with Steve Ellis, March 1, 2009.
3. Morris, Langdon. *Managing the Evolving Corporation.* Hoboken, NJ: John Wiley & Sons, 1994.
4. ———. "The Chief Innovation Officer." Unpublished manuscript, 2012. Microsoft Word file.
5. Strange, Adario. "Hands On with Apple's CarPlay Integration with Volvo." April 16, 2014. http://mashable.com/2014/04/16/hands-on-carplay-volvo.
6. Blank, Steve. "Why the Lean Start-up Changes Everything." *Harvard Business Review,* May 2013. http://hbr.org/2013/05/why-the-lean-start-up-changes-everything/ar/6.

Chapter 6 Reducing Innovation Risk

1. Kerber, Ross. "BlackRock CEO to US Companies: Don't Overdo Divs, Buybacks." *Reuters,* March 26, 2014. http://www.reuters.com/article/2014/03/26/blackrock-dividends-idUSL1N0MN0ZP20140326.
2. Mark Zuckerberg, CEO of Facebook, interview on October 29, 2011. http://www.cbsnews.com/news/facebooks-mark-zuckerberg-insights-for-entrepreneurs/.
3. Nixon, Richard M. *Six Crises.* Garden City, NY: Doubleday, 1962.

4. Morris, Langdon. *The Innovation Master Plan: The CEO's Guide to Innovation.* Walnut Creek, CA: Innovation Academy, 2011.

5. Barnett, William P. "Leading Innovation by Design." Webinar. May 17, 2014.

CHAPTER 7 ENGAGING WITH COLLABORATIVE TEAMS

1. Gerstner, Louis V. *Who Says Elephants Can't Dance? Leading a Great Enterprise through Dramatic Change.* New York: Harper Business, 2003.

2. Ibid.

3. Schlender, Brent. "The Lost Steve Jobs Tapes." *Fast Company*, April 17, 2012. http://www.fastcompany.com/1826869/lost-steve-jobs-tapes.

4. Isaacson, Walter. *Steve Jobs.* New York: Simon & Schuster, 2011.

5. Beckman, Sara, and Michael Barry. "Design and Innovation through Story-telling." *International Journal of Innovation Science* 1, no. 4 (December 2009).

6. Austin, Rob, and Lee Devin. *Artful Making: What Managers Need to Know About How Artists Work.* Upper Saddle River, NJ: Financial Times, 2003.

7. Mootee, Idris. *Design Thinking for Strategic Innovation: What They Can't Teach You at Business or Design School.* Hoboken, NJ: John Wiley & Sons, 2013.

8. This section is adapted from Morris, Langdon. *The Innovation Master Plan: The CEO's Guide to Innovation.* Walnut Creek, CA: Innovation Academy, 2011.

CHAPTER 8 BUILDING AGILE INNOVATION AS A CORE COMPETENCE

1. Lencioni, Patrick. *The Five Dysfunctions of a Team: A Leadership Fable.* San Francisco: Jossey-Bass, 2002.

2. Greenleaf, Robert K. *Servant Leadership: A Journey into the Nature of Legitimate Power and Greatness.* Edited by Larry C. Spears. 25th anniversary ed. Mahwah, NJ: Paulist, 2002.

3. Morris, Langdon. "The Chief Innovation Officer." Unpublished manuscript, 2012. Microsoft Word file.

4. Jacob, Oren. "The Inside Story: 5 Secrets to Pixar's Success." By Jump Associates. *Fast Company*, October 13, 2011. http://www.fastcodesign.com/1665008/the-inside-story-5-secrets-to-pixar-s-success.

PART III LEADING THE REVOLUTION: FROM PLANS TO ACTION

1. Mangold, James, Gill Dennis, Joaquin Phoenix, and Reese Witherspoon. *Walk the Line.* Directed by James Mangold. Beverly Hills, CA: 20th Century Fox Film Corporation, 2005. DVD.

Chapter 9 Developing Agile Leadership

1. Reprinted by permission from Miller, William L., and Langdon Morris. *Fourth Generation R&D: Managing Knowledge, Technology, and Innovation.* Hoboken, NJ: John Wiley & Sons, 1999.
2. Grint, Keith. "Wicked Problems and Clumsy Solutions: The Role of Leadership." *Clinical Leader* 1, no. 2 (December 2008): 54–68.
3. Mansfield, Guy. *Developing Your Leadership Skills: From the Changing World to Changing the World.* North Charleston, SC: CreateSpace, 2013.
4. Jobs, Steve. Commencement address, Stanford University, Stanford, CA, June 12, 2005.
5. Goble, Frank G. *The Third Force: The Psychology of Abraham Maslow.* New York: Viking Adult, 1970.
6. Jobs, commencement address.

Chapter 10 Cultivating Core Creativity

1. Davila, Tony, Marc J. Epstein, and Robert Shelton. *Making Innovation Work: How to Manage It, Measure It, and Profit from It.* Upper Saddle River, NJ: Pearson Education, 2006.
2. Point Forward. "Kimberly-Clark Pull-Ups." Accessed May 30, 2014. http://pointforward.com/case_kc_huggies.htm.
3. Gardner, Howard E. *Creating Minds: An Anatomy of Creativity as Seen through the Lives of Freud, Einstein, Picasso, Stravinsky, Eliot, Graham, and Gandhi.* New York: Basic Books, 1994.
4. Ackoff, Russell L. "System Thinking Master Class." Lecture at the Ackoff Center for the Advancement of Systems Thinking Seminar, Philadelphia, PA, August 2000.
5. Apple Inc. "WWDC. June 10, 2013." Video, 120:19. June 10, 2013.
6. Osborn, Alex F. *Applied Imagination: Principles and Procedures of Creative Thinking.* New York: Scribner, 1953.
7. Tischler, Linda. "Seven Secrets to Good Brainstorming." *Fast Company,* February 8, 2001. http://www.fastcompany.com/63818/seven-secrets-good-brainstorming.
8. Ma, Moses. "Innovation Throwdown." *The Tao of Innovation* (blog). *Psychology Today.* February 18, 2011. http://www.psychologytoday.com/blog/the-tao-innovation/201102/innovation-throwdown.
9. Minsky, Marvin. *The Society of Mind.* New York: Simon & Schuster, 1988.
10. Jobs, Steve. "Steve Jobs Speaks Out." By Betsy Morris. *CNNMoney,* March 7, 2008. http://money.cnn.com/galleries/2008/fortune/0803/gallery.jobsqna.fortune/7.html.
11. Drucker, Peter. *Innovation and Entrepreneurship: Practice and Principles.* New York: Harper & Row, 1985.

12. Colvin, Geoff. *Talent Is Overrated: What* Really *Separates World-Class Performers from Everybody Else.* New York: Portfolio, 2008.
13. Ericsson, K. Anders, Ralf Th. Krampe, and Clemens Tesch-Römer. "The Role of Deliberate Practice in the Acquisition of Expert Performance." *Psychological Review* 100, no. 3 (1993): 363–406.
14. Csikszentmihalyi, Mihaly. *Flow: The Psychology of Optimal Experience.* New York: Harper & Row, 1990.
15. Kaufman, Scott Barry. "The Real Neuroscience of Creativity." *Beautiful Minds* (blog). *Scientific American,* August 19, 2013. http://blogs.scientificamerican.com/beautiful-minds/2013/08/19/the-real-neuroscience-of-creativity/.

CHAPTER 11 ACHIEVING AN ICONIC BRAND

1. Mark, Margaret, and Carol S. Pearson. *The Hero and the Outlaw: Building Extraordinary Brands through the Power of Archetypes.* New York: McGraw-Hill, 2001.
2. Conlon, Jerome. *Soulful Branding,* 2014.
3. Keen, Sam. *In the Absence of God: Dwelling in the Sacred.* New York: Harmony Books, 2010.
4. Lin, Pei-Ying, Naomi Sparks Grewal, Christophe Morin, Walter D. Johnson, and Paul J. Zak. "Oxytocin Increases the Influence of Public Service Advertisements." *PLoS One* 8, no. 2 (February 2013): e56934. doi:10.1371/journal.pone.0056934.
5. The Business Panorama™ is a copyright of FutureLab Consulting, Inc.
6. Conlon, *Soulful Branding.*
7. Spear, Peter. "Steve Jobs Think Different Speech." *Peter Spear* (blog). http://peterspear.tumblr.com/post/67752673681/steve-jobs-think-different-speech-to.

CHAPTER 12 OPTIMIZING YOUR INFRASTRUCTURE

1. Allen, Thomas J., and Gunter W. Henn. *The Organization and Architecture of Innovation: Managing the Flow of Technology.* New York: Routledge, 2011.
2. Kleon, Austin. *Steal Like an Artist: 10 Things Nobody Told You about Being Creative.* New York: Workman, 2012.
3. Isaacson, Walter. *Steve Jobs.* New York: Simon & Schuster, 2011.
4. Jaruzelski, Barry, John Loehr, and Richard Holman. "The Global Innovation 1000: Why Culture Is Key." *Strategy + Business,* Winter 2011, 2–16.
5. Khalili, Ali, Sören Auer, Darya Tarasowa, and Ivan Ermilov. "SlideWiki: Elicitation and Sharing of Corporate Knowledge Using Presentations." Universität Leipzig, Germany.

Chapter 13 Advancing Open Innovation

1. Randers, Jorgen. *2052: A Global Forecast for the Next Forty Years.* White River Junction, VT: Chelsea Green, 2012.

2. Unilever. "Open Innovation." Accessed May 31, 2014. http://www.unilever .com/innovation/collaborating-with-unilever/open-innovation/index.aspx.

3. Procter & Gamble. "P&G Connect+Develop Launches New Open Innovation Website." February 7, 2013. http://news.pg.com/press-release/pg-corporate-announcements/pg-connectdevelop-launches-new-open-innovation-website.

4. Lindegaard, Stefan. *Making Open Innovation Work.* North Charleston, SC: CreateSpace, 2011.

5. Maxwell, Eliot. "Openness and the Digital Economy: Building on the Past, Shaping the Future." 2002 http://www.policyinnovations.org/ideas/policy_ library/data/OpenInnovations/_res/id%3Dsa_File1/INNOV0103_p119-176_ maxwell.pdf.

6. Rogers, Everett M. *Diffusion of Innovations.* 5th ed. New York: Free Press, 2003.

7. Rader, Michael. "IP: 3 strategies for beating patent trolls." *Inside Counsel,* November 22, 2011. http://www.insidecounsel.com/2011/11/22/ip-3-strategies-for-beating-patent-trolls.

Chapter 14 Traveling the Road to Revolution

1. Marx, Karl. Thesis 11. *Theses on Feuerbach.* Progress Publishers, 1845.

2. Duane, Ja-Naé. *How to Create a Revolution: A Step-By-Step Guide from History's Social Influencers.* N.p.: Ja-Naé Duane, 2012. Kindle edition.

Chapter 15 Using Agile Strategy to Shape Your Organization's Future

1. Rilke, Rainer Maria. *Letters to a Young Poet.* Translated by M. D. Herter Norton. New York: W. W. Norton, 2004.

2. Kurzweil, Ray. *The Singularity Is Near: When Humans Transcend Biology.* New York: Penguin Books, 2005.

3. Watson, Peter. *The Great Divide: Nature and Human Nature in the Old World and the New.* New York: Harper Perennial, 2011.

4. Kao, John. *Jamming: The Art and Discipline of Business Creativity.* New York: Harper Business, 1996.

5. Feynman, Richard P. "The Value of Science." Public address at the autumn meeting of the National Academy of Sciences, Pasadena, CA, November 1955. Quoted in Richard P. Feynman. *"What Do You Care What Other People Think?" Further Adventures of a Curious Character.* Edited by Ralph Leighton. New York: W. W. Norton, 1988.

6. Lee, Bruce. *Tao of Jeet Kune Do.* Burbank, CA: Ohara, 1975.

7. Musashi, Miyamoto. *The Book of Five Rings.* Shambhala Library, 2012.

8. Piel, Gerald. *The Acceleration of History.* Knopf, 1972.

9. Murphy, Michael. *The Future of the Body: Explorations into the Further Evolution of Human Nature.* New York: J. P. Tarcher, 1992.

10. Andreessen, Marc. "Why Software Is Eating the World." *Wall Street Journal,* August 20, 2011. http://online.wsj.com/news/articles/SB10001424053111903480904576512250915629460.

11. Kurzweil, *The Singularity Is Near.*

12. Vinge, Vernor. "The Coming Technological Singularity: How to Survive in the Post-Human Era." Paper presented at Vision 21 symposium, Westlake, OH, March 1993.

APPENDIX B RESOURCES FOR YOUR REVOLUTION

1. Moore, Geoffrey A. *Crossing the Chasm: Marketing and Selling Technology Products to Mainstream Customers.* New York: HarperCollins, 1991.

2. The de Bono Group. "Six Thinking Hats." Accessed June 2, 2014. http://www.debonogroup.com/six_thinking_hats.php.

APPENDIX C DEFINITIONS

1. Rogers, Everett M. *Diffusion of Innovations.* 5th ed. New York: Free Press, 2003; Moore, Geoffrey A. *Crossing the Chasm: Marketing and Selling Technology Products to Mainstream Customers.* New York: HarperCollins, 1991; Schwaber, Ken.

ACKNOWLEDGMENTS

Although writing is often a solitary endeavor, completing a book is an intensive collaborative effort. Many friends and colleagues have generously contributed feedback, ideas, suggestions, and inspiration that have made a tremendous difference in the book and our lives.

We offer our thanks to the principals, partners, and extended family of FutureLab, who contributed valuable thoughts and reflections, including Bob Bressler, Claire Rumore, Doug Glen, Dr. Ian Bennett, Jack Canfield, Jerome Conlon, and Dr. Stephen Kosslyn.

Our Agile Software development team also deserves special acknowledgment for their heroic efforts to turn concepts into working code in a genuinely agile way, including team leads Krunal Soni, Howard Shere, Chirag Gurav, and Pranay Patadiya, and architects Dr. Alyona Medelyan, Andy Hoskinson, Bill Simpson, and Steve Griffith. You guys have superpowers when it comes to overcoming impossible technical issues, and we're grateful for your skills and your commitment!

We are also grateful for the support, enthusiasm, and professionalism of the awesome team at John Wiley & Sons, including Shannon Vargo, Liz Gildea, and Lauren Freestone. Our thanks to you all!

• • •

I'd like to acknowledge the many colleagues and clients I've worked with over the years. It has been their insights, guidance, and support that led to so much of the learning that I hope is present here.

In particular, Bryan Coffman, Michael Kaufman, and Jay Smethurst have been great business partners, and Michael Barry, Sara Beckman, and Gary Waymire have been tremendous innovation mentors.

I'd also like to acknowledge Moses, for the brilliant insight that Agile + Innovation belong together, and Po Chi, for his gentle but firm guidance throughout this project. It has been a great pleasure working with you both.

—Langdon

I'm deeply indebted to a great number of friends, colleagues, and muses for their contributions of inspiration, knowledge, and support toward my writing this book. Your suggestions and wisdom have been incorporated into my thinking, and therefore into this book. Special thanks to Akira Hirai, Amber Schwab, Dr. Bathsheba Malsheen, Dan Greening, Elizabeth Estrada, Gaya Blair, Dr. Glenn Larsen, Dr. Harvey Stone, Jake Hsu, John Kao, Kirsten Sandberg, Kamal Ravikant, Malena Gamboa, Margarita Quihuis, Mark Resch, Dr. Marvin Greenberg, Paul Joyal, Paul To, Dr. Randy Sugawara, and Sue Kung. Also, just as Leonardo da Vinci had the Medici bank as a patron, I'm very grateful to Steve Ellis at Wells Fargo Bank for his encouragement and support— along with many others there, including Bipin Sahni, Kari Hovland, Kim Pugh, Lisa de Pashalis, Lori Crever, Margot Golding, Nathan Bricklin, and Paul Kizirian. Thanks so much for allowing us to nurture the ideas articulated in this book at a truly great company.

Finally, I must express gratitude to my family for teaching me to dream big, because that's the only way we can feel the passion necessary for a life worth living. Solomon and Heddy Ma were always happy to encourage the kids to reach for the stars, whether it's as a scientist and entrepreneur (me), an artist (my brother, Hamil), a writer (my sister Lybi), or the perfect mom (my sister Sophia). And a special thank you to Qian Li for her warm and invigorating support throughout this endeavor, and reminding me with every breath that life is a beautiful adventure.

—Moses

I am very grateful to the Hong Kong University of Science and Technology; its president, Tony Chan; executive vice president and provost, Wei Shyy; the dean of the School of Engineering, Khaled Ben Letaief; the acting dean of the School of Business and Management, Kalok Chan; former dean, Leonard Cheng; and many faculty colleagues, especially Matthew Yuen and Mitchell Tseng, for their support and guidance. They have given me the opportunity during the past several years to dedicate myself to a rigorous exploration of what innovation means.

A particularly important group of people deserves special mention: the thousands of entrepreneurs and would-be entrepreneurs, as well as corporate executives, who shared their business ideas and proposals with me when I was an active venture capitalist. The only way to repay them is to use the knowledge and insights I gained to help inspire the next generation.

The list of individuals who have been mentors and supporters is endless. Legendary venture capitalists, including Brook Byers, Bing Gordon, Randy Komisar, Dick Kramlich, and Don Valentine, helped shape my expectations of how innovation can change the world. My thanks to all of them, and to many others not named individually.

—Po Chi

ABOUT THE AUTHORS

LANGDON MORRIS

Langdon is one of the three principal founders of FutureLab.

He is also cofounder and senior partner of InnovationLabs, one of the world's leading innovation consultancies, with clients and affiliates on all continents.

His work focuses on helping leaders and their organizations implement the world's best innovation methods and tools and helping them solve very complex problems with high levels of creativity and effectiveness. His work has led to new breakthroughs and market-leading solutions.

The comprehensive innovation training program that Langdon designed is used worldwide and has been licensed to consulting partners as well as education ministries in multiple nations.

In addition, Langdon is well known as author or coauthor of some of the most important innovation books of the past decade, including *Permanent Innovation, The Innovation Master Plan*, and *4th Generation R&D*.

MOSES MA

Moses is one of the three principal founders of FutureLab.

He is an innovation consultant who works with senior executives at global companies and organizations and is the managing partner of Next Generation Ventures, a boutique, high-tech venture incubator with start-ups in enterprise, e-commerce, and e-learning technologies. You can follow him at his blog on the psychology of innovation at:

http://www.psychologytoday.com/blog/the-tao-innovation

He is also a tech visionary praised in *Time Magazine* and the *New York Times*. Over the years, he's been involved in the forefront of many exciting technologies—he was a legendary games designer who created two of the world's best-selling computer games, including the world's first commercially successful Internet game; he took an uncapitalized software start-up and built it into the ninety-seventh largest, seventh fastest growing, and eleventh most profitable in the country; he codeveloped the first specification for universal identity on the Internet; and he helped invent the concept of e-markets in business-to-business e-commerce.

Moses was trained as a scientist and received a bachelor of science degree from Caltech (1979) in physics, where he was lucky enough to learn from some of the most inspirational scientists of the twentieth century, including Richard Feynman and Eugene Shoemaker.

Po Chi Wu

Dr. Po Chi Wu is one of the three principal founders of FutureLab.

He is also adjunct professor in both the School of Business and Management and the School of Engineering at Hong Kong University of Science and Technology, where he has initiated educational programs in innovation and entrepreneurship at all levels: undergraduate, graduate, and professional training for corporate executives. Dr. Wu is currently serving as a vice chairman of Invotech, a new nonprofit organization. In this role, he is driving an initiative called *Smart Hong Kong,* which aims to inspire and motivate entrepreneurs, especially young people, to focus their energies on creating practical solutions that will make Hong Kong a better, smarter city, a place where people can be healthier, happier, and more productive.

Before coming to Hong Kong, he was a visiting professor and cofounding executive director of the Global Innovation Research Center, Peking University, and an adjunct faculty member at the University of San Francisco. Having been a highly successful international venture capitalist and entrepreneur based in Silicon Valley for more than 25 years, he brings a unique perspective and insight into the challenges of innovation and entrepreneurship.

Dr. Wu earned his doctorate in molecular biology from Princeton University (1972) and bachelor of arts degrees in mathematics and music from the University of California, Berkeley (1966).

INDEX

NOTE: Page references in *italics* refer to figures.